Policing
Organized Crime

Intelligence Strategy Implementation

Advances in Police Theory and Practice Series

Series Editor: Dilip K. Das

Policing Organized Crime: Intelligence Strategy Implementation
Petter Gottschalk

Security in Post-Conflict Africa: The Role of Nonstate Policing
Bruce Baker

Community Policing and Peacekeeping
Peter Grabosky

Community Policing: International Patterns and Comparative Perspectives
Dominique Wisler and Ihekwoaba D. Onwudiwe

Police Corruption: Preventing Misconduct and Maintaining Integrity
Tim Prenzler

Policing Organized Crime

Intelligence Strategy Implementation

Petter Gottschalk

CRC Press
Taylor & Francis Group
Boca Raton London New York

CRC Press is an imprint of the
Taylor & Francis Group, an **informa** business

CRC Press
Taylor & Francis Group
6000 Broken Sound Parkway NW, Suite 300
Boca Raton, FL 33487-2742

First issued in paperback 2019

© 2010 by Taylor and Francis Group, LLC
CRC Press is an imprint of Taylor & Francis Group, an Informa business

No claim to original U.S. Government works

ISBN: 978-1-4398-1014-9 (hbk)
ISBN: 978-0-367-86428-6 (pbk)

Library of Congress Cataloging-in-Publication Data

Gottschalk, Petter, 1950-
    Policing organized crime : intelligence strategy implementation / Petter Gottschalk.
        p. cm. -- (Advances in police theory and practice series ; 5)
    Includes bibliographical references and index.
    ISBN 978-1-4398-1014-9
    1. Police. 2. Criminal justice, Administration of. 3. Organized crime. I. Title. II. Series.

HV7921.G69 2009
364.1'06--dc22   2009010248

Visit the Taylor & Francis Web site at
http://www.taylorandfrancis.com

and the CRC Press Web site at
http://www.crcpress.com

Table of Contents

12   Performance Management in Policing   235

13   Performance Measurement in Policing   247

Series Preface

While the literature on police and allied subjects is growing exponentially, its impact upon day-to-day policing remains small. The two worlds of research and practice of policing remain disconnected even though cooperation between the two is growing. A major reason is that the two groups speak in different languages. The research work is published in hard-to-access journals and presented in a manner that is difficult to comprehend for a lay person. On the other hand the police practitioners tend not to mix with researchers and remain secretive about their work. Consequently, there is little dialogue between the two and almost no attempt to learn from one another. Dialog across the globe, amongst researchers and practitioners situated in different continents, are of course even more limited.

I attempted to address this problem by starting the IPES, www.ipes.info, where a common platform has brought the two together. IPES is now in its 15th year. The annual meetings which constitute most major annual event of the organization have been hosted in all parts of the world. Several publications have come out of these deliberations and a new collaborative community of scholars and police officers has been created whose membership runs into several hundreds.

Another attempt was to begin a new journal, aptly called *Police Practice and Research: An International Journal*, PPR, that has opened the gate to practitioners to share their work and experiences. The journal has attempted to focus upon issues that help bring the two on a single platform. PPR is completing its 10 years in 2009. It is certainly an evidence of growing collaboration between police research and practice that PPR which began with four issues a year, expanded into five issues in its fourth year and, now, it is issued six times a year.

Clearly, these attempts, despite their success, remain limited. Conferences and journal publications do help create a body of knowledge and an association of police activists but cannot address substantial issues in depth. The limitations of time and space preclude larger discussions and more authoritative expositions that can provide stronger and broader linkages between the two worlds.

It is this realization of the increasing dialogue between police research and practice that has encouraged many of us- my close colleagues and myself connected closely with IPES and PPR across the world- to conceive and implement a new attempt in this direction. I am now embarking on a book series, *Advances in Police Theory and Practice*, that seeks to attract writers from all parts of the world. Further, the attempt is to find practitioner contributors. The objective is to make the series a serious contribution to our knowledge of the police as well as to improve police practices. The focus is not only in work that describes the best and successful police practices but also one that challenges current paradigms and breaks new ground to prepare a police for the twenty-first century. The series seeks for comparative analysis that highlights achievements in distant parts of the world as well as one that encourages an in-depth examination of specific problems confronting a particular police force.

It is hoped that through this series it will be possible to accelerate the process of building knowledge about policing and help bridge the gap between the two worlds-the world of police research and police practice. This is an invitation to police scholars and practitioners across the world to come and join in this venture.

Dilip K. Das Ph.D.
Founding President, International Police Executive Symposium
IPES, www.ipes.info

Founding Editor-in-Chief, Police Practice and Research:
An International Journal
PPR, www.tandf.co.uk/journals

Introduction

Policing organized crime remains problematic. In the United Kingdom, Harfield (2008) argues that organized crime challenges long-held paradigms concerning policing infrastructure and operations. He argues that organized crime has developed to become an issue beyond the competence of conventional policing. In the United States and Canada, Beare and Martens (1998) pointed this out more than a decade ago. But Harfield (2008, 72) found that government "response will be based on trying to adapt a policing infrastructure intended for other policing functions rather than dealing with the problem of organized crime on its own."

An important element of dealing with the problem of organized crime is the interface between organized crime groups and the legitimate environment in society, which is of vital importance to the existence of organized crime. Contacts, relationships, and exchanges between criminal organizations and legal organizations are a threat to the legitimate environment, but they also offer opportunities for organized crime prevention. In The Netherlands, Bunt and Schoot (2003) identified three kinds of interfaces between organized crime groups and the legitimate environment. Firstly, the demand from the licit environment for illegal products and services forms a breeding ground for organized crime groups. Secondly, persons with the knowledge or skill can enable organized crime groups to carry out their criminal activities. Thirdly, criminal groups make use of other opportunities or tools present in the licit environment.

Policing criminal business enterprises requires police intelligence and police investigations. Police intelligence has to be based on an implemented intelligence strategy, which is important because failure to carry out strategy can cause lost opportunities and leave police officers reluctant to do strategic planning. Lack of implementation creates problems in maintaining priorities and reaching organizational goals. The strategy execution task is commonly the most complicated and time-consuming part of strategic management. Yet, strategy implementation suffers from a general lack of both academic and practical attention. *Policing Organized Crime: Intelligence Strategy Implementation* is intended as a research model to study the extent of intelligence strategy implementation, which will add to the police strategy and implementation literature already available.

This book makes a contribution to the emerging academic discipline of police science. According to Jaschke et al. (2007, 23),

> Police science is the scientific study of the police as an institution and of policing as a process. As an applied discipline, it combines methods and subjects of other neighboring disciplines within the field of policing. It includes all of what the police do and all aspects from outside that have an impact on policing and public order. Currently it is a working term to describe police studies on the way to an accepted and established discipline. Police science tries to explain facts and acquire knowledge about the reality of policing in order to generalize and to be able to predict possible scenarios.

The important topics of police science include strategies and styles of policing, police organizations and management, and policing specific crime types. This book gets to the core of police science by studying the serious types of organized crime in the context of intelligence strategy implementation.

References

Beare, M.E. and Martens, F.T. (1998). Policing organized crime. *Journal of Contemporary Criminal Justice* 14 (4): 398–427.

Bunt, H.G.v.d. and Schoot, C.R.A.v.d. (2003). *Prevention of organised crime—A situational approach.* Devon, U.K.: Willan Publishing.

Harfield, C. (2008). Paradigms, pathologies, and practicalities—Policing organized crime in England and Wales. *Policing* 2 (1): 63–73.

Jaschke, H.G., Bjørgo, T., Romero, F. del B., Kwanten, C., Mawby, R., and Pogan, M. (2007). *Perspectives of police science in Europe,* Final Report, European Police College, CEPOL, Collège Européen de Police, Hampshire, U.K.

About the Author

Petter Gottschalk, DBA, is one of Norway's leading experts on information technology management, electronic business, Internet issues, knowledge management, business strategy, police science, and organized crime. He has conducted research in the systems and technology strategy area and has published extensively on knowledge management technology. In recent years, Professor Gottschalk has focused on knowledge management in policing. He is professor of Information Systems and Knowledge Management in the Department of Leadership and Organization at the Norwegian School of Management in Oslo. In addition, he lectures at the Norwegian Police University College (also in Oslo) on knowledge management, criminal entrepreneurship, and organized crime.

He has extensive experience in technology management and executive management, including positions such as managing director of the Norwegian Computing Center and managing director of ABB Datacables. He has held numerous positions in public life, for example, as chairman of the Children's Ombudsman, where the Norwegian government appointed him to chair the ombudsman's position for four years. Professor Gottschalk provides regular expert advice on a broad range of technology, management, and policing issues to the media and has worked extensively with the Norwegian Broadcasting Corporation (NRK), newspapers, and journals. He received his MBA in Germany (Technische Universität Berlin), MSc in the United States (Dartmouth College and MIT), and DBA (Doctor of Business Administration) in the United Kingdom (Brunel University).

Theories of Organized Crime

1

Organized crime has received increased attention in recent years. To understand the what, how, and why of organized crime, to stimulate "know what," "know how," and "know why," there is a need for theory development. A theory might be a prediction or explanation, a set of interrelated constructs, definitions, and propositions that presents a systematic view of phenomena by specifying relations among variables with the purpose of explaining natural phenomena. The systematic view might be an argument, a discussion, or a rationale, and it helps to explain or predict phenomena that occur in the world.

In our context of organized crime, we search theoretical explanations in two streams of research, one of which we label *criminology theories* of organized crime where theories are developed explicitly to explain the phenomenon of organized crime. Another stream of research we label *management theories* of organized crime, where general management theories are applied to the phenomenon of organized crime (Gottschalk, 2008).

It is difficult to overstate the importance of theory to law enforcement's understanding of organized crime and criminal organizations. Theory allows analysts to understand and predict outcomes on a probabilistic basis (Colquitt and Zapata-Phelan, 2007). Theory allows analysts to describe and explain a process or sequence of events. Theory prevents analysts from being confused by the complexity of the real world by providing a linguistic tool for organizing a coherent understanding of the real world. Theory acts as an educational device that creates insights into criminal phenomena.

Criminology Theories

Traditionally, a criminal organization is often thought of as a monopolistic firm, and the *theory of monopoly* is predominantly used to analyze organized crime. The monopolistic model implies that potential criminals have no other choice, but are forced to join the criminal organization if they decide to commit a crime. Chang et al. (2005) find this perspective to be less than exhaustive in terms of describing criminal behavior. They argue that the determination of the market structure for crime should be endogenous, which has notable implications for the optimal crime enforcement policies and crime itself.

To recover the conventionally neglected facts and provide a more complete picture of organized crime, Chang et al. (2005) developed a model in

1

terms of a criminal decision framework in which individual crime and organized crime are coexisting alternatives to a potential offender. The model makes the size of a criminal organization a variable and explores interactive relationships among sizes of the criminal organization, the crime rate, and the government's law enforcement strategies. Model runs showed that the method adopted to allocate the criminal organization's payoffs and the extra benefit provided by this organization play crucial roles in an individual's decision to commit a crime and the way in which that crime is committed.

Gross (1978) argued in his classical article on the *theory of organizational crime* that more than some areas of sociology, studies of crime and delinquency, usually have a strong theoretical base. He suggested two important theoretical relationships. First, the internal structure and setting of organizations is of such a nature as to raise the probability that the attainment of the goals of the organization will subject it to the risk of violating societal laws of organizational behavior. Secondly, persons who actually act for the organization in the commission of crimes will, by selective processes associated with upward mobility in organizations, be persons likely to be highly committed to the organization and be, for various reasons, willing and able to carry out the crime, should it seem to be required in order to enable the organization to attain its goals, to prosper, or, minimally, to survive.

One of the most widely held theories of organized crime today in the United States is known as the *alien conspiracy theory*. This theory blames outsiders and outside influences for the prevalence of organized crime in American society. Over the years, unsavory images, such as well-dressed men of foreign descent standing in shadows with machine guns and living by codes of silence, have become associated with this theory. The alien conspiracy theory posits that organized crime (the Mafia) gained prominence during the 1860s in Sicily and that Sicilian immigrants are responsible for the foundations of U.S. organized crime, which is made up of twenty-five or so Italian-dominated crime families (Lyman and Potter, 2007).

Lombardo (2002) has challenged the alien conspiracy theory as an explanation for the origin of organized crime in America, as he reviewed the history of Black Hand (an organized crime group) activity in Chicago in the early twentieth century, arguing that the development of Black Hand extortion was not related to the emergence of the Sicilian Mafia, but rather to the social structure of American society.

The *rational choice theory* suggests that people who commit crimes do so after considering the risks of detection and punishment for the crimes as well as the rewards of completing these acts successfully. Examples of this theory include a man who discovers that his wife is having an affair and chooses to kill her, her lover, or both; the bank teller who is experiencing personal financial difficulty and decides to embezzle funds from the bank to substantially increase his/her earnings; and an inner-city youth who decides that social opportunities are minimal and that it would be easier to make money by dealing crack cocaine (Lyman and Potter, 2007).

Shvarts (2001) suggests that the rational choice theory can explain the growth of the Russian Mafia. Because of low income and financial difficulties at the individual level, combined with a corrupt police force, it seems rational to move into organized crime to improve the standard of living for members joining the criminal organization.

Some theorists believe that crime can be reduced through the use of deterrents. The goal of a deterrent (crime prevention) is based on the assumption that criminals or potential criminals will think carefully before committing a crime if the likelihood of getting caught and/or the fear of swift and severe punishment are present. Based on such a belief, *general deterrence theory* holds that crime can be thwarted by the threat of punishment, while the *special deterrence theory* suggests that penalties for criminal acts should be sufficiently severe that convicted criminals will never repeat these acts (Lyman and Potter, 2007).

Furthermore, *learning theories* have been used to explain the onset of criminal activity. The body of research on learning theory stresses the attitudes, ability, values, and behaviors needed to maintain a criminal career (Lyman and Potter, 2007).

Next, *cultural deviance theories* assume that slum dwellers violate the law because they belong to a unique subculture that exists in lower-class areas. The subculture's values and norms conflict with those of the upper class on which criminal law is based (Lyman and Potter, 2007).

Social control theory is yet another criminology theory where social control refers to those processes by which the community influences its members toward conformance with established norms of behavior. Abadinsky (2007, 22) remarked:

> Social control theorists argue that the relevant question is not, why do persons become involved in crime, organized or otherwise? But, rather, why do most persons conform to societal norms? If, as control theorists generally assume, most persons are sufficiently motivated by the potential rewards to commit criminal acts, why do only a few make crime a career? According to control theorists, delinquent acts result when an individual's bond to society is weak or broken. The strength of this bond is determined by internal and external restraints. In other words, internal and external restraints determine whether we move in the direction of crime or of law-abiding behavior.

Bruinsma and Bernasco (2004) used *social network theory* to describe and tentatively explain differences in social organization between criminal groups that perform three types of transnational illegal activities: smuggling and large-scale heroin trading, trafficking in women, and trading in stolen cars. Groups that operate in the large-scale heroin market tend to be close-knit, cohesive, and ethnically homogeneous. Groups active in the trafficking of women have a chain structure, while three clusters of offenders in a chain characterize those that operate in the market for stolen cars. Both groups are less cohesive than are criminal groups in the large-scale heroin market. The differences in social organization between the three types of illegal activities appear to be related to the legal and financial risks associated with the crimes in question and, thereby, to the required level of trust between collaborating criminals.

It is often argued that criminal organizations have a network structure. For example, similar to other forms of organized criminality (including weapons trafficking, immigrant smuggling, and prostitution), drug trafficking in Colombia occurs in fluid social systems where flexible exchange networks expand and retract according to market opportunities and regulatory constraints. This durable, elastic structure did not emerge overnight, but developed over many years as entrepreneurs built their enterprises through personal contacts and repeated exchanges and resources they accumulated gradually, while drawing on social traditions, such as contraband smuggling, that extend far back into Colombia's colonial past (Kenney, 2007).

Entrepreneurs and entrepreneurship are often found in organized crime. Casson (2008) defines an entrepreneur as someone who specializes in making judgmental decisions about the coordination of scarce resources. Coordination may be defined as a beneficial reallocation of resources. Thus, coordination is a dynamic concept, as opposed to allocation, which is a static concept. The concept of coordination captures the fact that the entrepreneur is an agent of change. He is not concerned merely with the perpetuation of the existing allocation of resources, but with improving upon it.

Krebs et al. (2003) applied noncooperative *game theory* to examine drug smuggling. The study tried to determine if fluctuations in key public policy variables have the potential to diminish the expected utility of smuggling drugs, thus encouraging lawful behavior. The study simulation indicated that decreasing the expected utility of smuggling drugs to a level where lawful behavior is likely to be chosen is an infeasible mission from a policy perspective. Additionally, a recent drug smuggling innovation, known as black powder, is likely to only increase the expected benefit of drug smuggling. Black powder is a simple industrial cloaking method that renders many surveillance strategies and chemical tests all but futile. The consequences of black powder and the exchange between drug control agents and drug smugglers are important in the simulation.

Based on the utility theory, game theory involves the mathematical representation of the decision-making process in situations where the interests of two or more players are interconnected and interdependent. A player may be either an individual or a group that operates as a single decision-making entity. Players in situations of uncertainty choose from a set of available actions called strategies, each of which offers a probability of producing a possible outcome. The choice a player makes is determined by the anticipated utility, viewed as an indication of the individual's beliefs and preferences, that each alternative behavioral strategy is expected to produce (Krebs et al., 2003).

It has been argued that some ethnic backgrounds are less qualified for organized crime. For example, law enforcement in the United States is somewhat reluctant to accept the existence of African American criminal organizations, based primarily on the opinion that such ethnic groups are incapable of structuring syndicates of any consequence, such as the Cosa Nostra. Such an opinion is based on the *theory of race*. Contrary to this opinion, Walsh (2004) found powerful black organized crime groups in the United States. For example, African Americans established connections with Asian drug dealers during the Vietnam War. Some of the heroin on the streets of American cities during this period had been smuggled from Vietnam inside the bodies of dead servicemen.

Profit-driven crime by criminal business enterprises should be understood mainly in economic terms rather than sociological or criminological terms. In an attempt to formulate a general *theory of profit-driven crime*, Naylor (2003) proposed a typology that shifts the focus from actors to actions by distinguishing between market crime, predatory crime, and commercial crime.

Management Theories

Agency theory has broadened the risk-sharing literature to include the agency problem that occurs when cooperating parties have different goals and division of labor. The cooperating parties are engaged in an agency relationship defined as a contract under which one or more persons (the principals) engage another person (agent) to perform some service on their behalf, which involves delegating some decision-making authority to the agent (Jensen and Meckling, 1976). Agency theory describes the relationship between the two parties using the metaphor of a contract.

According to Eisenhardt (1985), agency theory is concerned with resolving two problems that can occur in agency relationships. The first is the agency problem that arises when the desires or goals of the principal and the agent conflict and it is difficult or expensive for the principal to verify what the agent is actually doing. The second is the problem of risk-sharing that arises when the principal and agent have different risk preferences. The first agency problem appears when the two parties do not share productivity gains. The risk-sharing problem might be the result of different attitudes toward the use of new technologies. Because the unit of analysis is the contract governing the relationship between the two parties, the focus of the theory is on determining the most efficient contract governing the principal–agent relationship given assumptions about people (e.g., self-interest, bounded rationality, risk aversion), organizations (e.g., goal conflict of members), and information (e.g., information is a commodity that can be purchased).

Garoupa (2007) applied agency theory to criminal organizations. He models the criminal firm as a family business with one principal and several agents. He has in mind an illegal monopoly where it is difficult to detect and punish the principal unless an agent is detected. Furthermore, it is assumed that agents work rather independently, so that the likelihood of detection of one agent is fairly independent from another. An example of such agents is drug dealers on the street, with the principal being the local distributor. Another example would be agents as extortionists or blackmailers distributed across the city with the principal being the coordinator of their activities providing them information or criminal know-how.

Alliance theory is concerned with partnership, often referred to as an alliance, which has been noted as a major feature of criminal organizations. Partnership can reduce the risk of inadequate contractual provision. Trust is a critical success factor in partnerships, and criminal organizations are often based on trust between their members. von Lampe and Johansen (2003) identified four kinds of trust in organized crimes. First, individualized trust relates specifically to agreeable behavior of an individual. Next, trust based on reputation relates to the trust, which is based on publicly formed and held opinion about the ones to be trusted. This type of trust hinges on the flow of information. Information may be dispersed in a context associated with illegality, e.g., the underworld "grapevine system."

The third kind of trust is generalized trust, which comprises configurations in which trust is linked to social groups rather than to a particular individual. The trustor places trust in the trustee based on the presumption that the trustee conforms to some more general norms or patterns of behavior, for example, codes of conduct, such as mutual support and noncooperation with law enforcement that the trustee can be expected to share as a member of a subculture or association. Finally, there is abstract trust, which refers to trust that is placed in abstract systems that set and maintain certain basic conditions, e.g., the government, the monetary system, or the medical system in society at large (von Lampe and Johansen, 2003).

Das and Teng (2002) studied how alliance conditions change over the different stages of alliance development to understand the development processes. They defined the following stages in the alliance development process:

- *Formation Stage.* Partner firms approach each other and negotiate the alliance. They then carry out the agreement and set up the alliance by committing various types of resources. The alliance is initiated and put into operation. Alliances will be formed only under certain conditions. These conditions include a relatively high level of collective strengths, a low level of interpartner conflicts, and a high level of interdependencies.

- *Operation Stage.* Not only is the formation stage directly influenced by alliance conditions, the transition from the formation stage to the operation stage is also dictated by the same alliance conditions variables. During the operation stage, partner firms collaborate and implement all agreements of the alliance. The alliance will likely grow rapidly in size during this stage, somewhat akin to the growth stage of organizational life cycles. Other than the growth route, an alliance also may be reformed and/or terminated at this stage.

- *Outcome Stage.* During this stage, alliance performance becomes tangible and can thus be evaluated with some certainty. There are four possible outcomes for an alliance at this stage—stabilization, reformation, decline, and termination. A combination of outcomes is also possible, such as a termination after reformation. Alliance reformation and alliance termination do not necessarily signal alliance failure. Reformation and termination may be the best option under certain circumstances, such as the achievement of preset alliance objectives. Alliance condition variables continue to play a decisive role in the outcome stage. The particular alliance outcome will depend on the condition of the alliance.

Das and Teng (2003) discussed partner analysis and alliance performance in their journal article. An important stream of research in the alliance literature is about partner selection. It emphasizes the desirability of a match between the partners, mainly in terms of their resource profiles. The approach is consistent with the resource-based theory of the firm, which suggests that competitors are defined by their resources profiles.

Network theory argues that when locating transnational crime, it is often found that networks are the media through which individuals and groups move between the local and the global. According to Beare (2000), empirical research reveals that networks consist of a complex mix of criminals that range from the sophisticated specialists to the opportunists—all operating within the same crime field.

According to network theory, a network exhibits network externalities in terms of external effects. An organization exhibits network externalities when it becomes more valuable to members, as more people join and take advantage of it. A classic example from technology is the telephone, where the value for each subscriber increases exponentially with the number of network subscribers to whom you can talk and from whom you can receive services.

Lemieux (2003) argues that criminal organizations are both networks and businesses. Criminal organizations, when viewed as networks, have characteristics common to other social networks as well as specific characteristics associated with the fact that these organizations are criminal businesses. Common characteristics include size of networks, density, couplings, and ties.

In criminal networks, the core is generally composed of actors connected by strong ties, while the relationship between the core and the surrounding subnetworks is achieved through weak ties. These are ties through which information is transmitted in an upward direction and orders are transmitted in a downward direction (Lemieux, 2003).

Lemieux describes seven roles that can be found in all networks, and one individual can assume more than one role. They include:

1. *Organizers* are the core and determine the scale and scope of activities.
2. *Insulators* transmit information and orders between the core and the periphery while insulating the core from the danger posed by infiltration.
3. *Communicators* ensure feedback is obtained regarding orders and directives that they transmit to other actors in the network.
4. *Guardians* ensure network security and take necessary measures to minimize its vulnerability to infiltrations or external attack.
5. *Extenders* enlarge the network by recruiting new members and also by negotiating collaboration with other networks and encouraging collaboration with the business sector, government, and justice.
6. *Monitors* are dedicated to the network's effectiveness by providing information to organizers regarding weaknesses and problems within the network so that the organizers can resolve them.
7. *Crossovers* are part of a criminal network, but continue to work in legal institutions, whether governmental, financial, or commercial.

Several of the seven roles make it difficult to combat criminal networks. According to Lemieux (2003), this is particularly true for the roles of insulators, guardians, monitors, and crossovers.

Contractual theory is concerned with the role of contracts in social systems. von Lampe (2005) suggests that cooperation in a criminal group is typically based on some form of contract between criminals, which is connected to a criminal activity and might cover several elements, such as participation, tasks, responsibility, equipment, plans, profit sharing, escape routes, behavioral codes, and norms.

Luo (2002) examined how contract, cooperation, and performance are associated with one another. He argues that contract and cooperation are not substitutes but complements in relation to performance. A contract alone is insufficient to guide evolution and performance. Because organized crime often involves both intraorganizational as well as interorganizational exchanges that become socially embedded over time, cooperation is an important safeguard mechanism mitigating external and internal hazards and overcoming adaptive limits of contracts. The simultaneous use of both contractual and cooperative mechanisms is particularly critical to organized crime in an uncertain environment.

Relational contract theory was created by Macneil (2000), who has been doing relational contracts since the mid-1960s, and who by contract means relations among people who have exchanged, are exchanging, or expect to be exchanging in the future, in other words, exchange relations. He finds that experience has shown that the very idea of a contract as relations in which exchange occurs—rather than as specific transactions, specific agreements, specific promises, specific exchanges, and the like—is extremely difficult for many people to grasp. Either that or they simply refuse to accept that contract can be defined as relations among people in an exchange. Macneil (2000) searched for roots to summarize contract in a useful manner. He tried to distill what he found into a manageable number of basic behavioral categories growing out of these roots. Because repeated human behavior invariably creates norms, these behavioral categories are also normative categories. He identified the ten common contract behavioral patterns and norms: (1) role integrity—requiring consistency, involving internal conflict, and being inherently complex; (2) reciprocity—the principle of getting something back for something given; (3) implementation of planning; (4) effectuation of consent; (5) flexibility; (6) contractual solidarity; (7) the restitution, reliance, and expectation interests—the linking norms; (8) creation and restraint of power—the power norm; (9) proprietary of means; and (10) harmonization with the social matrix, i.e., with supracontract norms. Relational contract theory postulates that where the ten common contract norms are inadequately served, exchange relations of whatever kind will fall apart.

Neoclassical economic theory regards every business organization as a production function (Williamson, 1981), and where their motivation is driven by profit maximization. This means that companies offer products and services to the market where they have a cost or production advantage. For criminal organizations, this theory has an impact on the production function in organized crime.

Theory of core competencies is a popular theory in legal businesses. According to Prahalad and Hamel (1990), core competencies are the collective learning in the organization, especially how to coordinate diverse production skills and integrate multiple streams of technologies. Because core competence is about harmonizing streams of technology, it is also about the organization of work and the delivery of value. For criminal organizations, this theory has an impact on the in-house competencies for organized crime.

Resource-based theory implies that unique organizational resources of both tangible and intangible nature are the real source of competitive advantage. With resource-based theory, organizations are viewed as a collection of resources that are heterogeneously distributed within and across industries. Accordingly, what makes the performance of an organization distinctive is the unique blend of the resources it possesses. A firm's resources include not only its physical assets, such as plant and location, but also its competencies. The ability to leverage distinctive internal and external competencies relative to environmental situations ultimately affects the performance of the business (Hitt et al., 2001). For criminal organizations, there is a need for strategic resources, which are characterized by being valuable, nonimitable, nontransferable, exploitable, and combinable.

Relational exchange theory is based on relational norms. Contracts are often extremely imperfect tools for controlling opportunism. While relational contracts may mitigate some opportunistic behavior, significant residual opportunism may remain. It is possible that transactors using relational contracts may incur significant ex-post bargaining costs as they periodically negotiate contract adjustments (Artz and Brush, 2000). Relational norms concerned with behavior in critical situations are critical for criminal organizations.

Stakeholder theory implies that the identification of stakeholders and their needs is important for decision making in organizations. A stakeholder is any group or individual who can affect, or is affected by, the achievement of a corporation's purpose. Stakeholder theory is distinct because it addresses morals and values explicitly as a central feature of managing organizations. The ends of cooperative activity and the means of achieving these ends are critically examined in stakeholder theory in a way that they are not in many theories of strategic management (Phillips et al., 2003). Important stakeholders for a criminal organization might, for example, be the mafia boss and the mayor.

Theory of firm boundaries claims that the resource-based view, transaction costs, and options perspectives each explain only a portion of managerial motivation for decisions on firm boundaries. Firm boundaries are often determined by the scale and scope of activities found to be manageable. The rationale supporting the choices organizations make regarding member sourcing is multidimensional; firms are not only seeking potential sources of competitive advantage, but are also seeking to avoid opportunism and to preserve or create flexibility (Schilling and Steensma, 2002). There has been renewed debate on the determinants of firm boundaries and their implications for performance. According to Schilling and Steensma, the widely accepted framework of transaction cost economics has come under scrutiny as a comprehensive theory for firm scale and scope. At the heart of this debate is whether the underlying mechanism determining firm boundaries is a fear of opportunism (as posited by transaction cost economics), a quest for sustainable advantage (as posed by resource-based view theorists and others), a desire for risk-reducing flexibility (as has recently gained increased attention in work on options), or a combination of factors. Although perspectives on firm boundaries, such as transaction costs or the resource-based view, are based on fundamentally different motivations for pursuing hierarchical control over market contracts, they rely on common resource or context attributes as antecedents.

Social exchange theory was initially developed to examine interpersonal exchanges that are not purely economic. Several sociologists are responsible for the early development of this theory. These theorists view people's social behavior in terms of exchanges of resources. The need for social exchange is created by the scarcity of resources, prompting actors to engage one another to obtain valuable inputs. Social exchange can be defined as voluntary actions of individuals that are motivated by the return they are expected to obtain and typically, in fact, bring from others. Social exchange can be viewed as an ongoing reciprocal process in which actions are contingent on rewarding reactions from others. There are important differences between social exchanges and economic exchanges. Social exchanges may or may not involve extrinsic benefits with objective economic value. In contrast to economic exchanges, the benefits from social exchanges often are not contracted explicitly, and it is voluntary to provide benefits. As a result, exchange partners are uncertain whether they will receive benefits. Thus, social exchange theory focuses on the social relations among the actors that shape the exchange of resources and benefits. While its origins are at the individual level, social exchange theory has been extended to organizational and interorganizational levels (Das and Teng, 2002).

We have introduced above twelve management theories concerned with criminal organizations. These theories are compared in Table 1.1 in terms of what they imply for criminal organizations.

Alien Conspiracy Theory in the United States

As previously mentioned, one of the most widely held theories of organized crime today in the United States is known as the alien conspiracy theory. This theory blames outsiders and outside influences for the prevalence of organized crime in society. Over the years, unsavory images, such as well-dressed men of foreign descent standing in shadows with machine guns and living by codes of silence, have become associated with this theory. The alien conspiracy theory posits that organized crime (the Mafia) gained prominence during the 1860s in Sicily and that Sicilian immigrants are responsible

Table 1.1   Summary of Management Theories

#	Theory	What Is Important for Criminal Organizations?
1	Agency theory	The principal and agent(s) need to have common goals and the same degree of risk willingness and aversion
2	Alliance theory	Interdependence between the partners based on trust, comfort, understanding, flexibility, cooperation, shared values, goals and problem solving, interpersonal relations, and regular communication
3	Network theory	Network externalities and different roles in the network
4	Contractual theory	Common contract behavioral patterns include role integrity, reciprocity, implementation of planning, effectuation of consent, flexibility, contractual solidarity, reliance, restraint of power, proprietary of means, and harmonization with the social environment
5	Transaction cost theory	Frequent and standardized interactions
6	Neoclassical economic theory	More cost-effective production than competitors
7	Theory of core competencies	Improvement in core capabilities and competencies
8	Resource-based theory	Strategic resources are unique, valuable, difficult to imitate, exploitable, and difficult to substitute
9	Relational exchange theory	Norms determine behavior in three main dimensions: flexibility, information exchange, and solidarity
10	Stakeholder theory	Balance interests of powerful people
11	Theory of firm boundaries	Portfolio management
12	Social exchange theory	Only where each of the parties can follow their own self-interest when transacting with the other self-interested actor to accomplish individual goals that they cannot achieve alone and without causing hazards to the other party

for the foundations of U.S. organized crime, which is made up of twenty-five or so Italian-dominated crime families (Lyman and Potter, 2007).

The U.S. Federal Bureau of Investigation (FBI, 2008) argues that international organized crime poses eight strategic threats to the United States:

- *Threat 1: International organized criminals have penetrated the energy and other strategic sectors of the economy.* International organized criminals and their associates control significant positions in the global energy and strategic materials markets, which are vital to U.S. national security interests. They are now expanding their holdings in the U.S. strategic materials sector. Their activities tend to corrupt the normal workings of these markets and have a destabilizing effect on U.S. geopolitical interests.

- *Threat 2: International organized criminals provide logistical and other support to terrorists, foreign intelligence services, and governments.* Each of these groups is either targeting the United States or otherwise acting in a manner adverse to U.S. interests.
- *Threat 3: International organized criminals smuggle and/or traffic people and contraband goods into the United States.* Smuggling/trafficking activities seriously compromise U.S. border security and at times national security. Smuggling of contraband/counterfeit goods costs U.S. businesses billions of dollars annually, and the smuggling/trafficking of people leads to exploitation that threatens the health and lives of human beings.
- *Threat 4: International organized criminals exploit the U.S. and international financial systems to move illicit funds.* International organized criminals transfer billions of dollars of illicit funds annually through the U.S. financial system. To continue this practice, they seek to corrupt financial and nonfinancial intermediaries globally.
- *Threat 5: International organized criminals use cyberspace to target U.S. victims and infrastructure.* International organized criminals use an endless variety of cyberspace schemes to steal hundreds of millions of dollars at a cost to consumers and the U.S. economy. These schemes jeopardize the security of personal information, the stability of business and government infrastructures, and the security and solvency of financial investment markets.
- *Threat 6: International organized criminals are manipulating securities exchanges and perpetrating sophisticated frauds.* Increasingly, U.S. domestic and international securities markets have become ripe sectors for abuse by international organized criminals who seek to enrich themselves from the pockets of unsuspecting investors. Using the fast-paced securities markets, the Internet, and the wire services—where money, communications, and inducements can be exchanged in milliseconds—international organized criminals manipulate international borders and the limitations in law enforcement's detection capability to their advantage without the need to set up a base of operations in any one location.
- *Threat 7: International organized criminals corrupt and seek to corrupt public officials in the United States and abroad.* They corrupt public officials to operate and protect their illegal operations, and to increase their sphere of influence. In some countries, corrupt public figures and organized criminals have attained status, power, and wealth far outweighing those of legitimate authorities. In others, corruption occurs as an accepted means of doing business. Corrupt leaders in such countries who aid, support, and are beholden to organized crime cause substantial harm to their own people and often

to U.S. strategic interests. In the most serious instances, the corrupt official is himself or herself, for all practical purposes, the leader of an organized criminal group.

- *Threat 8: International organized criminals use violence and the threat of violence as a basis for power.* Violent tactics are one of the tools applied by organized crime groups. Violence is used as a threat to the physical security of individuals as well as to the economic well-being of people and neighborhoods, and as a threat to the ability of law enforcement to investigate their crimes when the threat of violence is used as a tool of coercion.

In summary, the FBI (2008) calls for an improved understanding of organized crime and criminal organizations to respond better in terms of policing and law enforcement.

The Organized Crime Control Act in the United States defines organized crime as "the unlawful activities of … a highly organized, disciplined association." The act of engaging in criminal activity as a group is referred to in the United States as racketeering, which is often prosecuted federally under the Racketeer Influenced and Corrupt Organizations Act. The FBI operates an organized crime section from its headquarters in Washington, D.C. and is known to work with other national law enforcement agencies, e.g., Polizia di Stato in Mexico and the Royal Canadian Mounted Police in Canada. The FBI works with federal (e.g., Drug Enforcement Administration and the U.S. Coast Guard), state (e.g., Massachusetts State Police Special Investigation Unit and New York State Police Bureau of Criminal Investigation), and city (e.g., New York Police Department Organized Crime Unit and Los Angeles Police Department Special Operations Divisions) law enforcement agencies.

Perhaps the best-known criminal organization supporting the alien conspiracy theory is the Sicilian mafia, which expanded into the United States as Cosa Nostra. The movie *The Godfather* had more influence on the public mind and the minds of many public officials than did any library filled with scholarly works that argued for the true nature of organized crime, noted Kenney and Finckenauer (1995). Don Corleone was the consigliori to the family. Between the head of the family, Don Corleone, who dictated policy, and the operating level of men who actually carried out the orders of the Don, there were three layers, or buffers. In that way, nothing could be traced to the top.

The Canada/U.S. organized crime threat assessment (FBI, 2006) seems to be inspired by the alien conspiracy theory as well. In the threat assessment from 2006, key findings are:

- A high level of criminal entrepreneurship distinguishes Asian Organized Crime (AOC) groups. They use both personal relationships and specific business and technological skills to maximize profit.
- AOC is active throughout Canada and the United States, from major metropolitan areas and their suburbs to isolated rural communities.
- Over the past decade, preexisting underground economies of the former Soviet Union (FSU) and its satellite states have transformed into fully realized transnational organized crime syndicates.
- Increasingly, Russian organized crime is characterized by fluid, cellular-type structures. Senior members/associates of Russian criminal groups appear to recognize and accept the hegemony of a single "criminal authority" who plays an important role in dispute resolution, decision making, and the administration of criminal funds.
- Italian Organized Crime/La Cosa Nostra (IOC/LCN) is the most mature form of organized crime in both Canada and the United States. Its ability to form alliances with and co-opt other organized crime groups gives it global influence.
- In both Canada and the United States, IOC/LCN is distinguished by its strict, vertically integrated, hierarchical structure. The resulting discipline and efficiency permit these groups to focus resources and maximize profit.
- African criminal enterprises are engaged in a variety of low- and midlevel criminal activities, which include a number of financial fraud schemes.
- Albanian criminal groups are engaged in a range of cross-border criminal activities, including drug smuggling and money laundering.
- U.S. authorities have reported a significant decrease in seizures and availability of Canadian pseudoephedrine. This development is attributable to joint Canada and U.S. law enforcement efforts and recent changes to legislation governing the sale of pseudoephedrine and ephedrine for export.
- Expanding financial, telecommunications, trade, and transportation systems that support global economies also provide abundant opportunities for criminal exploitation. Identity theft, money laundering, and Internet fraud are a few of the financial crimes that are growing in scale, scope, and sophistication.
- While there are few concrete linkages between Canadian and U.S. gangs, many street gangs appear to be evolving into significant criminal enterprises with international implications.
- Globally, human trafficking and migrant smuggling are the third largest sources of revenue for organized crime, after drugs and arms

trafficking. Women and children are particularly vulnerable to this form of exploitation.
- Middle Eastern/Southwest Asian criminal enterprises are typically loosely organized theft or financial fraud rings that increasingly use small, legitimate cash businesses to facilitate their activities.

Case: National Intelligence Strategy of the United States

The National Intelligence Strategy of the United States of America was published in October 2005 under the heading *Transformation through Integration and Innovation* by the Office of the Director of National Intelligence (ODNI) in Washington, D.C. (www.odni.gov). The new concept of national intelligence codified by the Intelligence Reform and Terrorism Prevention Act passed by Congress in 2004 has its origins in the tragedy of September 11, 2001, and the President's National Security Strategy of the United States of America, first issued on September 17, 2002.

The *vision* of the National Intelligence Strategy is to become a unified enterprise of innovative, intelligence professionals, whose common purpose in defending American lives and interests and advancing American values and draws strength from U.S. democratic institutions, diversity, and intellectual and technological prowess.

The *mission* is formulated in terms of what the United States must do:

- Collect, analyze, and disseminate accurate, timely, and objective intelligence, independent of political considerations, to the president and all who make and implement U.S. national security policy, fight U.S. wars, protect the nation, and enforce U.S. laws.
- Conduct the U.S. government's national intelligence program and special activities as directed by the president.
- Transform U.S. capabilities in order to stay ahead of evolving threats to the United States, exploiting risk while recognizing the impossibility of eliminating it.
- Deploy effective counterintelligence measures that enhance and protect our activities to ensure the integrity of the intelligence system, U.S. technology, U.S. armed forces, and U.S. government's decision processes.
- Perform national duties under law in a manner that respects the civil liberties and privacy of all Americans.

While the vision tells what the United States will become, the mission tells what the United States must do, and the *strategy* tells how the United States will succeed. The fifteen strategic objectives in the intelligence strategy are differentiated as mission objectives and enterprise objectives. While mission objectives relate to efforts to predict, penetrate, and preempt threats, enterprise objectives relate to the capacity to maintain competitive advantages over states and forces that threaten U.S. security.

Mission *objectives* include defeating terrorists, preventing spread of weapons of mass destruction, and sustaining a peaceful and democratic United States. Enterprise objectives include building an integrated intelligence capability, strengthening analytic expertise, strengthening foreign intelligence relationships, creating uniform security practices, and eliminating redundancy.

Intelligence is concerned with information collection and analysis. In terms of information collection, the National Intelligence Strategy (ODNI, 2006, 12) stresses that:

> Our technical means of collecting information must remain unmatched. They allow us to avert conflict, expand peace, and win wars. The nation gains when our technical systems are developed for multiple purposes, but long development schedules and changing requirements undermine our agility and resources. Accordingly, the Intelligence Community must:
>
> - Expand collection and analysis from open sources, and manage them as integrated intelligence activities.
> - Establish a national clandestine service to integrate all the elements of human source collection in accord with the highest traditions of professionalism and intellectual prowess.
> - Rebalance the technical collection architecture to improve responsiveness to user requirements; enhance flexibility and survivability; and provide new sources and methods for current and emerging targets.
> - Expand the reporting of information of intelligence value from state, local, and tribal law enforcement entities and private sector stakeholders.

The next step for this intelligence strategy was to develop a strategic planning and evaluation process as well as performance guidance to reflect vision, mission, strategy, and objectives (ODNI, 2006).

In 2008, the ODNI published *Vision 2015*, which expands upon the notion of an intelligence enterprise, first introduced in the National Intelligence Strategy and later in the 100- and 500-Day Plans (ODNI, 2008). It charts a new path forward for a globally networked and integrated intelligence enterprise for the twenty-first century, based on the principles of integration, collaboration, and innovation.

The vision is focused on knowledge management (ODNI, 2008, 15):

> By 2015, the focus should shift from information sharing (e.g., interoperable systems, information discovery and access) to knowledge sharing (e.g., capturing and disseminating both explicit and tacit knowledge). Just as we are dismantling today's

information "silos", we will need to bridge the knowledge "archipelagos" of tomorrow in a systematic way that combines both content and context in an on-demand environment. Robust social networking capabilities will be required – expertise location, ubiquitous collaboration services, integrated e-learning solutions, visualization tools, and enterprise content management systems. More importantly, a strategic approach to knowledge sharing and management must be incorporated that includes lessons learned and concept and doctrine development.

When discussing implementation, ODNI (2008) stresses the importance of adaptability, alignment, and agility. Adaptability is an organization's aptitude for anticipating, sensing, and responding successfully to changes in the environment. Alignment is the degree of consistency and coherence among an institution's core strategy, systems, processes, and communications. Agility is an organization's ability to reconfigure processes and structures quickly—with minimal effort and resources—to seize opportunities and address strategic risks.

References

Abadinsky, H. 2007. Organized crime, 8th ed., Belmont, CA: Thomson/Wadsworth.

Artz, K.W. and Brush, T.H. 2000. Asset specificity, uncertainty and relational norms: An examination of coordination costs in collaborative strategic alliances. *Journal of Economic Behavior & Organization* 41: 337–362.

Beare, M.E. 2000. Structures, strategies and tactics of transnational criminal organizations: Critical issues for enforcement. Paper presented at the *Transnational Crime Conference* convened by the Australian Institute of Criminology in association with the Australian Federal Police and Australian Customs Service and held in Canberra, March 9–10.

Bruinsma, G. and Bernasco, W. 2004. Criminal groups and transnational illegal markets. *Crime, Law and Social Change* 41 (1): 79–94.

Casson, M. 2008. *The entrepreneur: An economic theory*, 2nd ed., Cheltenham, U.K.: Edward Elgar Publishing.

Chang, J.J., Lu, H.C., and Chen, M. 2005. Organized crime or individual crime? Endogenous size of a criminal organization and the optimal law enforcement. *Economic Inquiry* 43 (3): 661–675.

Colquitt, J.A. and Zapata-Phelan, C.P. 2007. Trends in theory building and theory testing: A five-decade study of the *Academy of Management Journal, Academy of Management Journal* 50 (6): 1281–1303.

Das, T.K. and Teng, B.S. 2002. The dynamics of alliance conditions in the alliance development process. *Journal of Management Studies* 39 (5): 725–746.

Das, T.K. and Teng, B.S. 2003. Partner analysis and alliance performance. *Scandinavian Journal of Management* 19: 279–308.

Eisenhardt, K.M. 1985. Control: Organizational and economic approaches. *Management Science* 31 (2): 134–149.

Federal Bureau of Investigation (FBI) 2006. *Canada/U.S. organized crime threat assessment*, Washington D.C.: Government Printing Office.

Federal Bureau of Investigation (FBI) 2008. *Department of justice launches new law enforcement strategy to combat increasing threat of international organized crime*, Press Release: April 23, www.fbi.gov. *Overview of the law enforcement strategy to combat international organized crime*, Washington, D.C.: U.S. Department of Justice.

Garoupa, N. 2007. Optimal law enforcement and criminal organization. *Journal of Economic Behavior & Organization* 63: 461–474.

Gottschalk, P. 2008. How criminal organizations work: Some theoretical perspectives. *The Police Journal* 81 (1): 46–61.

Gross, E. 1978. Organizational crime: A theoretical perspective. *Studies in Symbolic Interaction* 1: 55–85.

Hitt, M.A., Bierman, L., Shumizu, K., and Kochhar, R. 2001. Direct and moderating effects of human capital on strategy and performance in professional service firms: A resource-based perspective. *Academy of Management Journal* 44 (1): 13–28.

Jensen, M.C. and Meckling, W.H. 1976. Theory of the firm: Managerial behavior, agency costs and ownership structures. *Journal of Financial Economics* 3 (4): 305–360.

Kenney, D. and Finckenauer, J. 1995. *Organized crime in America*, New York: Wadsworth Publishing.

Kenney, M. 2007. The architecture of drug trafficking: Network forms of organization in the Colombian cocaine trade. *Global Crime* 8 (3): 233–259.

Krebs, C.P., Costelloe, M., and Jenks, D. 2003. Drug control policy and smuggling innovation: A game-theoretic analysis. *Journal of Drug Issues* 33 (1): 133–160.

Lemieux, V. 2003. *Criminal networks*. Ottawa, Canada: Royal Canadian Mounted Police.

Lombardo, R.M. 2002. Black hand: Terror by letter in Chicago. *Journal of Contemporary Criminal Justice* 18 (4): 394–409.

Luo, Y. 2002. Contract, cooperation, and performance in international joint ventures. *Strategic Management Journal* 23 (10): 903–919.

Lyman, M.D. and Potter, G.W. 2007. *Organized crime*, 4th ed. Upper Saddle River, NJ: Pearson Prentice Hall.

Macneil, I.R. 2000. Relational contract theory: Challenges and queries. *Northwestern University Law Review* 94 (3): 877–907.

Naylor, R.T. 2003. Towards a general theory of profit-driven crimes. *British Journal of Criminology* 43: 81–101.

Office of the Director of National Intelligence (ODNI). 2006. *The National Intelligence Strategy of the United States of America*. Washington, D.C.: Government Printing Office. Web site: www.odni.gov.

Office of the Director of National Intelligence (ODNI). 2008. *Vision 2015: A globally networked and integrated intelligence enterprise*. Washington, D.C.: Government Printing Office. Web site: www.odni.gov.

Phillips, R., Freeman, R.E., and Wicks, A.C. 2003. What stakeholder theory is not. *Business Ethics Quarterly* 13 (4): 479–502.

Prahalad, C.K. and Hamel, G. (1990). The core competence of the corporation. *Harvard Business Review* 76 (3): 79–91.

Schilling, M.A. and Steensma, H.K. 2002. Disentangling the theories of firm boundaries: A path model and empirical test. *Organization Science* 13 (4): 387–401.

Shvarts, A. 2001. The Russian mafia: Do rational choice models apply? *Michigan Sociological Review* 15: 29–63.

von Lampe, K. 2005. Organized crime in Europe. In *Handbook of transnational crime and Justice*, Ed. P. Reichel, 403–417. London: Sage Publications.

von Lampe, K. and Johansen, P.O. 2003. *Criminal networks and trust*. Paper presented at the 3rd annual meeting of the European Society of Criminology, Helsinki, Finland, August 29.

Walsh, A. 2004. *Race and crime*. New York: Nova Science Publishers.

Williamson, O.E. 1981. The modern corporation: Origins, evolution, attributes. *Journal of Economic Literature* (December) 1537–1568.

Entrepreneurship in Organized Crime

2

Organized crime by criminal entrepreneurs is not a new phenomenon. Felsen and Kalaitzidis (2005) describe historical cases, such as piracy, slavery, and opium smuggling. The most famous and far-reaching pirates in medieval Europe were the Vikings—warriors and looters from Scandinavia. They raided the coasts, rivers, and inland cities of all Western Europe as far as Seville in Spain. While being admired as entrepreneurial heroes at home, they were the most feared enemy abroad.

Organized Crime

There are numerous definitions in the literature about what constitutes organized crime; however, many are confusing, puzzling, or simply contradictory. As Abadinsky (2007) states, there is no generally accepted definition of organized crime. To further emphasize this point with regard to European attempts to define organized crime, von Lampe (2005) notes that the overall picture is murky, fragmented, and often contradictory because of culturally induced differences in perceptions and conceptualizations. Lyman and Potter (2007) summed up the definitional problem when they commented that the greatest problem in understanding organized crime is not the word *crime,* but the word *organized.*

Furthermore, part of the definitional problem is the idiosyncratic use of a range of different terms like mafia, mob, gang, syndicate, outfit, network, cell, club, cartel, and so forth, which are often used to characterize organized crime. In an attempt to somewhat overcome the definitional and theoretical challenge surrounding the meaning, nature, and conceptualization of organized crime, we have drawn on Albanese's (2004) work in which he has produced a definition of organized crime based on a consensus of writers, scholars, and researchers over the past 35 years regarding organized criminal activity. Albanese's (2004, 4) definition is:

> Organized crime is a continuing criminal enterprise that rationally works to profit from illicit activities that are often in great public demand. Its continuing existence is maintained through the use of force, threats, monopoly control, and/or the corruption of public officials.

This consensus definition of organized crime, while not perfect, is at least adequate for our purposes. It captures the essence very clearly of our thesis in this work, which is that first and foremost organized crime is an entrepreneurial business enterprise, regardless of what else it may be and/or what it involves. For our purposes, the central dynamic we are interested in exploring in this book is the notion of organized crime as entrepreneurship. Entrepreneurship involves risk-taking individuals who undertake industrial and commercial activities (businesses) with a view to making a profit. In the case of organized crime, such entrepreneurial risk-taking focuses on illegal activities as the core business strategy for profit making by those involved in the enterprise.

An organized crime is any crime committed by persons occupying, in an established division of labor, positions designed for the commission of crime. Organized crime is crime committed by criminal organizations whose existence has continuity over time and across crimes, and that may use systematic violence and corruption to facilitate their criminal activities. These criminal organizations have varying capacities to inflict economic, physical, psychological, and societal harm. The greater their capacity to harm, the greater the danger they pose to society. Organized crime involves a continuing enterprise in a rational fashion, geared toward profit achieved through illegal activities (van Duyne et al., 2003, 2005; Wright, 2006).

It is an ongoing criminal conspiracy, with a structure greater than any single member, and the potential for corruption and violence to facilitate the criminal process. When the U.S. Federal Bureau of Investigation (FBI, 2008) adds the word *international* in their new law enforcement strategy to combat increasing threat of international organized crime, they describe these groups as "self-perpetuating associations of individuals who operate internationally for the purpose of obtaining power, influence, monetary, and commercial gains, wholly or in part by illegal means, while protecting activities through a pattern of corruption and violence.

In order to speak about organized crime, according to the European Union, at least six out of a set of eleven characteristics need to be present, four of which must be those numbered 1, 3, 5, and 11 out of this list (Elvins, 2003):

1. *Collaboration of more than two people*
2. Each with own appointed tasks
3. *For a prolonged or indefinite period of time*
4. Using some form of discipline or control
5. *Suspected of the commission of serious criminal offences*
6. Operating at an international level
7. Using violence or other means suitable for intimidation
8. Using commercial or business-like structures

9. Engaged in money laundering
10. Exerting influence on politics, the media, public administration, judicial authorities, or the economy
11. ***Determined by the pursuit of profit and/or power***

Characteristic 8 suggests commercial or business-like structures, as assumed and explored in terms of managing organizations in this book. Several other characteristics are similar to those of traditional legal projects. For example, a project is normally a collaboration of more than two people (1), each with his/her own appointed tasks (2), and for a prolonged, not indefinite period of time (3). While an organized crime seldom will be for an indefinite period of time, the criminal organization might very well be. Compared to legal business projects, we suggest that criminal projects have a tighter control structure.

A typical criminal organization is the Russian Mafia group that was discovered by law enforcement on Mallorca in 2008. The Russian criminal entrepreneur is Genadijus Petrov, who set up a criminal enterprise on the Spanish island several years before the police discovered the group. The organization was a collaboration of twenty Russian criminals. The criminal organization on Mallorca was set up to launder money from criminal activities in the Russian Federation. After some time, the criminal enterprise expanded its business activities into other kinds of organized crime.

Symeonidou-Kastanidou (2007) argues that there is a need for a new definition of organized crime, where entrepreneurial structure is included as an important element. An entrepreneur is a person who operates a new enterprise or venture and assumes some accountability for the inherent risks. The view on entrepreneurial talent is a person who takes the risks involved to undertake a business venture. Entrepreneurship is often difficult and tricky, as many new ventures fail. In the context of the creation of for-profit enterprises, entrepreneur is often synonymous with founder. Business entrepreneurs often have strong beliefs about a market opportunity and are willing to accept a high level of personal, professional, or financial risk to pursue that opportunity.

An organization is considered to have entrepreneurial structure when the following elements cumulate: allocation of roles, hierarchy, and concrete structure. Allocation of roles within an organization occurs when a group of members is exclusively tasked with planning and preparation activities, a second is tasked with the implementation and execution of the plan, while a third is responsible for securing the proceeds. Hierarchy occurs when a predetermined superior–inferior relationship exists among members of the organization. Concrete structure is considered to exist when a group possesses its own assets, which enables the group to make a profit (Symeonidou-Kastanidou, 2007).

It is primarily the first and third of the above criterion that are perceived as harmful to society. These two ensure the organization's continuity and survival. Criminal organizations invest money and other resources so as to achieve power at a political level and to intervene in emerging markets (Symeonidou-Kastanidou, 2007).

Illegal Business

As indicated by our definition of organized crime drawn from Albanese (2004) above, this book is based on the enterprise paradigm of organized crime (Liddick, 1999, 404):

> The enterprise paradigm is really an approach to studying the problem of organized crime, grounded in the structural-functional school of sociology, general systems theory, and the theories of formal legal organizations.

Currently, a considerable number of academics and practitioners exist that perceive organized crime as networks rather than structured and rational hierarchies. In that school of thought, criminal activities are often driven by rational choice or entrepreneurship. This does not automatically lead to a rational organization of the criminal activities according to a rational business model. However, in our view, it is not at all the case that legal businesses are rational organizations. On the contrary, corporations are social systems filled with political and other nonrational activities. Hence, we argue that to apply the business enterprise paradigm, there is no need to assume either rationality or hierarchy in the criminal organization. We agree with Albanese (2004) who argues that the enterprise model of organized crime grew out of dissatisfaction with both the hierarchical and ethnic models that have dominated the criminological literature about how organized crime is structured.

A common view in the literature, according to Albanese (2004), is that research should focus on the factors that cause illicit relationships and, hence, criminal gangs to form. It is the conspiratorial gang-like nature of organized crime that sets it apart from individual criminal behavior. It is not the individual drug dealer and illegal casino operator or money lender that is the primary concern, but rather how these individuals entrepreneurially form an enterprise to organize links to customers and suppliers as well as their foot soldiers to provide illicit goods and services for profit.

Because many criminal organizations operate according to the network model rather than the hierarchical model, functions, such as marketing, logistics, and finance, may be spread to several places in the network. For example, in the American Mafia, a place might be a family (Abadinsky, 2007, 8):

> The member of the American Mafia, acting as a patron, controls certain resources as well as strategic contacts with people who control other resources directly or who have access to such persons. The member-as-patron can put a client "in touch with the right people." He can bridge communication gaps between the police and criminals, between businessmen and syndicate-connected union leaders; he can transcend the world of business and the world of the illegitimate entrepreneur. He is able to perform important favors and be rewarded in return with money or power. There is a network surrounding the patron, a circle of dyadic relationships orbiting the OC [organized crime] member in which most clients have no relations with another except through the patron.

Albanese (2004) argues that the realization that organized crime operates as a business spurred a series of studies in an effort to isolate those factors that contribute most significantly to the formation of criminal enterprises. For example, when applying general organization theory to criminal activity, it was found that organized crime stems from the same fundamental assumptions that govern entrepreneurship in the legitimate marketplace—a necessity to maintain and extend one's share of the market. According to this finding, organized crime groups form and thrive in the same way that legitimate businesses do—they respond to the needs and demands of suppliers, customers, regulators, and competitors. The only difference between organized crime and legitimate business is that organized criminals deal in illegal products, whereas legitimate businesses generally do not.

The supply of illegal goods and services does not seem to be marked by a tendency toward the development of large-scale criminal enterprises, due to the illegal nature of the product. Instead, smaller, more flexible, and efficient enterprises characterize this type of organized crime. While criminal entrepreneurship is focused on both establishing and growing the business over time, a decentralized structure may be chosen to avoid law enforcement, thereby creating more competition and economic rivalry.

We assume there is an evolutionary nature in criminal business enterprises. An entrepreneurial account of the nature of organized crime is inherently dynamic, in that it encourages the future to intrude on the explanation of the enterprise. The explanation of the enterprise lies not, or at least not solely, in forces that are visible today, it lies instead in how criminals organize to deal with an uncertain future.

Evolution in criminal business enterprise might be exemplified by Marzola's Studio. As a pedophile, Sergio Marzola discovered there was money to be made in the market. As an entrepreneur, he set up a secret Internet service for trading in images of children being raped by adults. The typical supplier of new images was a father raping his daughter. Marzola paid 250 euro for a daughter filmed in lingerie, 500 euro filmed naked, and, subsequently, 750 euro filmed being raped. Marzola was selling the images through Internet bulletin boards whose existence was known only to pedophiles. They spend only minutes or even seconds on these boards before making contact and then disappearing into private chat rooms to conduct business. Marzola is an Italian, but moved to Ukraine, where he bought a house and a studio in the city of Karkov. Young Ukrainian girls were raped and filmed in the Marzola's Studio. Marzola was arrested in 2006, sparking an international investigation that led to the arrests of 92 others.

Evolution might be defined as change in the characteristics of an organization over time. Evolution is a process that happens to an organization. An organization is not a stable entity, as it changes due to internal dynamics and reactions to the environment. Evolution is not a random process, it has a certain direction.

Langlois (2007, 1115) identified three factors that determine organizational change and development in firms:

1. *The pattern of existing capabilities in the firm and market.* Are existing capabilities distributed widely among many distinct organizations or are they contained importantly within the boundaries of large firms?
2. *The extent of the market and the level of development of market-supporting institutions.* To what extent can the needed capabilities be tapped through existing arrangements and to what extent must they be created from scratch? To what extent are there relevant standards and other market-supporting institutions?
3. *The nature called for by the economic change.* When technological change or changes in relative prices generate a profit opportunity, does seizing that opportunity require a systemic reorganization of capabilities (including the learning of new capabilities) or can change proceed in autonomous fashion along the lines of an existing division of labor?

Evolution will occur in several combinations of these factors. For example, when an entrepreneurial opportunity arises, a systemic rearrangement of capabilities and development of new capabilities will occur, especially when existing capabilities are dispersed and market-supporting institutions are weak.

The entrepreneurial theory of the criminal firm argues that entrepreneurship is a crucial element in explaining the nature and boundaries of the criminal enterprise. According to this theory, a criminal enterprise exists because of entrepreneurship. Here, entrepreneurship is the professional examination of how, by whom, and with what effects opportunities to create future profit are discovered, evaluated, and exploited. Entrepreneurship involves the study of sources of opportunities; the processes of discovery, evaluation, and exploitation of opportunities; and the set of individuals who discover, evaluate, and exploit them (Langlois, 2007).

The entrepreneurial theory of the criminal firm suggests that the criminal enterprise represents a realization of entrepreneurial vision. Setting up a firm organization means hiring staff whose services are not completely specified in advance by the employment or network arrangement. This incompleteness is compensated by entrepreneurial vision. An essential contribution from entrepreneurial vision to firm organizing of resources is the provision of a cognitive input in the form of a business conception. A business conception consists of subjective, sometimes highly idiosyncratic imaginings in the mind of an entrepreneur of what business is to be created and how to do it. Like a business frame, Witt (2007, 1127) argues that "a business conception is the basis for the entrepreneur's interpretation of incoming information with respect to its relevance and meaning for the imagined business venture."

An entrepreneurship perspective on the nature of the firm rests on two fundamental assumptions about the nature of business activity: profit-seeking individuals and asymmetrically dispersed knowledge across economic actors. The quest for profit, wealth, and power plays an important motivational role in the criminal entrepreneur's pursuit of new criminal business opportunities. Asymmetrically dispersed knowledge implies differentiated sets of knowledge held by decision makers, which in the business context causes variation in the ability to identify and assimilate new information and events. Individual decision makers tend to notice new information that relates to and can be combined with knowledge they already have (Zander, 2007).

When criminal entrepreneurs engage in knowledge-intensive ventures, the need for human and social capital exceeds the need for physical assets. Human capital might be defined as the abilities individuals possess and their demographic characteristics. Social capital might be defined as a network contributing to entrepreneurial goals, where resources are obtained through the social network of actors (Madsen et al., 2008).

Criminal Entrepreneurship

As already mentioned, an entrepreneur is a person who operates a new enterprise or venture and assumes some accountability for the inherent risk (Symeonidou-Kastanidou, 2007). The modern view on entrepreneurial talent is a person who takes the risks involved to undertake a business venture. Entrepreneurship is often difficult and tricky, as many new ventures fail. In the context of the creation of for-profit enterprises, entrepreneur is often synonymous with founder. Most commonly, the term *entrepreneur* applies to someone who creates value by offering a product or service in order to obtain certain profit.

Except for criminal entrepreneurs' readiness to use personal violence and the ability to shield oneself from it, other social or individual constrictions and qualities do not seem to differ that much from those encountered in successful legal businessmen, for example, among successful drug entrepreneurs in Colombia, is described by Zaitch (2002, 49):

> Opportunities to become a successful drug entrepreneur in Colombia have remained, of course, unequally distributed. Except for the readiness to use personal violence and the ability to shield oneself from it, other social or individual constrictions and qualities do not seem to differ that much from those encountered in successful legal businessmen: sex, age, personal or family contacts, entrepreneurial skills of all sorts, personal attributes such as creativity, alertness or charisma, skills to both exercise power and deal with existing power pressures, and luck.
>
> However, access to the entrepreneurial levels of cocaine business has been remarkably open to a wide and heterogeneous range of people. The social origins of cocaine entrepreneurs cannot be traced to one social, economic or ethnically specific group. Although some backgrounds and patterns can be observed according to regional differences and historic events, they far from constitute general trends.

Entrepreneurship is the practice of starting new organizations or revitalizing mature organizations, particularly new businesses, generally in response to identified opportunities. Entrepreneurship is sometimes labeled entrepreneurialism. Entrepreneurship is often a difficult undertaking, as a vast majority of new businesses fail. Entrepreneurial activity is substantially different from operational activity, as it is mainly concerned with creativity and innovation. Entrepreneurship ranges from small individual initiatives to major undertakings creating many job opportunities.

The majority of recent theories in the business and managerial economic literature assume that the economic performance of small- and medium-sized firms depends largely on the entrepreneur's (or team's) capacities. Even so, economists still do not fully understand the relationship between an entrepreneur and firm performance. The entrepreneurial process is the result of a complex interaction between individual, social, and environmental factors. Taken separately, neither the personality of the entrepreneur nor the structural characteristics of the environment can, on its own, determine an organization's performance (Thomas and Mancino, 2007).

In order to provide an example of the relationship between entrepreneurs' subjective characteristics/traits and organizational performance, Thomas and Mancino (2007) carried out an empirical study. It aimed to explain how the presence of entrepreneurs' specific subjective characteristics can influence an organization's strategic orientation and, as a consequence, local development. By analyzing several subjective characteristics taken from a sample of 101 successful entrepreneurs from southern Italy, certain issues emerge regarding the link between the economic performance of the ventures launched in this area and the weak level of growth. Successful entrepreneurs' behavior and decisions are heavily influenced by family support. The entrepreneurial culture of the family also tends to substitute the protective role played by public institutions. The entrepreneurial decisions of local entrepreneurs are triggered both by their need to rid themselves of poverty and their feeling that they are destined to continue the family business, the majority of them being the children of entrepreneurs. Most of the interviewees were classified as "necessity" rather than "opportunity" entrepreneurs.

An entrepreneur might be driven by a compulsive need to find new ways of allocating resources. He or she might be searching for profit-making opportunities and engineer incremental changes in products and processes. While strongly innovative entrepreneurs tend to champion radical changes in resource allocation by making new product markets and pioneering new processes, weakly innovative entrepreneurs tend to seek small changes in resource allocation to explore profit-making opportunities among already established activities (Markovski and Hall, 2007).

Founders of new legal firms tend to be experienced professionals who pursue opportunities closely related to their previous employment. Entrepreneurs often have several years of work experience in the same industry as their own start-up enterprises. This suggests that entrepreneurs do not come from out of the blue, but build their human intellectual capital through work experience in established firms. Similarly, criminal entrepreneurs might be experienced professionals before establishing their own criminal business enterprise.

Jacobides and Winter (2007) phrased the question: How do entrepreneurs choose the boundaries of their own ventures? To answer this question, they started from the premise that while entrepreneurs believe themselves to have superior ideas in one or multiple parts of value creation arenas, they are characteristically short of cash and of the ability to convince others to provide it. This premise motivates a simple model in which the entrepreneur has a value-adding set of ideas for parts of a value creation arena (e.g., smuggling of cocaine from Colombia to Germany via The Netherlands). Assuming that the entrepreneur's objective is to maximize criminal wealth, it might be observed that initial scope depends not only on available cash, but also on how much value the entrepreneur's ideas add to each participant in the organized crime. Entrepreneurs will focus on the areas that provide the maximum profit and minimum risk per available cash.

Audretsch and Keilbach (2007) operationalized entrepreneurship in terms of entrepreneurial behavior, which involves the activities of individuals who are associated with creating new organizations rather than the activities of individuals who are involved with maintaining or changing the operations of on-going established organizations. Accordingly, entrepreneurial thinking and the cognitive process associated with the identification of an opportunity can be viewed in conjunction with the decision to engage in entrepreneurial action.

Motivation and personality traits are part of an entrepreneurial initiative. Motivational needs of entrepreneurs typically include needs for achievement, affiliation, dominance, and autonomy. Personality traits of entrepreneurs typically include sociable, decisive, authoritative, goal-oriented, self-confidence, anxious, risk-taking, intuitive, internal locus of control, self-confident, and leadership (Seet et al., 2008).

Because motivation and personality traits often are an important part of an entrepreneurial initiative, Jayasinghe et al. (2008, 250) deem rationality and bounded rationality approaches as inappropriate for a comprehensive analysis of the entrepreneur:

> Such approaches marginalize the influence of emotions and the entrepreneur's private life and assume that entrepreneurial behavior is conditioned to rational and calculative self-interest. Treating the entrepreneur as an "integrated self," characterized by rationality and bounded rationality in her/his behavior, disguises the "unconscious motivations" of agential actions, while viewing emotions as operating outside her/his consciousness disregards their contribution to the entrepreneur's "practical consciousness."

Jayasinghe et al. (2008) argue that a framework is needed to define the entrepreneur as a socially situated agent exercising his or her own agency. In fact, entrepreneurs have many of the same characteristics as leaders, where social aspects are more focused than rational decision making. Entrepreneurship is a kind of leadership focusing on creativity and innovation. As leaders are sometimes contrasted with managers, so also are entrepreneurs. Managers tend to be administrators who are more methodical and less prone to risk-taking. The entrepreneur has an enthusiastic vision, the driving force of an enterprise. The entrepreneur's vision tends to be supported by a set of related ideas not spelled out before. The overall blueprint to realize the vision is clear; however, specific actions may be incomplete, flexible, and evolving.

Similarly, Williams (2006) argues that even if there are frequent debates whether specific ones should be included as entrepreneurs or not, the widespread agreement is that what is being defined and delineated is essentially a wholesome and virtuous subject. Entrepreneurs typically have several of the following characteristics: a need for independence, a need for achievement, internal locus of control, the ability to live with uncertainty and take measured risks, opportunistic, innovative, self-confident, proactive and decisive with higher energy, self motivated, and have vision and flair.

von Lampe (2007) made some observations on the social microcosm of illegal entrepreneurs. He examined the patterns of interaction of offenders involved in the importation and wholesale distribution of contraband cigarettes in Germany. He assumed that under normal circumstances offenders would prefer to operate alone and in complete isolation, but found that smugglers and wholesale distributors of contraband cigarettes came into contact with a number of individuals in the course of their illegal activities.

The social microcosm of an illegal entrepreneur includes all those individuals he or she encounters in the course of his or her criminal activities who are in a position to influence the success or failure of that particular criminal enterprise (von Lampe, 2007, 132):

> The concept of the "social microcosm of illegal entrepreneurs" encompasses three aspects that have variously been addressed in the criminological and organized crime literature: co-offending, the social embeddedness of criminal networks, and the interaction between illegal and legal spheres of society.

Co-offending includes the joint execution of criminal activity. Social embeddedness includes relatives, friends, and others in the personal network that participate in social transactions that do not have a criminal connotation as such, but do nevertheless have some bearing on the criminal activity. Interaction between illegal and legal institutional environments is typically visible in terms of corruption and infiltration.

von Lampe (2007) found that cigarette smugglers, like any other offender, do not operate in a social vacuum. As the stakes increase, cigarette smugglers increasingly rely on actors from outside their immediate social milieu. Contacts with legitimate third parties are established ad hoc.

Entrepreneurial orientation varies among criminal entrepreneurs as among legal entrepreneurs. Entrepreneurial orientation refers to the processes, practices, and decision-making activities used by entrepreneurs that lead to the initiation of an entrepreneurial enterprise. Proactiveness, risk-taking, and innovativeness are typical conceptualizations of entrepreneurial orientation. Proactiveness refers to an opportunity-seeking, forward-looking initiative that involves introducing new methods ahead of the competition. Risk-taking represents a behavior of taking bold actions with uncertain outcomes. Innovativeness refers to an ability to identify and stimulate creativity and experimentation in introducing new methods (Kropp et al., 2008).

Entrepreneurial Capital

When a criminal entrepreneur decides to set up a criminal enterprise, he or she will need capital to do so. Capital, in the financial sense, is the money that gives the business the power to buy goods and services to be used in the production of other goods or the offering of a service. For example, if the enterprise is to begin smuggling drugs, there will be a need for capital to buy drugs because smugglers have to pay their suppliers before they get paid from their customers.

In the legal sector of the economy, the corporate finance sector has the task of providing the funds for a corporation's activities. It generally involves balancing risk and profitability while attempting to maximize an entity's wealth and the value for its stakeholders. Long-term funds are provided by ownership equity and long-term credit. Banks that are extending a line of credit mostly provide short-term funding in terms of working capital. The balance between these forms is the company's capital structure.

To start up a criminal business enterprise, some of these options are not available to a criminal entrepreneur. Typically, the entrepreneur will need to search for funding from crime money, which will be available if the potential profit is high and the potential risk is low.

According to van Duyne (2007), in many cases, the money handled is in the form of cash and is carried around personally by criminals in their clothes, suitcases, on or in the body, boot of the car, or some other hiding place. Banking transactions are much less frequent. Dealing with crime money is different from dealing with clean money.

van Duyne (2007, 87) studied what wealthy criminals do with their ill-gotten money, their criminal money management as well as what they actually did with their money in economic terms:

> The criminal money-management (or laundering in common parlance) was carried out with a sophistication geared to the available acumen as well as what was required in the given circumstances. In general, the sophistication hardly mirrored the imagery of criminals-getting-smarter and always-"ahead-of-us." Ethnic minority crime-entrepreneurs with a social-economic home elsewhere used to take their money cash out of the country, while indigenous entrepreneurs faced always the requirement of justifying the acquired registered assets, like cars, boats, real estate and, of course, well-filled bank accounts. Apart from a few complicated and well thought out exceptions, extensive chains of financial cross-border transactions had a low frequency.

van Duyne (2007) found that the field of criminal finances and related activities (money laundering and the total set of countermeasures) is far from clear. The range and reach of crime markets is so large that no law enforcement agency seems capable of identifying all kinds of crime money transactions. Both origin and destination are hard to determine. In many official presentations, crime money flows are projected from tax haven to tax haven and to unstable states, but the evidence is not clear.

An important part in criminal finances of start-up enterprises is corruption. To get into a market, corruption is often required. Markovska (2007) tells the story how legal Western firms are able to start up in Ukraine if they bribe at different levels and in different sectors. For example, to get involved in the medical sector, the following actors need to be bribed by pharmaceutical companies:

- Pharmaceutical Committee in Kiev (the main absorbent of bribes, the first contact of Western pharmaceutical companies with Ukrainian reality). Most corrupt practice is tender purchase.
- Major hospitals (paid for clinical trials)
- Specialized hospitals (paid for research results and general publication)
- Local surgeries (basic equipment, torches, pens, and paper)

Markovska's (2007) study considered the systemic nature of corruption in Ukraine. The transition from Soviet rule and communism to independence and capitalism enabled many successful criminal enterprises to become established. Financing criminal enterprises became easy, as illegal privatization enabled criminals to quickly gain control over enormous wealth.

Corruption requires the presence of entrepreneurial capital. According to Pinto et al. (2008), corruption is a persistent feature of human societies, with the earliest references dating back to the fourth century BCE. Receivers of the funds can be corrupt individuals or corrupt organizations. When an individual is the beneficiary of the corrupt activity, the individual behaves as an agent by favoring the source at the expense of a third party. By applying agency theory, we label the corrupt individual an agent and the corrupting individual a principal, and the principal achieves a favor from the agent because of the benefit. When an organization is the beneficiary of the corrupt activity, the benefit results in unlawful organizational behavior and corporate crime.

The Case of Terrence "Terry" Adams*

Terrence "Terry" Adams is the head of Britain's most enterprising, and feared, organized crime gang—the Adams family, otherwise known as the A-Team, or the Clerkenwell Crime Syndicate. Terry was the oldest of eleven children, born to a law-abiding, working-class, Irish Catholic family. He grew up in Islington, north London. Terry was the closest to his younger brothers Patrick (a.k.a. Patsy) and Sean (a.k.a. Tommy) with whom he would go into a life of crime. That life of crime began by extorting money from traders and stallholders at street markets close to their home in the Clerkenwell area,

---

* This case was written by David Amoruso and published on the Internet (Amoruso, 2007).

before moving on to armed robberies. Patrick served seven years in prison for armed robbery in the 1970s.

Terry was the brain behind their criminal operations, Sean dealt with financial matters, and Patrick was the muscle. A former associate of the Adams brothers said: "Terry was always the most levelheaded one out of the bunch. His brother Tommy was wild and the other brother, Patsy, could be very wild and crazy. A lot of the people involved in this kind of business don't have a lot going on up top. But Terry and his brothers were different. They were a real class act. Terry was always well dressed and in charge of whatever was going on. When he walked into a room, everyone stood up. He was like royalty."

Terrence Adams was a criminal entrepreneur who initiated and operated a new enterprise and assumed some accountability for the inherent risks. As observed by Symeonidou-Kastanidou (2007), a criminal entrepreneur is a person who has the talent of taking risks involved in a new business venture. Terry was the founder who recruited his own brothers. Thomas and Mancino (2007) stated that successful entrepreneurs' behavior and decisions are heavily influenced by family support. The entrepreneurial culture of the family also tends to substitute the protective role played by public institutions. The criminal enterprise represented a realization of Terry's entrepreneurial vision.

By the 1980s, the Adams family moved into the drug trade. There was a huge demand for cocaine and cannabis in the 1980s, and then for the drug ecstasy during the 1990s. They built up links with Yardie groups and the Colombian cocaine cartels. The money made was laundered through various corrupt financiers, accountants, lawyers, and other professionals, and subsequently invested in property and other legitimate businesses.

Like most criminal groups (van Duyne et al., 2003, 2005; Wright, 2006), the Adams family ruled through intimidation and violence. They are rumored to have been involved in thirty murders. An accountant, Terry Gooderham, allegedly skimmed £250,000 of drug money from the Adams brothers. He was found dead, alongside his girlfriend, in Epping Forest in 1989.

A rival Irish family, the Reillys, challenged the Adams family's dominance of Islington. Patrick Adams and an associate went into a pub controlled by the Reillys. There the Adams associate insulted a Reillys member. The Reillys went away to arm themselves and returned to the pub. It was an ambush; their BMW was fired on repeatedly by members of the Adams gang. No one was killed, but the incident sent out a clear message: the Adams family runs Islington.

By the late 1990s, the heat was on. In 1998, Sean "Tommy" Adams was convicted of organizing an £8 million hashish-smuggling operation, and was sentenced to seven years imprisonment. When a judge ordered that he surrender some of his profits or face a further five years, his wife turned up twice to the court, carrying £500,000 in cash inside a briefcase on each occasion.

In May 2003, Terry Adams was arrested and charged with money laundering, tax evasion, and handling stolen goods. He was released on £1 million bail. And in February 2007, he pleaded guilty to conspiracy to launder £1.1 million. The judge said, "Your plea demonstrates that you have a fertile, cunning, and imaginative mind capable of sophisticated, complex, and dishonest financial manipulation." On March 9, 2007, Terry Adams at the age of 52 was sentenced to seven years in prison.

As a criminal entrepreneur, Terry is probably driven by a compulsive need to find new ways of allocating resources in organized crime while in prison. He has probably championed radical changes in resource allocation and pioneered new processes, as described by Markovski and Hall (2007).

The Case of Frank and Peter Lowy*

The U.S. Senate accused billionaire Frank Lowy of hiding millions of dollars to dodge taxes. A report from a U.S. Senate committee investigating the use of offshore tax havens has claimed that the billionaire Lowy family "used transfer companies and a foundation with a Delaware corporation to help … hide their beneficial interest in a foundation with US$68 million in assets."

Frank Lowy, founder of "the global shopping center," has been identified by the U.S. Senate Committee on Homeland Security and Governmental Affairs as a client of LGT (Liechtenstein Global Trust) Group, the secretive Liechtenstein bank owned by UBS (Union Bank of Switzerland) and the Liechtenstein royal family.

The Senate committee alleges LGT helped thousands of people avoid paying taxes thanks to its secretive systems and procedures. The names of LGT clients and the inner workings of the bank were exposed in 2008 when a disgruntled clerk at LGT, Heinrich Kieber, downloaded all the bank's names and secret accounts onto two CDs and turned them over to tax authorities in the United States and Europe.

The committee's report, which cites internal LGT memos and recorded telephone conversations, claims that Lowy wanted to shelter assets from the Australian Tax Office by setting up a foundation in Liechtenstein called Luperla Foundation.

The report further claims that LGT internal memos "note that Mr. Lowy had reached a settlement with the Australian Tax Office (and) did not want to bring new funds into Australia, and was concerned that if the Australian

---

* This case was written by James Thomas and published on the Internet (Thomson, 2008).

tax authorities learned of his having additional assets, the government might try to subject them to additional claims." Lowy paid $25 million in 1995 to settle a protracted dispute with the Australian tax office.

Lowy issued a statement confirming the tax office was conducting an audit of his affairs in relation to the Liechtenstein allegations. But he denied he had done anything improper. "No attempt was made to save any Australian tax. Nor is it considered that any Australian tax was in fact saved."

The statement also criticized the committee for relying on information stolen from the bank, and the subcommittee "failed to give Frank Lowy or his family any meaningful opportunity to be heard or otherwise have the true position stated. This amounts to a denial of natural justice."

References

Abadinsky, H. 2007. *Organised crime*, 8th ed. Belmont, CA: Thomson Wadsworth.

Albanese, J.S. 2004. *Organised crime in our times*, 4th ed. Cincinnati: LexisNexis, Anderson Publishing.

Amoruso, D. 2007. Terrence "Terry" Adams, *Gangsters Inc.* Online at: http://gang-stersinc.tripod.com/TerryAdams.html.

Audretsch, D.B. and Keilbach, M. 2007. The theory of knowledge spillover entrepreneurship. *Journal of Management Studies* 44 (7): 1242–1254.

Elvins, M. 2003. Europe's response to transnational organised crime. In *Crime: Perspectives on global security*, Eds. A. Edwards and P. Gill, 29–41. London: Routledge.

Federal Bureau of Investigation (FBI). 2008. *Department of Justice launches new law enforcement strategy to combat increasing threat of international organised crime*, Press Release April 23, Federal Bureau of Investigation. Online at www.fbi.gov "Overview of the Law Enforcement Strategy to Combat International Organised Crime," U.S. Department of Justice, Washington, D.C.

Felsen, D. and Kalaitzidis, A. 2005. A historical overview of transnational crime. In *Handbook of Transnational Crime and Justice*, Ed. P. Reichel, 3–19. London: Sage Publications.

Jacobides, M.G. and Winter, S.G. 2007. Entrepreneurship and firm boundaries: The theory of a firm. *Journal of Management Studies* 44 (7): 1213–1241.

Jayasinghe, K., Thomas, D., and Wickramasinghe, D. 2008. Bounded emotionality in entrepreneurship: An alternative framework. *International Journal of Entrepreneurial Behaviour & Research* 14 (4): 242–258.

Kropp, F., Lindsay, N.J., and Shoham, A. 2008. Entrepreneurial orientation and international entrepreneurial business venture startup. *International Journal of Entrepreneurial Behaviour & Research* 14 (2): 102–117.

Langlois, R.N. 2007. The entrepreneurial theory of the firm and the theory of the entrepreneurial firm. *Journal of Management Studies* 44 (7): 1107–1124.

Liddick, D. 1999. The enterprise "model" of organised crime: Assessing theoretical propositions, *Justice Quarterly* 16 (2): 404–430.

Lyman, M.D. and Potter, G.W. 2007. *Organised crime*, 4th ed. Upper Saddle River, NJ: Pearson Prentice Hall.

Madsen, H., Neergaard, H., and Ulhøi, J.P. 2008. Factors influencing the establishment of knowledge-intensive ventures. *International Journal of Entrepreneurial Behaviour & Research* 14 (2): 70–84.

Markovska, A. 2007. The bitter pill of a corrupt heritage: Corruption in Ukraine and developments in the pharmaceutical industry. In *Crime business and crime money in Europe. The dirty linen of illegal enterprise*, Eds. P.D. van Duyne, A. Maljevic, M. van Dijck, K. von Lampe, and J. Harvey, 227–246. Nijmegen, The Netherlands: Wolf Legal Publishers.

Markovski, S. and Hall, P. 2007. Public sector entrepreneurship and the production of defence. *Public Finance and Management* 7 (3): 260–294.

Pinto, J., Leana, C.R., and Pil, F.K. 2008. Corrupt organizations or organizations of corrupt individuals? Two types of organization-level corruption. *The Academy of Management Review* 33 (3): 685–709.

Seet, P.S., Ahmad, N.H., and Seet, L.C. 2008. Singapore's female entrepreneurs: Are they different? *International Journal of Entrepreneurship and Small Business* 5 (3/4): 257–271.

Symeonidou-Kastanidou, E. 2007. Towards a new definition of organised crime in the European Union. *European Journal of Crime, Criminal Law and Criminal Justice* 15 (1): 83–103.

Thomas, A. and Mancino, A. 2007. The relationship between entrepreneurial characteristics, firms' positioning and local development. *Entrepreneurship and Innovation* 8 (2): 105–114.

Thomson, J. 2008. *US senate accuses billionaire Frank Lowy of hiding millions to dodge tax*. smartcompany, online at: www.smartcompay.com (published July 18).

van Duyne, P.C. 2007. Crime finances and state of the art. Case for concern? In *Crime business and crime money in Europe—The dirty linen of illicit enterprise*, Eds. P.D. van Duyne, A. Maljevic, M. van Dijck, K. von Lampe, and J. Harvey, 69–95. Nijmegen, The Netherlands: Wolf Legal Publishers.

van Duyne, P.C., von Lampe, K., and Newell, J. 2003. *Criminal finances and organising crime in Europe*. Nijmegen, The Netherlands: Wolf Legal Publishers.

van Duyne, P.C., von Lampe, K., van Dijck, M., and Newell, J. 2005. *The organised crime economy: Managing crime markets in Europe*. Nijmegen, The Netherlands: Wolf Legal Publishers.

von Lampe, K. 2005. Organised crime in Europe. In *Handbook of transnational crime and justice*, Ed. P. Reichel, 403–417. London: Sage Publications.

von Lampe, K. 2007. Criminals are not alone. Some observations on the social microcosm of illegal entrepreneurs. In *Crime business and crime money in Europe. The dirty linen of illegal enterprise*, Eds. P.D. van Duyne, A. Maljevic, M. van Dijck, K. von Lampe, and J. Harvey, 131–156. Nijmegen, The Netherlands: Wolf Legal Publishers.

Williams, C.C. 2006. *The hidden enterprise culture—Entrepreneurship in the underground economy*. Cheltenham, U.K.: Edward Elgar Publishing.

Witt, U. 2007. Firms as realizations of entrepreneurial visions. *Journal of Management Studies* 44 (7): 1125–1140.

Wright, A. 2006. *Organised crime*. Devon, U.K.: Willan Publishing.

Zaitch, D. 2002. *Trafficking cocaine—Colombian drug entrepreneurs in The Netherlands*. Studies of Organized Crime, Kluwer Law International, The Hague, The Netherlands.

Zander, I. 2007. Do you see what I mean? An entrepreneurship perspective on the nature and boundaries of the firm. *Journal of Management Studies* 44 (7): 1141–1164.

Developing Intelligence Strategy

3

Strategy can simply be defined as principles (a broad-based formula) to be applied in order to achieve a purpose. These principles are general guidelines steering the daily work in order to reach organizational goals. Strategy is both a plan for the future and a pattern from the past; it is the match an organization makes between its internal resources and skills (sometimes collectively called competencies) and the opportunities and risks created by its external environment. Strategy is the long-term direction of an organization. Strategy is the course of action for achieving an organization's purpose. Strategy is the pattern of resource allocation decisions made throughout the organization. Strategy is the direction and scope of an organization over the long term, which achieves advantage for the organization through its configuration of resources within a changing environment and to fulfill stakeholders' expectations (Johnson and Scholes, 2002).

When Italian police developed a new intelligence strategy against Mafia-type organized crime, the ambition was to change social conduct based on intelligence and analysis of extortionists, politicians linked to the Mafia, eyewitness testimony, illegal favors by white collar workers, anti-Mafia activists, and potential police collaborators (Spina, 2008, 197):

> Consider a context like Sicily, Calabria, or Campania. If most entrepreneurs and shopkeepers refused to pay extortionists but rather reported them to police, if citizens stopped voting for political figures who are known to be directly or indirectly linked to the [M]afia, if eyewitnesses decided to give their testimony regardless of retaliation, if all the "white collars" (professionals, civil servants, politicians, entrepreneurs, opinion makers) avoiding favoring the [M]afia in any way, if enough ordinary citizens engaged in grassroots anti [M]afia activities, and if enough [M]afia men chose to collaborate with the police and public prosecutors, then after some time the [M]afia would disappear, because its members would frequently be exposed and apprehended, and the organization would lose its sources of income and eventually collapse.

Indirect actions by Italian police based on intelligence and analysis is intended to supplement and complement repressive actions. Repressive actions are aimed at discouraging people from crime by punishing them afterward, while indirect actions are aimed at reinforcing and spreading attitudes and behaviors that can pose serious obstacles to the day-to-day activities of Mafia men and women (Spina, 2008).

Strategic criminal intelligence analysis aims to weigh a variety of crimes against each other in order to base priorities on a relative calculation of social harm. According to Sheptycki (2007), this implies that strategic analysis attempts to compare different types of criminal activity including violence, drug distribution and consumption, intellectual property theft, car theft and burglary, smuggling of guns, child pornography, trafficking in humans, stock market fraud, and avoidance of health and safety legislation in food production.

Strategic Planning Process

Strategic planning represents the extent to which decision makers look into the future and use formal planning methodologies. Planning is something we do in advance of taking action. It is anticipatory decision making. We make decisions before actions are required. According to Mintzberg (1994), planning is future thinking, it is about controlling the future, it is decision making, and it is a formalized procedure to produce an articulated result in the form of an integrated system of decisions. The result of strategic planning manifests itself in a strategic plan, such as in the document *National Strategy for Intelligence and Analysis* (POD, 2007).

Zhao et al. (2008, 3) argue that:

> Strategic planning in police departments represents a significant departure from a traditionally reactive orientation to one that is more proactive in nature.

This chapter belongs to the planning school of strategy, where strategy is documented as a plan. According to Mintzberg (1994), planning has these characteristics:

- *Planning is future thinking*. It is taking the future into account. Planning denotes thinking about the future. Planning is action laid out in advance.
- *Planning is controlling the future*. It is not just thinking about it, but achieving it—enacting it. Planning is the design of a desired future and of effective ways of bringing it about. It is to create controlled change in the environment.
- *Planning is decision making*. Planning is the conscious determination of courses of action designed to accomplish purposes. Planning is those activities which are concerned specifically with determining in advance what actions and/or human and physical resources

are required to reach a goal. It includes identifying alternatives, analyzing each one, and selecting the best ones.

- *Planning is integrated decision making.* It means fitting together of ongoing activities into a meaningful whole. Planning implies getting somewhat more organized; it means making a feasible commitment around that which already available courses of action get organized. This definition may seem close to the preceding one, but, because it is concerned not so much with the making of decisions as with the conscious attempt to integrate different ones, it is fundamentally different and begins to identify a position for planning.
- *Planning is a formalized procedure to produce an articulated result in the form of an integrated system of decisions.* What captures the notion of planning above all—most clearly distinguishes its literature and differentiates its practice from other processes—is its emphasis on formalization, the systemization of the phenomenon to which planning is meant to apply. Planning is a set of concepts, procedures, and tests. Formalization here means three things: (1) to decompose, (2) to articulate, and (3) to rationalize the process by which decisions are made and integrated into organizations.

Given that this is planning, the question becomes: Why do it? Mintzberg (1994) provides the answers:

- Organizations must plan to coordinate their activities.
- Organizations must plan to ensure that the future is taken into account.
- Organizations must plan to be rational in terms of formalized planning.
- Organizations must plan to control.

Zhao et al. (2008, 20) found in a survey of strategic planning in U.S. police forces:

A second dimension refers to the number of ranks involved in the strategic planning process. In some departments, only top administrators (the chief or deputy chief) were involved in the plan. Alternatively, there were law enforcement agencies in which patrol officers were expected to also fully participate in strategic planning. Hierarchical involvement reflects the extent of employee involvement.

Zhao et al. (2008, 23) compared four models of strategic planning, as illustrated in Figure 3.1, and found model 4 to be the best one because:

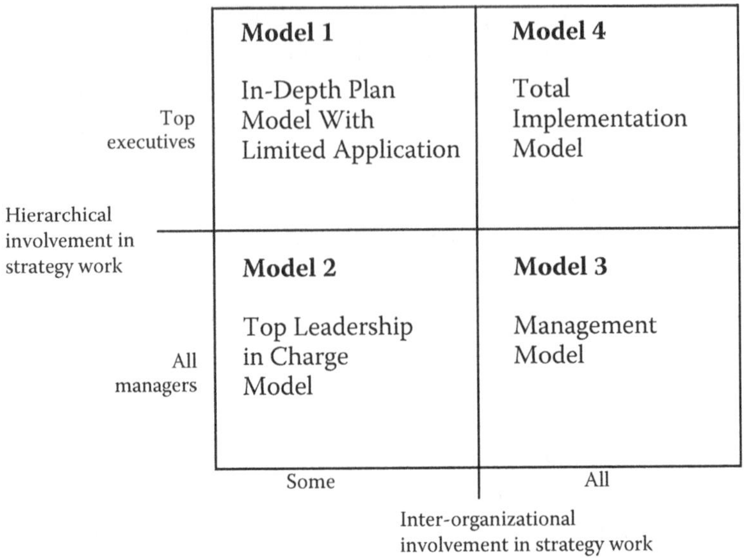

		Model 1 In-Depth Plan Model With Limited Application	Model 4 Total Implementation Model
Top executives			
Hierarchical involvement in strategy work		Model 2 Top Leadership in Charge Model	Model 3 Management Model
All managers			
		Some	All

Inter-organizational
involvement in strategy work

Figure 3.1 Four models for strategic planning in policing. (Adapted from Zhao et al. 2008. *Police Quarterly* 11 (1): 3–26.)

- The strategic plan becomes the driving force for departmental change. Every organization needs to change to adapt to a changing environment. It is reasonable to argue that planned and proactive change is better than unplanned and reactive change. In this sense, strategic planning under this model represents planned change in an organization. The implementation of this model requires a fundamental change in many areas, such as planning, organizational change, and performance evaluation.
- Sworn officers at every rank are held accountable for their assignments. New evaluation methods are developed to hold employees accountable. For example, problem-solving activities can be incorporated into performance evaluation. Community surveys can also be used to indicate the performance of patrol beats, etc.
- The community is familiar with the agency's strategic plan.
- Organizational change can be formally documented and updated in accordance with the plan. There is a good fit between strategic planning and community policing because they share very similar principles of organizational change.
- Consensus exists among employees with regard to where the department is headed. If the plan is written with the participation of employees in the development of goals, objectives, and specific measures, the plan derives legitimacy from employees.

- The level of change is significant and risks associated with conflict and turmoil and even failure are elevated because substantial change (and especially cultural change) is difficult.

Intelligence Strategy Characteristics

Traditionally, intelligence was understood to mean information from criminals about criminal activity by a covert source. Today, intelligence is a systematic approach to collecting information with the purpose of tracking and predicting crime to improve law enforcement (Brown et al., 2004). Intelligence analysts investigate who is committing crimes, how, when, where, and why. They then provide recommendations on how to stop or curb the offenses. As part of this, analysts produce profiles of crime problems and individual targets, and produce both strategic (overall, long-term) and tactical (specific, short-term) assessments within the confines set by the police force.

The aim of intelligence strategy is to continue to develop intelligence-led policing in all parts of a nation and in all regions of the world. An intelligence strategy provides a framework for a structured problem solving- and partnership-enhanced approach, based around a common model. For example, the National Intelligence Model in the United Kingdom is a structured approach to improve intelligence-led policing both centrally and locally in policing districts, such as the South Yorkshire Police (SYPIS, 2007).

Intelligence-led policing is carried out in many law enforcement areas. For example, intelligence-led vehicle crime reduction was carried out in the West Surrey police district in the United Kingdom. Analysis of vehicle crime included identifying (Brown et al., 2004):

- Locations (hot spots, streets, car parks, postcodes, wards, etc.) of vehicle crime
- Sites where vehicles were dumped
- Times of offenses
- Prolific vehicle crime offenders
- Areas where prolific offenders were identified as offending
- Models of vehicles targeted for vehicle crime
- Type of property stolen in theft from vehicle offenses

The analysis resulted in problem profiles, which identified emerging patterns of crime. These patterns included vehicle crime occurring in special car parks and the theft of badges from cars. Such information was disseminated to local officers for action.

Intelligence-led policing is defined as a business model and a management philosophy, according to Ratcliffe (2008, 89):

> Intelligence-led policing is a business model and managerial philosophy where data analysis and crime intelligence are pivotal to an objective, decision-making framework that facilitates crime and problem reduction, disruption and prevention through both strategic management and effective enforcement strategies that target prolific and serious offenders.

An interesting case of intelligence-led policing in the United Kingdom was the project called Operation Gallant that led to a reduction of 17 percent in car thefts in 2003. Operation Gallant involved all basic command units (BCU) in the collection and analysis of information (Brown et al., 2004, 2):

> In the case of Operation Gallant, the intelligence-led vehicle crime reduction approach involved the activity of officers from across a BCU. A crime analyst, dedicated solely to examine vehicle crime patterns and trends, developed a detailed picture of vehicle crime in the area, including analysis of time, location, vehicle type, and known offenders. As a result of this strategic analysis, a number of interventions were planned, drawing heavily upon the Operation Igneous tactical menu. The most significant, in terms of resources devoted to the operation, involved a program of prolific offender targeting and crime prevention advice targeted toward the owners of high-risk vehicles.

The substantial decline in car crimes was explained by the increased attention paid to this crime sector (Brown et al., 2004, 16):

> Given the fact that the first reduction coincides with the commencement of the planning process for Operation Gallant, this may also reflect an anticipatory effect in which the very act of planning and talking about an operation leads to a decline.

Is Strategy Always Strategy?

Strategy is a label frequently applied to a wide variety of activities, thoughts, initiatives, and documents in industry and government. There seems to be no limit to the use of this popular term. Yet a number of definitions of strategy might lead to some borderlines for the use and misuse of this label. Today, anecdotal evidence suggests that strategy is used as a label every time something is considered to be "important." Often, executives, suppliers, and others use the term to achieve attention. So, if an initiative, a project, or a plan is important, is it then always strategy?

This section attempts to clarify some criteria and characteristics of strategy in terms of documents carrying this term. The recent national strategy for police intelligence and analysis (a twenty-page document) in Norway is used as a case for discussion (POD, 2007).

To determine whether or not a document might be characterized as "strategy" is useful in many respects. First, strategy implementation follows strategy planning. If the content is not intended for implementation, then it might be misleading to label it strategy. Next, strategy expects priority. If the content is not important, then again it might be misleading to label it strategy. Furthermore, strategy is perceived as some kind of direction. However, if nobody knows what the organization wants to achieve, then there is hardly any identifiable direction.

Strategic planning takes many different forms in different organizations. However, Boyd and Reuning-Elliott's (1998) study of strategic planning provides strong support for the measurement properties of the strategic planning construct. In particular, the study results indicate that strategic planning is a concept that can be reliably measured through seven indicators: mission statement, trend analysis, competitor analysis, long-term goals, annual goals, short-term action plans, and ongoing evaluation. This evidence is important because previous researchers rarely tested for dimensionality of the planning construct nor did most studies report tests of the reliability of their measures.

Similarly, Grant (2002) found that the resulting strategic plan after a planning process typically comprises these elements:

- *Time.* A statement of the planning period or planning horizon.
- *Goal.* A statement of the goals the organization seeks to achieve over the planning period.
- *Forecast.* A set of assumptions or forecasts about key developments in the external environment to which the organization must respond.
- *Change.* A qualitative statement of how the shape of the organization will be changing in relation to activities, procedures, and priorities.
- *Action.* Specific action steps with regard to decisions and projects, supported by a set of milestones, stating what is to be achieved by specific dates.
- *Finance.* A set of financial projections, including operating budgets to implement the plan.

A *well-formulated* strategy helps to *allocate* an organization's *resources* into a unique and viable posture based on its relative internal competencies and shortcomings. Strategy is at a different *level* than tactical or operational plans. Strategy is about decision making, and strategy names certain persons as decision makers. Strategy also describes the most significant *policies* guiding or limiting actions, as well as the major *action sequences* to be accomplished, which are the defined goals within the limits set. A strategy includes an *analysis* of the past, present, and future.

Based on the current Norwegian document entitled *National Strategy for Police Intelligence and Analysis* and requirements of the strategy construct, it is now possible to conduct a content analysis of the strategy document.

By simple count, there are two Yeses and five Nos in Table 3.1. This result indicates that the Norwegian document is not necessarily a strategy, as it claims.

From an implementation point of view, police districts in Norway find it difficult to implement the "strategy." While the National Police Directorates demand that they comply, many police districts in 2008, one year after the strategy launch, seemed reluctant to do so. So far, the explanation has been local resistance to change. This research suggests another explanation: The strategy document is not good enough to guide implementation.

This was minor exploratory research, exploring the possibility of determining whether a document claiming to be a "strategy" really is just that. More research is needed to clarify the issues and establish a consistent set of characteristics and strategy construct requirements. While some characteristics may be classified as requirements, other may be classified as recommendations.

More research is also needed to evaluate strategy documents in terms of thorough content analysis (Riffe and Freitag, 1997). As an alternative to the application of predefined categories for classification, grounded theory might be applied. Grounded theory involves the systematic collection and analysis of data for the purpose, ultimately, of generating theory (Mactavish et al., 2007). Within grounded theory, we find axial coding, which is the process of relating codes to each other via a combination of inductive and deductive thinking. For example, Phillips and Noble (2007) clustered statements that appeared to pertain to similar ideas into categories. Grounded theory might be applied in future research on the collected characteristics of strategy documents.

Table 3.1   Evaluation of National Strategy for Police Intelligence (POD, 2007) in Terms of Strategy Construct Requirements

Strategy Construct Requirements	POD Strategy Evaluation
Analysis of the present intelligence situation?	No
Analysis of the future intelligence situation?	No
Description of actions based on strategy?	Yes: Measurement criteria
Financing actions to enable implementation?	No
Time frame for strategy implementation?	No
Goals to be achieved based on the strategy?	Yes: Decision support in policing
Intelligence and analysis defined and described?	No

Not all documents labeled *strategy* are actually strategy in the sense of the common strategy construct. Too many documents seem to misuse this label to attract attention. This section reported from early research the evaluation of documents claiming to be strategies. More research is needed in terms of the strategy construct, characteristics, and requirements as well as relevant content analysis of strategy documents.

Case: National Intelligence Model in the United Kingdom

In the United Kingdom, the National Intelligence Model (NIM) was introduced in 2000 to focus on how intelligence is used and where it is sourced. According to John and Maguire (2004), NIM provides a cohesive intelligence framework across the full range of levels of criminality and disorder. NIM has inspired intelligence strategy in many countries, such as the Police Intelligence Model in Sweden (Polisen, 2006) and the National Strategy for Intelligence and Analysis in Norway (POD, 2007).

NIM is a model for policing that should ensure information is fully researched, developed, and analyzed to provide intelligence. Intelligence enables senior managers to provide strategic direction, make tactical resource decisions about operational policing, and manage risk. The model works at three levels: (1) local/basic command unit, (2) force and/or regional, and (3) serious and organized crime that is usually national or international.

The organization of information within NIM starts with the creation of a strategic assessment, which identifies issues that are likely to affect service delivery. All partners within crime- and disorder-reduction partnerships in England commit resources and coordinate activity to deal with these issues. An accurate and thorough assessment will allow managers to make informed decisions concerning service delivery, which will assist them in achieving performance targets (SYPIS, 2007).

The national intelligence model in the United Kingdom by which the Norwegian strategy was simulated is a business model for law enforcement. It became the policy of the Association of Chief Police Officers (ACPO), and many forces underwent major restructuring and were allocated new resources in order to implement it. NIM takes an intelligence-led approach to policing. The U.K. government acknowledged its benefits, and all forces in England and Wales were required to implement NIM to national minimum standards beginning in 2004.

NIM consists of nine individual parts (Centrex, 2005):

1. *Crime Pattern Analysis* is a generic term for a number of related analytical disciplines, such as crime (or incident series identification), crime trend analysis, hot spot analysis, and general profile analysis.

2. *Market Profile* is an assessment, continually reviewed and updated, that surveys the criminal market around a particular commodity, such as drugs or stolen vehicles, or of a service, such as prostitution, in an area.

3. *Demographic/Social Trend Analysis* is centered on an examination of the nature of demographic changes and their impact on criminality, as well as on the deeper analysis of social factors, such as unemployment and homelessness, which might underlie changes or trends in offenders or offending behavior.

4. *Criminal Business Profile* contains detailed analysis of how criminal operations or techniques work, in the same way the legitimate businesses may be explained.

5. *Network Analysis* describes not just the linkages between people who form criminal networks, but also the significance of the links, the roles played by individuals, and the strengths and weaknesses of a criminal organization.

6. *Risk Analysis* assesses the scale of risks posed by individual offenders or organizations to individual potential victims, the public at large, and also to law enforcement agencies.

7. *Target Profile Analysis* embraces a range of analytical techniques that aim to describe the criminal, his or her criminal activity, lifestyle, associations, the risk the person poses, and personal strengths and weaknesses in order to give focus to the investigation targeting each person.

8. *Operational Intelligence Assessment* maintains the focus of an operation on the previously agreed objectives, particularly in the case of a sizeable intelligence collection plan or other large-scale operations.

9. *Results Analysis* evaluates the effectiveness of law enforcement activities, e.g., the effectiveness of patrol strategies, crime reduction initiatives, or a particular method of investigation.

Part 4 in NIM is of particular interest when focusing on criminal organizations. This component acknowledges the enterprise paradigm of organized crime, where legal and illegal businesses share some common features. A criminal business profile might focus on primary and secondary activities of criminal organizations similar to noncriminal organizations. The profile might examine all aspects of activities, such as how victims are selected; the technical processes involved in the crimes; methods of removing, disposing of, or laundering proceeds; and weaknesses in systems or procedures that the criminal business exploits. Similarly, element 5 supports the enterprise paradigm for criminal organizations.

Part 3 in NIM is often concerned with designing geodemographic classification, which is a field of study that involves the classification of persons according to the type of neighborhood in which they live. As a method of segmenting people, it has long been of value to direct marketers who, being often unable to identify the age, marital status, or occupational status of people in mailing lists, found it a useful means of applying selectivity to their telemarketer mailings. By analyzing the behavioral characteristics of consumers in different types of neighborhoods, they found they could improve business performance by targeting promotional activities to names and addresses falling within specific types of postal codes (Webber, 2004).

Case: National Strategy for Intelligence and Analysis in Norway

In May 2007, the Norwegian Police Directorate concluded a strategy process with the *National Strategy for Intelligence and Analysis* document. According to the document, all police districts in Norway needed to implement the strategy (POD, 2007).

The Norwegian *National Strategy for Intelligence and Analysis* developed by the Norwegian Police Directorate in 2007 (POD, 2007) was very much stimulated by the development of NIM in the United Kingdom. It defines three levels for intelligence and analysis in Norway: (1) local police districts, (2) cooperation between police districts, and (3) and international intelligence and analysis.

The vision for the national strategy is that "the police shall always make the right decision at the right time," while "the main goal of strategic intelligence and analysis is to provide decision makers with the best possible basis for prioritizing commitment areas, preparing operations, collaborating with external partners, planning efficient use of resources, developing strategies for prevention, and assessment and evaluation." At the operational level, strategy goals include initiating and supporting investigation, initiating and supporting operative action, preventing incidents, planning efficient use of resources, collaborating with external partners, and assessment and evaluation.

According to the strategy document, there are several prerequisites to achieve strategic and operational goals:

- *Management responsibilities.* It is important that the management has a comprehensive view of the organization and involves stakeholders and problem owners.
- *Measurement criteria.* Police work is traditionally measured in terms of detection rate, processing time, and backlog of cases. Parameters

should be developed to capture citizen satisfaction with police work, extent of safety, crime level, and threat level.

- *Evaluation.* Both strategy effect and strategy process should be evaluated.
- *Professional values.* The intelligence and analysis work of the police shall be characterized by a high degree of professional ethics.

The main focus of the Norwegian strategy document seems to be organization in terms of responsibility for intelligence at the national, regional, and local level, as illustrated by Table 3.2. The document does not define or describe intelligence or analysis, which are important terms in this strategy.

Chapter 7 in the document is concerned with competence and training (POD, 2007, 18):

> The basic characteristics of all analysis work are critical thinking and curiosity. The analyst should be humble and at the same time have integrity. He/she should be creative. At the same time, the work requires a structured approach in order to handle vast volumes of data without losing sight of the purpose of the work. The analyst is to monitor and follow social development in those areas that may be of significance for the development of criminality.
>
> A professional police background and experience are important for operative analysts. They must have ample knowledge of and experience from investigation and intelligence. For strategic analysis, a social science background is considered more important. Social science methodology may better enable the analyst to use information-based theories from the academic literature and thus have a broader perspective of sources—understanding and explaining trends and development features. A social science background also provides expertise regarding quantitative methodology that deals with variables and values (descriptive statistics, deduction statistics) and qualitative methodology that deals with concepts and categories (techniques for reduction and understanding of textual material).

Case: New York State Intelligence Strategy

At the core of the New York State Intelligence Strategy is a fusion center that unifies law enforcement (Johnson and Dorn, 2008):

> Creating one center for intelligence and terrorism information—to combine and distribute that information to law enforcement agencies statewide—prevents duplication of effort by multiple agencies. Additionally, one state fusion center serving the entire New York law enforcement community provides a comprehensive picture of criminal and terrorist networks, aids in the fight against future terrorist events, and reduces crime. Agencies throughout New York are not only invited to provide information to the NYSIC [New York State Intelligence Center] and to make requests for case assistance, but are also encouraged to contribute

Table 3.2   Table of Contents in the Document *National Strategy for Police Intelligence and Analysis* (POD, 2007)

National Strategy for Police Intelligence and Analysis

Preface

1. Introduction
    1.1 The Working Party's terms of reference
    1.2 The Working Party's work
2. Summary
3. Purpose
4. Vision and goals
    4.1 Vision
    4.2 Main goals
        4.3.1. Strategic main goals
        4.3.2 Operative main goals
5. Prerequisites for goal attainment
    5.1 Management responsibility
    5.2 Measurement criteria
    5.3 Evaluation
    5.4 Professional conduct values for intelligence and analysis work
6. Organization
    6.6 National, regional, and local responsibility
        6.6.1 Level 1 – Police district level
        6.6.2 Level 2 – Regional level
        6.6.3 Level 3 – National level
        6.6.4 Level 4 – Paramount level
7. Competence and training
8. Recommendations

personnel to staff the center. This state-of-the-art facility pools the resources of many agencies by gathering law enforcement information and data from upstate New York and combining it in a centralized location. Access to an extensive array of databases through a single contact point is provided by the various components, facilitating criminal information and intelligence exchange. This fusion center unifies the efforts of state, local, and federal analysts to compile, analyze, and disseminate terrorism and intelligence data.

The mission of the New York State Intelligence Center (NYSIC) is to improve the efficient, timely, and accurate exchange of information among all New York State law enforcement agencies. Working in close partnership with the New York City Police Department (NYPD) Intelligence Division when investigations cross into the boroughs of New York City, the NYSIC focuses on all aspects of criminal activity in the counties outside New York City. The NYSIC augments law enforcement operations by acting as a centralized, comprehensive intelligence fusion center, specifically producing and coordinating the statewide exchange of criminal intelligence. Intelligence analysts at the NYSIC have daily interaction with law enforcement agencies across the United States. Together, the NYPD Intelligence Division and the NYSIC provide a seamless sharing of criminal intelligence for all law enforcement agencies throughout the state.

References

Boyd, B.K. and Reuning-Elliott, E. 1998. A measurement model of strategic planning. *Strategic Management Journal* 19: 181–192.

Brown, R., Cannings, A., and Sherriff, J. 2004. *Intelligence-led vehicle crime reduction: An evaluation of Operation Gallant*, Home Office online Report 47/04: http://www.homeoffice.gov.uk/rds/pdfs04/rdsolr4704.pdf.

Centrex. 2005. *Guidance on the national intelligence model*, Centrex, National Centre for Policing Excellence, Bedford, U.K.: Bedford Publishing Co.

Grant, R.M. 2002. *Contemporary Strategy Analysis*, 4th ed. Oxford, U.K.: Blackwell Publishing.

John, T. and Maguire, M. 2004. *The National Intelligence Model: Key lessons from early research*, Home Office online Report 30/04: http://www.homeoffice.gov.uk/rds/pdfs04/rdsolr3004.pdf.

Johnson, B.R. and Dorn, S. 2008. Fusion centers: New York intelligence strategy unifies law enforcement. *The Police Chief* (November). Online: www.policechiefmagazine.org.

Johnson, G. and Scholes, K. 2002. *Exploring corporate strategy*. Harlow, Essex, U.K.: Pearson Education, Prentice Hall.

Mactavish, J.B., MacKay, K.J., Iwasaki, Y., and Betteridge, D. 2007. Family caregivers of individuals with intellectual disability: Perspectives on life quality and the role of vacations. *Journal of Leisure Research* 39 (1): 127–155.

Mintzberg, H. 1994. Rounding on the managers' job. *Sloan Management Review* 36 (1): 11–26.

Phillips, J. and Noble, S.M. 2007. Simply captivating: Understanding consumers' attitudes toward the cinema as an advertising medium. *Journal of Advertising* 36 (1): 81–94.

POD. 2007. *Nasjonal strategi for etterretning og analyse (National strategy for intelligence and analysis)*. Politidirektoratet (Norwegian Police Directorate), Oslo, Norway.

Polisen. 2006. *Polisens underrättelsemodell (Police Intelligence Model)*, Rikspolisstyrelsen, Stockholm, Sweden.

Ratcliffe, J.H. 2008. *Intelligence-led policing*. Devon, U.K.: Willan Publishing.

Riffe, D. and Freitag, A. 1997. A content analysis of content analyses, twenty-five years of journalism quarterly. *Journalism Mass Communication Quarterly* 74: 873–882.

Sheptycki, J. 2007. Police ethnography in the house of serious and organized crime. In *Transformations of policing*, Eds. A. Henry and D.J. Smith, 51–77. Oxford, U.K.: Ashgate Publishing.

Spina, A.L. 2008. Recent anti-Mafia strategies: The Italian experience. In *Organized crime: Culture, markets and policies*, Eds. D. Siegel and H. Nelen, 195–206. New York: Springer.

SYPIS. 2007. *South Yorkshire Police Intelligence Strategy 2007: Breaking the chain*, South Yorkshire Police, U.K.: www.policereform.gov.uk.

Webber, R. 2004. Designing geodemographic classifications to meet contemporary business needs. *Interactive Marketing* 5 (3): 219–237.

Zhao, J.S., Thurman, Q.C., and Ren, L. 2008. An examination of strategic planning in American law enforcement agencies. *Police Quarterly* 11 (1): 3–26.

Implementing Intelligence Strategy

4

Strategy implementation suffers from a general lack of academic attention. Despite the importance of the strategy execution process, much more attention is paid to strategy formulation than its implementation. As one of several reasons put forward for this discrepancy, Atkinson (2006) suggests that researchers, when starting work on this subject, often underestimate the difficulties involved in studying such a topic.

In May 2007, the Norwegian Police Directorate concluded a strategy process with the document *National Strategy for Intelligence and Analysis*. According to the document, all police districts in Norway had to implement the strategy (POD, 2007). This is the implementation case to be studied in this book. Our research question might be formulated as: What are determinants of law enforcement strategy implementation?

Implementation Process

Both scholars and practitioners have emphasized the need for improved implementation of strategies in law enforcement and policing. Implementation is important for four reasons. First, the failure to carry out a strategy can cause lost opportunities, duplicated efforts, incompatible organizational units, and wasted resources. As well, the extent to which a strategy meets its objectives is determined by implementation. Further, the lack of implementation leaves police officers dissatisfied and reluctant to continue doing strategic planning work. Finally, the lack of implementation creates problems establishing and maintaining priorities in future strategic planning.

The strategy execution task is commonly the most complicated and time-consuming part of strategic management. In contrast, strategy formulation is primarily an intellectual and creative act involving analysis and synthesis. Implementation is a hands-on operation and action-oriented human behavioral activity that calls for executive leadership and key managerial skills. In addition, implementing a new strategy often requires a change in organizational direction and frequently entails a focus on effecting strategic change. Therefore, strategic change often needs a sense of urgency and effective communication.

More than half of the strategies devised by organizations are never actually implemented (Atkinson, 2006). As a consequence, discussions of whether managers "walk their talk," "show word–deed alignment," or "adhere to their plans" have emerged. One approach in these discussions is to study strategy implementation consistency, i.e., the alignment of an organization's resource allocation decisions with its articulated strategy over time (Brauer and Schmidt, 2006). Sometimes, phased implementation of police strategy is an alternative (Quinton and Olagundoye, 2004), where some police districts test out the strategy before it is rolled out into the entire nation.

Atkinson (2006) reports six silent killers of strategy implementation: (1) top-down senior management style; (2) unclear strategic intentions and conflicting priorities; (3) an ineffective management team; (4) poor vertical communication; (5) weak coordination across functions, businesses, or borders; and (6) inadequate down-the-line leadership skills development. In addition, another inhibitor to successful strategy implementation that has been receiving a considerable amount of attention is the impact of an organization's existing management controls and particularly budgeting systems.

Strategic control systems ensure that the immense effort put into preparing lengthy and detailed strategic plans is, in fact, translated into action. Strategic control systems provide the short-term targets that deliver long-term goals. Therefore, successful strategy implementation is substantially dependent on effective strategic, as well as management, control systems (Atkinson, 2006).

The term *implementation* is given a variety of meanings in the literature. Implementation is a procedure directed by management to install planned change in an organization. Implementation is the process of gaining targeted organizational members' appropriate and committed use of an innovation. Implementation is the extent to which an innovation becomes ingrained within organizational behaviors. Some authors find implementation to be completed when change is occurring, while others find it continues until intended benefits have been realized (Gottschalk, 1999).

When a crime reduction strategy was implemented in the United Kingdom, the barriers that affected implementation were separated into three themes (Harrington et al., 2006):

1. How the strategy was constructed and managed centrally—tensions between high ambitions when selling the strategy and low ambitions for delivered results.
2. The development and rollout of the strategy—confusion locally over how the new strategy connected with existing programs.
3. The impact of local circumstances—competition between high priority strategies and tasks.

According to Bullock et al. (2002, 33), "... effective implementation of crime reduction projects is essential if the aims are going to be achieved. There is a long history of partial implementation failure in crime reduction projects."

When an earlier crime reduction strategy was implemented in the United Kingdom, these implementation lessons were learned (Homel et al., 2004):

- *Invest to deliver*: It requires continuous development work. It goes beyond the routine processes of basic planning and priority setting. It requires a raft of preparatory work including assessments of capacity for implementation, options based on realistic risk assessments, and the development of viable and flexible management systems, including performance management loops.
- *Organize centrally to deliver locally*: To support efficient local implementation, the central agency must be an active part. This means that the center itself must be appropriately staffed with competent personnel capable of providing direct support to local initiatives.
- *Separate research and evaluation from program delivery*: The problem here is the different timetables for operational versus research and evaluation issues. Therefore, action to research and develop the evidence base should be undertaken as a separate, but related, parallel activity to the delivery of the main strategy.
- *Build and maintain a knowledge management system*: The management and dissemination of knowledge about implementation failures and successes and practices and policies should be in place to stimulate learning. Effective knowledge management is basic to the continuing development and evolution of strategy implementation.
- *Create flexible fund management models*: Often, strategy implementation requires funding. The crime reduction strategy suffered from a variety of funding and budgeting problems. Many of these difficulties appear to have been the result of changes in the operations of central financial management in the Home Office.

When three different strategies for combating burglary were implemented in the Metropolitan Police, Gloucestershire Constabulary, and Hampshire and Isle of Wright Constabulary in the United Kingdom, the enablers that affected implementation were separated into three themes (Stockdale and Gresham, 1995):

1. *Publicity*: A high profile-named operation brings a number of advantages. It provides a unifying focus to a range of activities and it makes police operations understandable to the public.
2. *Internal communication*: An effective communication and consultation system is vital in ensuring the successful implementation of any strategy and in encouraging officers' commitment and support.
3. *Training*: Consideration should be given at the planning stage to training needs.

Y Model for Strategy Work

In all kinds of strategy work, there are three steps. The first is concerned with analysis, the second is concerned with choice (selection and decision), while the final step is concerned with implementation.

We now introduce a model for strategy work (Figure 4.1). A graphical representation of the Y model is shown in the figure. It is called the Y model as it looks like the letter Y. There is one feedback-arrow to compare the evaluation with the desired situation. In this chapter, we will follow the Y model in our discussions.

The model consists of seven stages covering analysis, choice, and implementation. When using intelligence strategy as an example, the stages include:

1. *Describe the current situation.* The current intelligence situation in the business can be described using several methods. The benefits method identifies benefits from use of intelligence within the business. Distinctions are made between rationalization, control, organizational, and market benefits. Other methods include the three-era model, management activities, and stages of growth.

2. *Describe the desired situation.* The desired business situation can be described using several methods depicted in the first chapter: value configurations, competitive strategy, management strategy, business process redesign, knowledge management, the Internet and electronic business, and information technology benefits.

3. *Analyze and prioritize needs for change.* After descriptions of the current situation and the desired situation have been analyzed, needs for change can be identified. The gap between the desired and current situation is called "needs for change." The analysis will provide details on needs, what change is needed, and how changes can take place. "What" analysis will create an understanding of vision and goals, knowledge strategy, market strategy, and corporate problems and opportunities. "How" analysis will create an understanding of technology trends and applications. These analyses should result in proposals for new intelligence approaches in the organization.

4. *Seek for alternative actions.* When needs for change have been identified and proposals for filling gaps have been developed, alternative actions for improving the current situation can be developed. New intelligence approaches can be developed, acquired, and implemented in alternative ways. For example, company staff can develop an information system in-house that can be purchased as a standard application from a vendor or leased from an application systems provider (ASP).

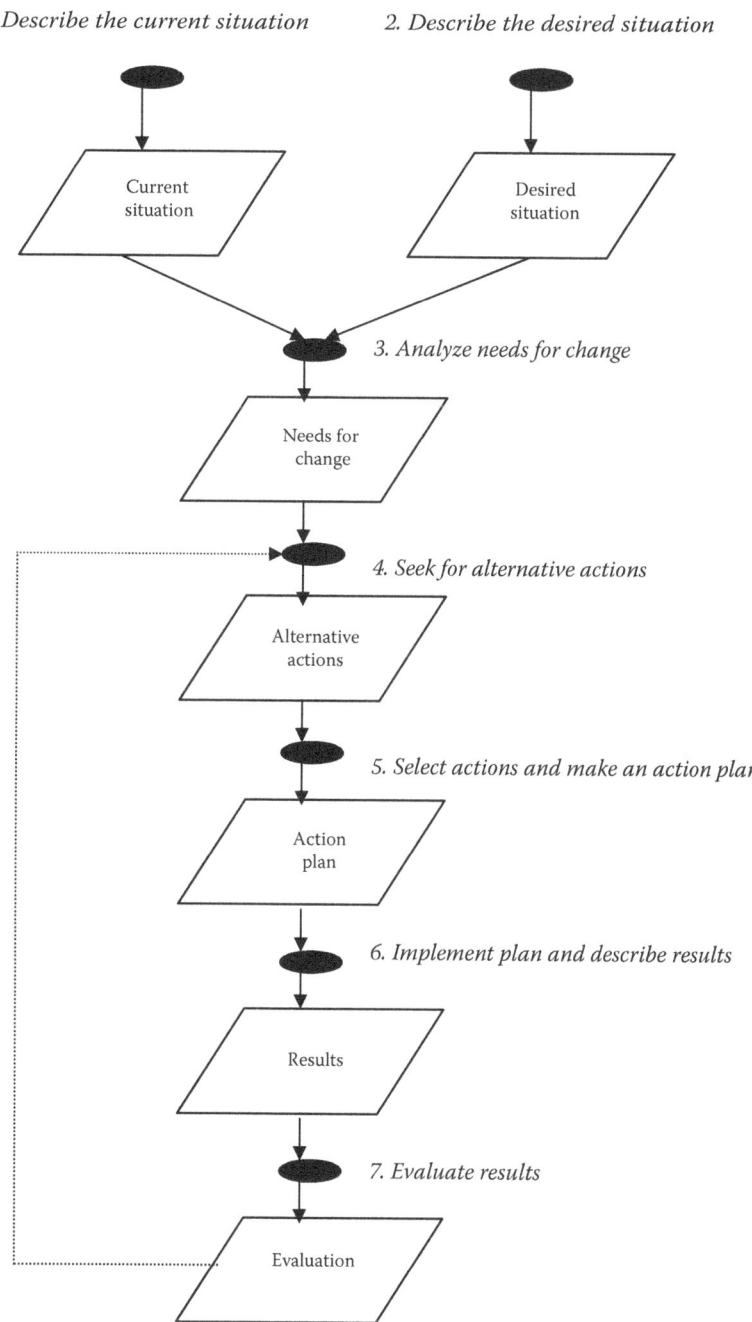

Figure 4.1 The Y model for strategy work.

5. *Select actions and make an action plan.* When needs for change and alternative actions have been identified, several choices have to be made and documented in an action plan. Important issues here include development process, user involvement, time frame, and financial budget for intelligence projects.

6. *Implement a plan and describe results.* This is the stage of action. Technical equipment, such as servers, PCs, printers, and cables, are installed. Operating systems are installed. Application packages, software programs, programming tools, end user tools, and database systems are installed. Development projects are organized. Management and user training takes place. A segment of the implementation is to document results over time.

7. *Evaluate results.* Implementation results are compared with needs for change. It is determined by what extent gaps between desired and current situation have been closed. This is the beginning of the intelligence strategy revision process where a new process through the Y model takes place. Typically, a new intelligence strategy process should take place every other year in business organizations.

While stages 1 to 3 cover *analysis*, 4 and 5 cover *choice*, and 6 and 7 cover *implementation*. In some strategy models, stage 2 is listed as the first stage. It is here recommended to do stage 1 before stage 2. It is easier to describe the ideal situation when you know the current situation. If you start out with stage 2, it often feels difficult and abstract to describe what you would like to achieve. Having completed stage 1 first makes the work more relevant. Stage 3 is a so-called gap analysis, looking at the difference between the desired and actual situation. This stage also includes prioritizing. Stage 4 is a creative session, as it calls for ideas and proposals for alternative actions. Stages 5 and 6 are typical planning stages. The final stage 7 is important because we can learn from performing an evaluation.

Implementation at the End of the Y Model

Stages 6 and 7 in the section above cover strategy implementation in the Y model for strategic planning (Gottschalk, 2007). While stage 6 is concerned with implementing the plan and describing results, stage 7 is concerned with evaluating results, as illustrated in Figure 4.2.

The creation of intelligence strategy has become a major challenge for police executives and intelligence executives in recent years. Investments in information technology have been large, and many failed investments reflect this challenge. The impact of intelligence on organizational performance has grown in strategic importance, and thus the significance of failed intelligence

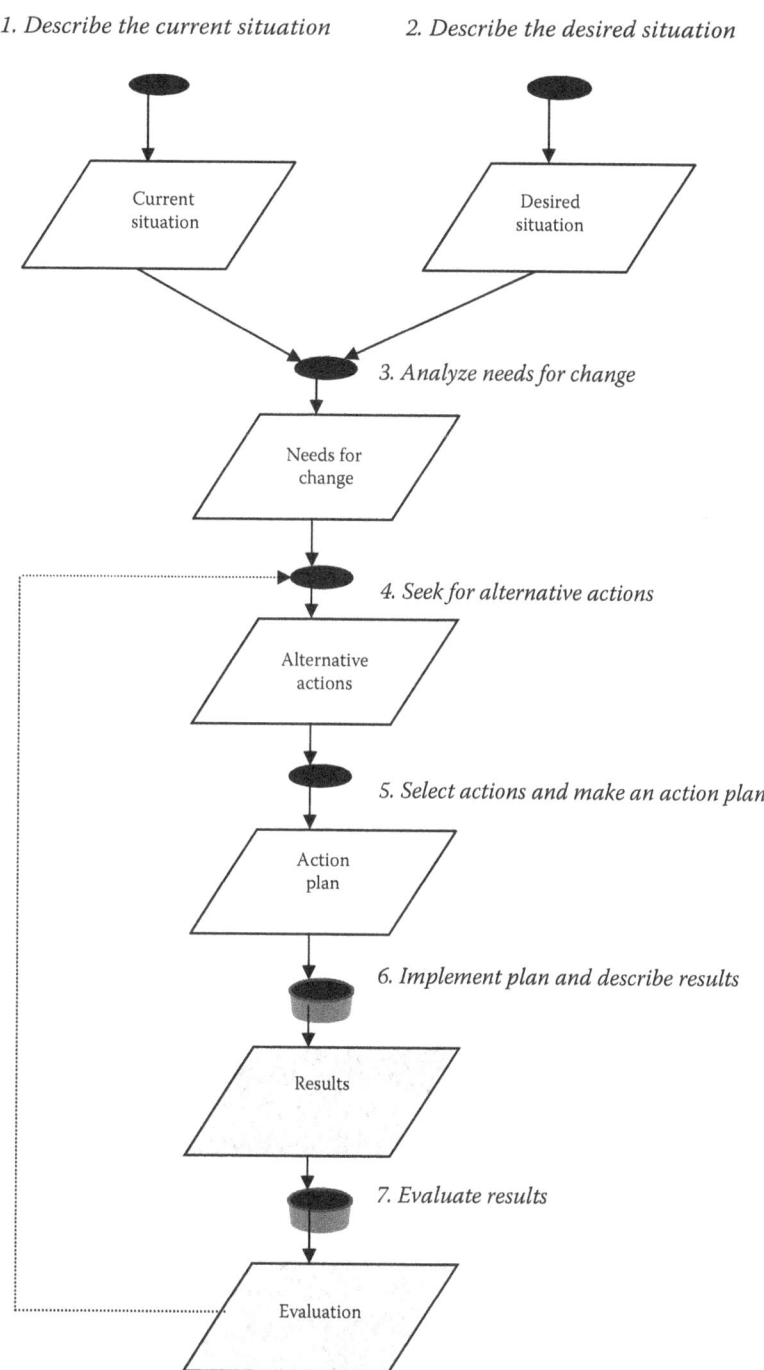

Figure 4.2 The two stages of implementation.

investments is even greater. Information processing and information technology (IT) are becoming critical to many business and government operations, and the technology itself is changing at a rapid rate. New information technology will continue to transform organizations, and changes in how industry participants use IT can alter established relationships in an industry. Strategic intelligence planning can play a critical role in helping organizations increase efficiency, effectiveness, and competitiveness. Although organizations use different methods in their analysis of current and desired situations, the resulting plans need to be implemented.

The importance of the implementation of strategic intelligence plans is illustrated by the significant attention paid to them in recent years. Studies show that implementation is important for four reasons. First, the failure to carry out the strategic intelligence plan can cause lost opportunities, duplicated efforts, incompatible systems, and wasted resources. Second, the extent to which strategic intelligence planning meets its objectives is determined by implementation. Third, the lack of implementation leaves police executives and officers dissatisfied with and reluctant to continue their strategic planning. Fourth, the lack of implementation creates problems establishing and maintaining priorities in future strategic intelligence planning.

Plan Implementation

Intelligence strategy implementation can be defined as "the process of completing the projects for application of intelligence and analysis to assist an organization in realizing its goals." However, implementing an intelligence strategy is not simply the act of executing many projects and individual systems. Instead, implementing such a plan demands a gestalt view in the planning of individual systems. A gestalt view represents the implementation of the plan philosophy, attitudes, intentions, and ambitions associated with intelligence use in the organization. It may include decisions about the intelligence work organization and the implementation of intelligence architecture.

The term *implementation* is given a variety of meanings in the literature. It can be described as a procedure directed by a manager to install planned change in an organization. Change is an empirical observation of difference in form, quality, or state over time in an organizational entity. Implementation can be the process of gaining targeted organizational members' appropriate and committed use of an innovation. Information technology implementation from strategic intelligence planning is a typical innovation.

When is an intelligence approach implemented? Is it implemented when top management as part of the intelligence strategy approves it? When it is installed on a company computer? When it is put into its first use? When it is widely accepted by people in the company? When it is modified as a result of

Figure 4.3 Implementation of an IS/IT intelligence application.

use, based on both detected errors and needs for improvement? When do the benefits of the intelligence strategy finally appear? There is no unified answer to this question when implementation has occurred, but most scholars agree that installation of a system is too early, while benefits are too late to wait for. This is illustrated in Figure 4.3. Most scholars agree that an intelligence application is implemented when it is used and accepted by users. So, in the example in Figure 4.3, we would say that implementation occurred in 2009.

Using the gestalt view, we can say that an intelligence strategy implementation is defined by the degree of implementation. If the complete intelligence strategy is implemented, we can talk about 100 percent implementation. If nothing is implemented, we can talk about zero implementation. A strategic intelligence plan is implemented over time, as illustrated in Figure 4.4. The process of implementation can follow different paths. In the figure, there are two examples of early and late implementation, both ending at an implementation degree of 60 percent.

There is no optimal extent of implementation. It depends on the situation in the company over time. If the intelligence strategy has an excellent match with a desired business situation and an actual business development, then more of the strategy is likely to be implemented. If the intelligence strategy consists of a few large, focused projects that, when first started, have to be finished, then more of the strategy is likely to be implemented. If the organization has a culture of walk and talk consistency, then more of the strategy is likely to be implemented. (Walk and talk consistency implies that management actually does what it says it is going to do.) If the intelligence strategy has a short time horizon, then more of the strategy is likely to be implemented. If management is able to predict the future, then more of the strategy is likely to be implemented.

While there is no optimal extent of implementation, generally, we would be surprised to find either everything or nothing implemented. If everything is implemented, then it creates an impression of ignoring changes over time that should influence implementation. If nothing is implemented, then it creates an impression that the organization is completely unable to create change, and there is complete inconsistency between talk and walk. For example, an empirical study of Norwegian business organizations tells us that, on average, 60 percent of a system's strategy was implemented (Gottschalk, 1999). Whether this is good or bad is hard to tell. We may suggest a rule of thumb

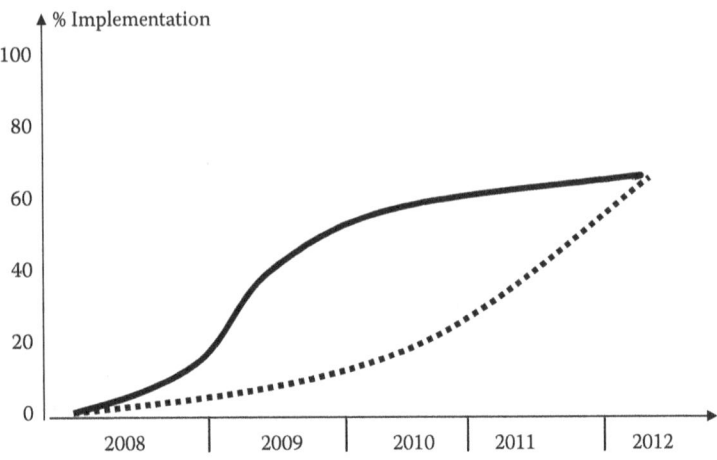

Figure 4.4 Implementation of strategy over time.

that two-thirds should be implemented over time, as illustrated by alternative paths in Figure 4.4.

We have to remind ourselves that initially, at the start of implementation, the complete intelligence strategy is to be implemented. All actions were written into the plan to be executed. Nothing was written into the plan without the intention of being executed. What we are saying about implementation extent is that environmental changes, as well as internal changes over time, may create a situation where some of the plan contents are not smart to do anymore. Such evaluation of the plan after some time, often after one or two years, can cause revision of the plan.

At this stage 6 in the Y model of implementing the plan, all attention should be focused on implementation of the entire plan. This is the stage of action. In the case of a systems strategy, technical equipment, such as servers, PCs, printers, and cables, are installed. Operating systems are upgraded. Application packages, software programs, programming tools, end user tools, and database systems are installed. Development projects are initiated. And management and user training takes place.

Implementation Factors

At this stage, we should focus on the tackling of implementation challenges. The literature on implementation challenges is steadily growing. A series of factors influencing implementation have been identified. In the following, we will discuss some important factors for implementation of strategy, where we use the case of IS (information systems)/IT (information technology) strategy as an example:

- Resources needed for the implementation
- User involvement during the implementation
- Solutions to potential resistance during the implementation
- Responsibility for the implementation
- Management support for the implementation
- Information technology needed for implementation

Resources Needed for the Implementation

One reason for the lack of implementation is that resources often are not made available. The answer to the simple question: Can it be done? is dependent on competence and resources. It is important to identify the resources and actions needed to implement new applications and development tools. Resource mobilization for implementation is an effective mechanism to secure the quality of the process. An important resource issue in the field of strategic IS/IT is the difficulty of recruiting IS specialists and defining their role in projects. In an IS/IT strategy written in English in a Norwegian organization, this problem was confirmed: "Technological expertise is a precondition for development and migration of new and complicated technology in the institution, but the dependence on such expertise also represents a problem to management" (Gottschalk, 1999). Some information systems professionals are systems rationalists preoccupied with new capabilities of technology, tending to ignore goal incongruence and assuming consensus on goals. Generally speaking, information systems innovations are dependent on an IS professional environment. Just as important, there is a need for users who will champion the new systems and have the drive and vision to push the projects forward. In addition, many businesses are dependent on external expertise, such as consultants, for implementation. In summary, these resources are important:

- Financial resources needed for the implementation
- Technical abilities needed for the implementation
- Human resources needed for the implementation
- Project team time needed for the implementation
- External consultants needed for the implementation
- A project champion needed for the implementation

User Involvement during the Implementation

Both resources for and extensive performance of user training are necessary to secure implementation of IS/IT strategy. Education, training, and other implementation activities are generally viewed as outside the IS role, in part because formal authority for training usually is assigned elsewhere.

Training may consist of both formal and informal training. Formal training can be long-term as well as short-term instruction received through seminars, classes, conventions, and private lessons, while informal training can be on-the-job training received from co-workers and supervisors as the need arises. Many training efforts are based on needs analysis, needs assessment, or performance analysis. User involvement in implementation is an effective mechanism to secure quality of implementation. It is usually better to use a high-involvement process that utilizes the knowledge and creativity of the people who actually do the work. Implementation represents a situation of transition in which users experience a threat to their sense of control over their work, if not direct loss of control. Interventions, which restore the users' sense of control, will reduce the threatening quality of the implementation experience and, as a result, heighten the users' satisfaction with the new systems. In this view, the active ingredient for user involvement is the perceived control. User needs are the source of benefits that motivate the use of an information technology application, and user satisfaction increases the implementability. In summary, these user involvement issues are important:

- Training of information systems users
- Users' understanding of systems' functional features
- Users' participation in systems projects
- Users' involvement in the operation of information systems
- Participation in the ongoing development of information systems
- Users' support for the implementation

Solutions to Potential Resistance during the Implementation

Solutions to potential resistance during the implementation are methods and processes of solving problems created by latent opposition to the implementation. Resistance involves a stubbornness in fulfilling the expectations of others. Resistance to implementation may have many facets, such as quiet ignorance, active argumentation, low priority put on implementation compared with other assignments, etc. Potential bases of resistance to the adoption of the plan should be identified, and the plan should define solutions needed for avoiding and/or dampening potential resistance to the necessary changes. Resistance may be caused by uncertainty, lack of competence, or commitment to the status quo. Some may find their influence threatened, while others feel that implementation may be harmful to the organization, and then some sense that the plan should be improved before implementation. In summary, these resistance issues are important:

- Solutions to potential resistance caused by job security
- Solutions to potential resistance caused by change of position

- Solutions to potential resistance caused by new skills requirements
- Solutions to potential resistance caused by skepticism about results
- Solutions to potential resistance caused by functional units' interests
- Solutions to potential resistance of our customers

Responsibility for the Implementation

During implementation, the senses of implementers (those responsible for the introduction of the technology to prospective users) will influence the extent of implementation. Most IS units do not have responsibility for key organizational results. Line managers are increasingly assuming responsibility for planning, building, and running information systems that affect their operation. It is important to identify the IT departments' actions necessary to expedite adoption of the plan. A monitoring system to review implementation and provide feedback is an effective implementation mechanism. For each benefit desired from the implementation, specific responsibility for realizing benefits should be allocated within the business. Only when specific people are responsible for implementation actions is implementation likely to occur. Responsibility has to be defined in such detail that responsible people take expected initiatives when problems occur during implementation. It may also be valuable to consider whether the chief executive responsible for strategy is willing to accept the personal risk involved. If not, the strategy may be good, but is unlikely to be implemented. Implementation participants must accept responsibility for their own behavior, including the success of the actions they take to create change. Responsibility as such may take on two forms: negative duty and positive duty. Negative responsibility implies that action be taken due to threats and is often motivated by loyalty, while positive responsibility implies that action be taken due to commitment. In summary, these responsibility issues are important:

- Responsibility for implementation on time
- Responsibility for implementation within budget
- Responsibility for implementation with intended benefits
- Responsibility for step-wise implementation of large projects
- Responsibility for implementation of high-priority projects
- Responsibility for short-term benefits from initial projects
- Personnel rewards from successful implementation

Management Support for the Implementation

Management support is widely recognized as an important factor in the implementation of information systems. Management may be hesitant when it comes to the implementation of IS/IT strategy, hence, representing a problem.

Some top executives, in reality, are committed to the status quo. Both middle management attitudes and senior management attitudes toward implementation are important influences on the extent of plan implementation. It may be difficult to secure top management commitment for implementation (commitment being defined as acceptance of plan values and willingness to exert effort on its behalf). The planning methodology itself may require too much top management involvement. The output of planning is not necessarily in accordance with management expectations. Top management monitoring of implementation may represent an effective implementation mechanism. Management control systems provide a comprehensive mechanism for implementing plans. Management monitoring and control of the implementation may be organized through a steering committee. Management support is pivotal to the adoption of innovations. Chief executive officers (CEOs), in particular, have a major impact on changes in their organizations. A plan must be a call for action, one that recognizes management's responsibility to fix what is broken proactively and in real time. It is imperative that IT personnel educate their top managers and make them aware of the importance of their support in major IT initiatives. Top management support is a key recurrent factor critical for effective implementation. In summary, these management issues are important:

- Management expectations of the implementation
- Management participation in the implementation
- Management monitoring of the implementation
- Management knowledge about the implementation
- Management time needed for the implementation
- Management enthusiasm for the implementation

Information Technology Needed for Implementation

Information technology to be implemented is composed of the hardware and software to be developed, acquired, installed, used, and modified. Information technology is developing rapidly, but in many organizations, IT is still lagging behind users' needs. For example, artificial intelligence is still in its infancy as a technology. This implies that a firm that wants to implement advanced knowledge management systems may have problems finding suitable technology. It is, therefore, important that the IS/IT strategy has identified available technology. It is seldom smart to trust vendors' promises concerning future features of new technology when developing the IS/IT strategy. Instead, technological constraints should be identified and accepted. It is often emphasized that information architecture is not enough unless data access issues can be resolved. In summary, this technology is important:

- Hardware to be implemented
- Communications technology to be implemented
- Databases to be implemented
- Applications software to be implemented
- Operating systems to be implemented
- A data infrastructure for the organization

Resources needed for the implementation, user involvement during the implementation, solutions to potential resistance during the implementation, responsibility for the implementation, management support for the implementation, and information technology needed for the implementation are all considered important factors for IS/IT strategy implementation. These factors were empirically evaluated first in Norway and then in Australia (Gottschalk, 1999).

In addition to the six factors listed above, four more factors were added in the empirical studies: (1) analysis of the organization, (2) anticipated changes in the external environment, (3) projects' relevance to the business plan, and (4) clear presentation of implementation issues.

In Norway, two factors were significant: responsibility for the implementation and user involvement during the implementation. In Australia, one factor was significant: the projects' relevance to the business plan.

The average extent of strategic IS/IT plan implementation in Australia was 3.4, while the average plan implementation in Norway was 3.3, on a scale from 1 (little extent) to 5 (great extent). These results indicate that in both Australia and Norway, roughly 60 percent of a strategic IS/IT plan is implemented on average.

In Australia, responding organizations had an extensive description of projects' relevance to the business plan (3.7), while they had a limited description of solutions to potential resistance (1.9). In Norway, responding organizations had an extensive description of technology to be implemented (3.6), while they had a limited description of solutions to potential resistance (2.0).

The significant predictor in Australia was projects' relevance to the business plan, which had the highest overall description rating (3.7), indicating that relevance is both important and taken care of in many Australian firms. The two significant predictors in Norway were responsibility of implementation and user involvement during implementation, which had high overall description ratings of 2.7 and 3.0.

The interesting difference between Australia and Norway lies in the finding that strategic descriptions are more important for implementation in Australia, while resource descriptions are more important for implementation in Norway. Given that both have about the same extent of plan implementation, 3.4 and 3.3, there is little reason to argue that firms in one nation are more successful than firms in the other.

One emerging proposition is that smaller organizations will tend to be more dependent on resources to get a plan implemented, while larger organizations will tend to be more dependent on strategic relevance to get a plan implemented. This proposition is relevant as responding Australian firms were much larger than were the Norwegian respondents. However, no significant relationship was found between organization size and the extent of relevance description.

Another emerging proposition is related to cultural differences. According to the Scandinavian research on information systems development (Gottschalk, 1999), Scandinavia has high living standards and educational levels, an advanced technology infrastructure, an open community, and key innovative leaders. This tradition seems different from research in other countries, such as the United Kingdom with control structures, which may imply different strategic IS/IT plan implementation problems.

Research Model to Explain Implementation Extent

The dependent variable in this conceptual research is the extent of strategy implementation, as illustrated in Figure 4.5. Implementation might be measured in four different ways: completion of tasks thus far, tasks to be completed, completion of the overall strategy, and improved organizational performance from the strategy (Gottschalk, 1999).

Specifically, implementation might be measured using these alternative definitions (Gottschalk, 1999):

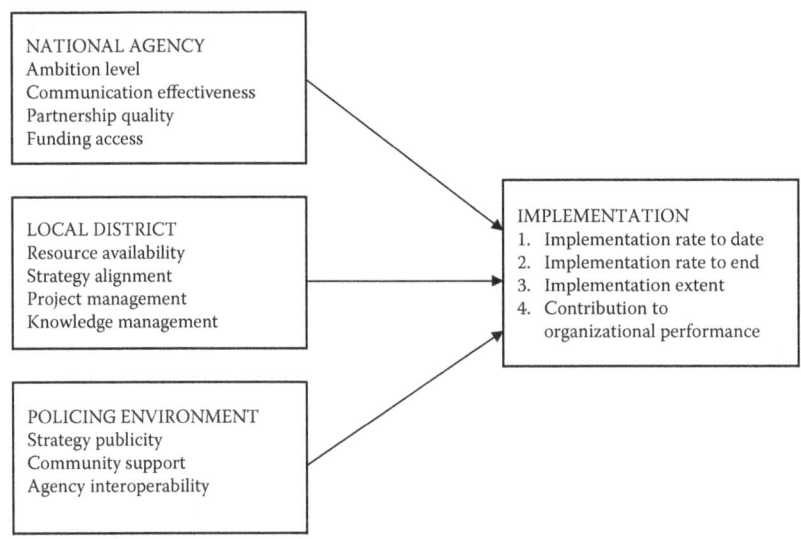

Figure 4.5 Research model to study the extent of strategy implementation.

1. *Implementation rate to date*: Divide projects actually completed to date by projects scheduled to be implemented.
2. *Implementation rate to end*: Divide projects actually implemented to date by projects in the strategy, and divide by percent of expired time horizon.
3. *Implementation extent*: The extent to which the strategy has been completed on time, within budget, as expected, with desired results without deviations during implementation, with satisfaction of stakeholders.
4. *Contribution to organizational performance*: Reduced crime, increased success rate, reduced resource consumption, and improved knowledge sharing.

As illustrated in Figure 4.5, three independent variables are introduced in the research model. First, the national agency, such as the Norwegian Police Directorate, has to be an active part in the implementation based on realistic ambitions and effective communications. The national agency has to secure required funding for strategy implementation (Homel et al., 2004). Next, the local district should have available resources and align strategies that compete for resources (Harrington et al., 2006). Finally, the strategy should enjoy publicity both internally and in society because a high profile operation brings a number of advantages (Stockdale and Gresham, 1995).

Agency operability is one of the items in the policing environment where the mobilization of electronic information across organizations has the potential of modernizing and transforming information exchanges. High-ranking issues among the defining purposes of e-government are highly agile, citizen-centric, accountable, transparent, effective, and efficient government operations and services (Scholl and Klischewski, 2007).

Based on the research model, three research hypotheses can be formulated:

1. The extent of local strategy implementation is positively related to the central agency's support for local implementation.
2. The extent of local strategy implementation is positively related to the local police district's readiness for implementation.
3. The extent of local strategy implementation is positively related to the environment's support for implementation.

Case: National Intelligence Model in the United Kingdom

In the United Kingdom, strategy implementation took place by adapting the it to local police strategy. As an example, the South Yorkshire Police intelligence strategy (SYPIS, 2007) is a combination of the National Intelligence

Model (NIM) and the South Yorkshire Policing Model (SYPM), as illustrated in Figure 4.6.

Projects are created within the strategy. Action managers have been appointed for these projects, and they report to the Intelligence Strategy Management Board on a quarterly basis. The board directs, sets targets, and reviews progress of these actions; completed ones may be discharged and new ones added.

Case: National Strategy for Intelligence and Analysis in Norway

Similar to the approach in the United Kingdom, Norwegian police districts are responsible for implementing the strategy (POD, 2007). In a survey conducted in 2008 (one year after the strategy was developed), police districts were asked about the extent of implementation. The average response was 34 percent implementation, varying from 0 to 100 percent.

An intelligence meeting was held outside Oslo in May 2008 to enhance strategy implementation through knowledge exchange among participants at the meeting. Out of a national police force of 12,500, 324 police officers participated at the meeting. Important topics at the conference were knowledge-based and intelligence-led policing.

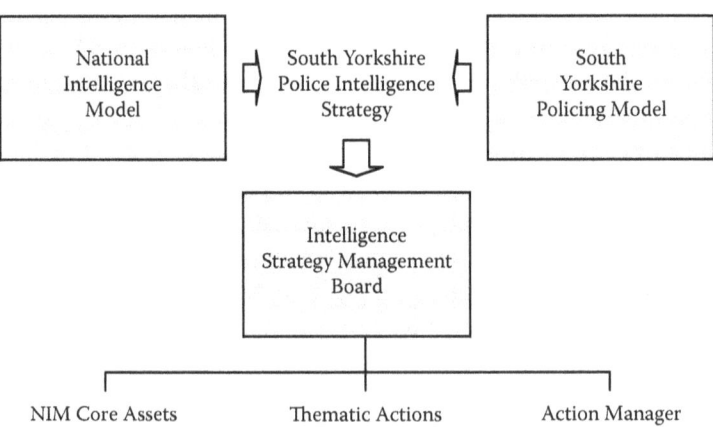

Figure 4.6 Intelligence Strategy Management Structure in South Yorkshire Police. (Adapted from SYPIS. 2007. *South Yorkshire Police Intelligence Strategy 2007–Breaking the chain*, South Yorkshire Police, U.K.: www.policereform.gov. uk)

Case: Police Intelligence Model in Sweden

While both British and Norwegian central law enforcement agencies left it to local police districts to find ways to implement intelligence strategy, Swedish police developed a specific implementation procedure (Polisen, 2006). According to the procedure, each police district would establish projects that were aligned with the strategy. Projects were to be defined in terms of tasks, responsibilities, and deadlines.

Here are some examples of projects to be carried out in support of the strategy (PUM, 2005):

1. Create understanding, in the entire organization, for changes in operations to support the new strategy: Information to all employees by May 31, 2006.
2. Establish strategic management according to the new strategy: Management meetings twice a year, the first by September 1, 2006.
3. Develop responsibility for intelligence services according to the new strategy: Mobilize resources by May 30, 2007.
4. Implement analysis methodology according to the new strategy: Learning process for new methodology completed by September 30, 2007.

References

Atkinson, H. 2006. Strategy implementation: A role for the balanced scorecard? *Management Decision* 44 (10): 1441–1460.

Brauer, M. and Schmidt, S.L. 2006. Exploring strategy implementation consistency over time: The moderating effects of industry velocity and firm performance. *Journal of Management Governance* 10: 205–226.

Bullock, K., Farrell, G., and Tilley, N. 2002. *Finding and implementing crime reduction initiatives*, Policing and Reducing Crime Unit, Research Development and Statistic Directorate, Home Office, London: www.policereform.gov.uk.

Gottschalk, P. 1999. Strategic information systems planning: The IT strategy implementation matrix. *European Journal of Information Systems* 8: 107–118.

Gottschalk, P. 2007. *Knowledge management in law enforcement: Technologies and techniques*. Hershey, PA: Idea Group Publishing.

Harrington, V., Trikha, S., and France, A. 2006. *Process and early implementation issues: Emerging findings from the On Track evaluation*, Home Office Online Report 06/04, London: www.policereform.gov.uk.

Homel, P., Nutley, S., Webb, B., and Tilley, N. 2004. *Investing to deliver: Reviewing the implementation of the UK Crime Reduction Programme*, Home Office Research, Development and Statistics Directorate, London: www.policereform.gov.uk.

POD. 2007. *Nasjonal strategi for etterretning og analyse (National strategy for intelligence and analysis)*, Politidirektoratet (Norwegian Police Directorate), Oslo, Norway.

Polisen. 2006. *Polisens underrättelsemodell (Police Intelligence Model)*, Rikspolis-styrelsen, Stockholm, Sweden.

PUM. 2005. *Prosjektdirektiv PUM—Polisens underrättelsesmodell (Project Directive PUM—The Police Intelligence Model)*, Police Authority of Västra Götaland, Sweden.

Quinton, P. and Olagundoye, J. 2004. An evaluation of the phased implementation of the recording of police stops. *Home Office Development and Practice Report*, London: www.blink.org.uk/docs/homeoffice/dpr23pdf.

Scholl, H.J. and Klischewski, R. 2007. E-government integration and interoperability: Framing the research agenda. *International Journal of Public Administration* 30 (8): 889–920.

Stockdale, J.E. and Gresham, P.J. 1995. Combating burglary: An evaluation of three strategies. *Crime Detection & Prevention Series*, Paper 59. Police Research Group, London: www.policereform.gov.uk.

SYPIS. 2007. *South Yorkshire Police Intelligence Strategy 2007—Breaking the chain*, South Yorkshire Police, UK: www.policereform.gov.uk.

Organizational Structure

5

Barriers to strategy implementation are often found in the organizational structure in law enforcement. Organizational structure is the formal decision-making framework by which job tasks are divided and coordinated (Birkinshaw et al., 2002; Markides and Williamson, 1996). The purpose of the organizing function is to make the best use of the organization's resources to achieve organizational goals. Formalization is an important aspect of structure, as it is the extent to which the units of the organization are explicitly defined and its policies, procedures, and goals are clearly stated.

The new ways of gathering information in terms of intelligence and analysis may crash with the old structures— the way activities are traditionally organized and carried out. Crime does not obey the boundaries between police districts or police departments. Crime does not obey the boundaries between authorities. Economic crime, for example, may burden authorities in such entities as the tax office, the enforcement office, customs, and the prosecutor, in addition to the police districts. Information exchange should be the minimum of collaboration, but often there is a need to work closer together and create new knowledge in multiprofessional and multiorganizational groups (Puonti, 2007).

It is often argued that the police have a bureaucratic and functional organization. Bureaucratic structures have a certain degree of standardization, and functional structures have specialized groups, such as homicide, narcotics, and organized crime. Such structures may represent barriers to interorganizational knowledge management based on intelligence and analysis.

It has long been argued that organizational structure is the result of organizational choices. This idea was developed by Mintzberg (1979) and applied by scholars, such as van Donk and Molloy (2008). According to this concept, the structure of organizations is the result of choices based on nine design parameters, which are used by organizations to divide and coordinate their work to establish desired patterns of behavior.

Organizational Design

The choices about each of the design parameters mentioned above represent the building blocks of the organizational structure. The nine design parameters are (van Donk and Molloy, 2008; Mintzberg, 1979):

1. *Design of positions in terms of job specialization*: The amount of tasks to be executed and the amount of control over that work. Jobs can be specialized in two dimensions. First, job specialization in the *horizontal dimension* represents division of labor. At one extreme, the police officer is a jack-of-all-trades, forever jumping from one broad task to another. At the other extreme, he focuses his efforts on the same highly specialized task, repeated day in and day out, even minute in and minute out. Second, job specialization in the *vertical dimension* represents separation of work from the administration. At one extreme, the police officer merely does the work without any thought as to how or why. At the other extreme, he controls every aspect of the work in addition to doing it. In the first dimension, we find narrowness by horizontal job specialization (in that it deals with parallel activities) and breadth by horizontal job enlargement. In the second dimension, we find depth by vertical job specialization and closeness by vertical job enlargement.

2. *Design of positions in terms of behavioral formalization*: Regulating the behavior of individuals by formalization of job, workflow, or rules. No matter what the means of formalization (job, workflow, or rules), the effect on the person doing the job is the same—his behavior is regulated. Power over how that work is to be done passes from the police officer to the person who designs the specification, often a manager in the police district or in the national police directorate. Organizations formalize behavior to reduce its variability, ultimately to predict and control it. One prime motive for doing so is to coordinate activities. The fully formalized organization, as far as possible, is the completely controllable, precise, and predictable organization. There should be no confusion in the organization. Everyone knows exactly what to do. The alternative is a completely informal organization, where neither jobs nor workflows nor rules are specified.

3. *Design of positions in terms of training and indoctrination*: Training is the process by which job-related skills and knowledge are taught, while indoctrination is the process by which organizational norms are acquired. Professionals are trained over long periods of time, before they ever assume their positions. Often, this training takes place outside the organization, frequently in a police academy. The training itself usually requires a particular and extensive expertise, beyond the capacity of the organization to provide. Indoctrination is the way an organization formally socializes its members for its own benefit, and is the process by which organizational norms are acquired.

4. *Design of superstructure in terms of unit grouping*: Establishing the formal lines of authority by combining people into units and

departments. Grouping establishes a system of common supervision among positions and units, and requires positions in the same group to share common tasks and resources. Grouping creates common measures of performance. When positions are to be allocated to groups, several criteria are applied, such as knowledge and skill, work process, and function. Positions may be grouped according to specialized knowledge and skills that police officers bring to the job. Alternatively, positions may be grouped according to functions. When grouped according to knowledge, the same kinds of experts are organized in the same group. When grouped according to function, different kinds of personnel are organized in the same group to carry out all tasks in that function.

5. *Design of superstructure in terms of unit size*: The span of control (distinguishing between a narrow and a wide span). This design of superstructure determines how large each unit or work group should be. This is a question of span of control. While a tall organizational structure will be the result of small groups, a flat structure will be the result of large groups. A linkage focusing on *planning* involves future thinking. A linkage focusing on *control* involves correcting actions as they occur.

6. *Design of lateral linkages in terms of planning and control systems*: The specification of the desired output and the assessment if the desired outputs or standards have been achieved. The purpose of a plan is to specify a desired output in the future. The purpose of performance control is to regulate the overall results of a given unit.

7. *Design of lateral linkages in terms of liaison devices*: Positions bypassing normal vertical channels to establish contacts between two units to coordinate the work of these units. Examples of liaison positions are task forces and standing committees. The standing committee is a more permanent interdepartmental grouping. It meets regularly to discuss issues of common interest. Another example of lateral linkage is the matrix structure. A weak liaison device would be a coordinator who attempts to make different parts of the organization aware of the needs of the other parts. A strong liaison device would be a board with power to make decisions influencing several parts of the organization.

8. *Design of decision-making systems in terms of vertical decentralization*: The power to make decisions down the chain of authority. When all power for decision making rests at a single point in an organization with a single individual, the structure is completely centralized. When the power is dispersed among many individuals, the structure is decentralized. Centralization is the tightest means of coordinating decision making in an organization. Vertical decentralization is

concerned with the delegation of decision power down the chain of command.

9. *Design of decision-making systems in terms of horizontal decentralization*: Refers in general to the extent to which nonmanagers control decision processes. Decentralization implies transfer of power out of the line structure. Power is transformed into informal power, for example, control over knowledge resources and information gathering and advice.

A comparison of these organizational structure parameters for criminal (C) versus legal (L) organizations is illustrated in Figure 5.1. We suggest that horizontal job specialization is applied to a greater extent in criminal organizations, while a deeper vertical job specialization is found in legal organizations. An example of a legal organization might be a police investigation unit (Figure 5.1 illustrates the two sides of policing organized crime).

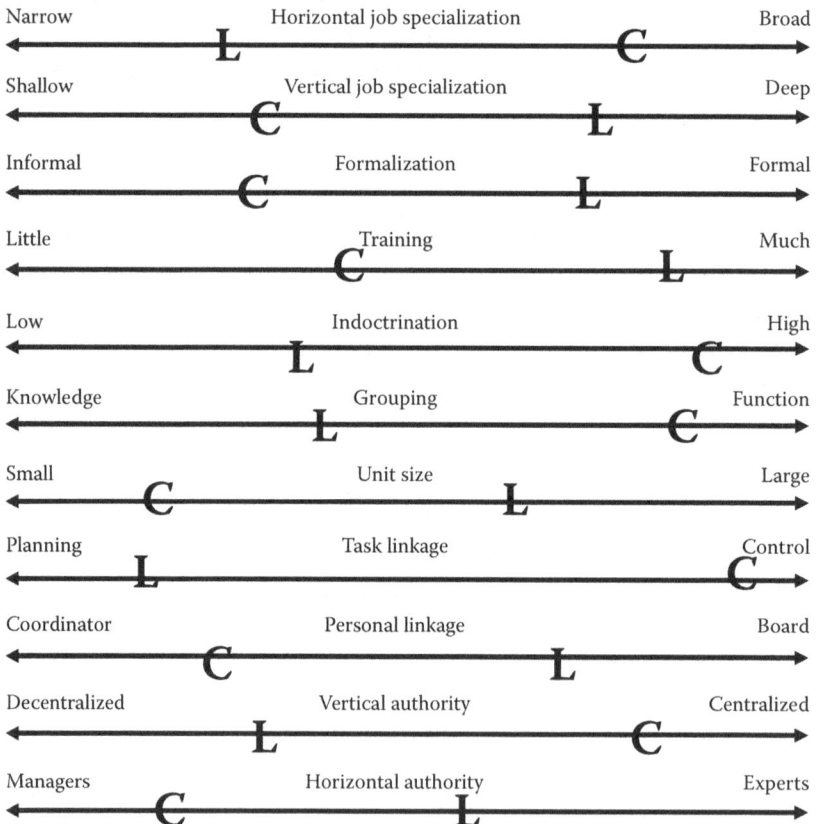

Figure 5.1 Organizational structure parameters for criminal versus legal organizations (C: criminal, L: legal).

In addition to the above nine design parameters, the shape of the organizational structure is influenced by contingency factors. Examples of contingency factors are age and size of the organization, regulation in the environment, stability in the environment, and power in terms of external control and internal control (van Donk and Molloy, 2008).

Organizational design in policing is concerned with resilience, which is the capacity of a system, potentially exposed to hazards, to adapt by resisting or changing in order to reach and maintain an acceptable level of functioning and structure. Resilience represents the capacity of an organization, where the desired situation is characterized by enough staff with enough skills to perform in the face of unforeseen or strenuous circumstances (Loveday, 2008).

Organizational Configuration

A slightly different approach to organizational structure is organizational configuration, which is defined as a multidimensional constellation of conceptually distinct characteristics that commonly occur together. In this perspective, organizations are understood as clusters of interconnected structures and practices. It represents a systemic and holistic view of organizations, where patterns or profiles, rather than design parameters, are related to an outcome, such as performance (Fiss, 2007). Ketchen et al. (1997) found that an organization's performance is partially explained by its configuration.

When studying criminal organizations, organizational structures are often identified as either economic–bureaucratic structures or independent–network structures. Criminal networks have the merit of capturing the flexible and dynamic nature of interpersonal interaction. When studying Colombian cocaine firms, Zaitch (2002, 297) found a mixture of the two structures:

> By studying internal business and labor relations, I tried to capture both the economic and dynamic dimensions of cocaine enterprises. I found that Colombian cocaine firms are informal, small, mutating and decentralized. Some are individual enterprises; others adopt the form of temporary partnerships between two or three people. These coalitions are often formed solely for a single project, with some of the people involved also engaging in legal activities or in other coalitions. In many cases, a percentage system is used to divide profits, and payments in kind are not rare. A further conclusion of this study is that despite the importance of kinship ties and the frequent use of relatives, none of these enterprises are "family businesses." Brokers (people with contacts) play a central role in bringing about these coalitions and transactions.

Organizational configuration in police, which is our concern here, has changed lately by including international relations. Generally, police configuration has recently expanded its reach and range. An analysis of organizational change in the policing sector in fifteen European countries revealed that the extent of Europeanization of national law enforcement structures, however, was still very limited. There is yet no one standard model for policing being rolled out across Europe. Well-established national characteristics continue to shape organizational change within the various countries (Sheptycki, 2007).

However, the evidence also revealed that the increased emphasis on national coordination of international information flows between police agencies about serious organized crime had caused significant changes in the structure of the police sector across the continent. Luxembourg, for example, merged its two police forces, the police and the Gendarmerie Grand-Ducale, into a single national force. In Belgium, the three principal police-type agencies (the gendarmerie, the judicial police, and the municipal police) were integrated into one police force structured on two levels (federal and local). In Norway, the number of police districts was cut in half, and the national police management was moved out of the department of justice and into an independent police directorate. The Netherlands reorganized its 148 police constabularies into an integrated national structure with twenty-five regions and has continued to refine and centralize its national system for the management of intelligence. Also, in Sweden, a national criminal intelligence service has been created (Sheptycki, 2007).

Organizational Architecture

Yet, another slightly different approach to organizational structure is organizational architecture (Auteri and Wagner, 2007; Ethiraj and Levinthal, 2004; Moussavou, 2006). The issue of structuring organizational effort became popular in the 1990s with the promotion of the concept organizational architecture. The architecture of an organization provides the framework through which an organization aims to realize its core qualities as specified in its ambitions. It provides for the infrastructure where business processes are deployed. It ensures that the organization's core qualities are realized across the business processes deployed within the organization.

According to most authors, organizational architecture is a metaphor; like traditional architecture, it shapes the organizational space where life will take place. It also represents a concept which implies a connection between the organizational structures and other systems inside the organization in order to create a unique synergistic system, which will be more than just the sum of its parts.

Some systems are effective and efficient, while others are not. Successful systems may be attributable to the skill exercised in designing the system or to the quality of management practiced during operations, or both. Successful systems are characterized by their simplicity, flexibility, reliability, economy, and acceptability:

- *Simplicity.* An effective organizational system need not be complex. On the contrary, simplicity in design is an extremely desirable quality. Consider the task of communicating information about the operation of a system and the allocation of its inputs. The task is not difficult when components are few and the relationships among them are straightforward. However, the problems of communication multiply with each successive stage of complexity.
- *Flexibility.* Conditions change and managers should be prepared to adjust operations accordingly. There are two ways to adjust to a changing operating environment: (1) to design new systems or (2) to modify operating systems. An existing system should not be modified to accommodate a change in objectives, but every system should be sufficiently flexible to integrate changes that may occur either in the environment or in the nature of the inputs.
- *Reliability.* System reliability is an important factor in organizations. Reliability is the consistency with which operations are maintained, and may vary from zero output (a complete breakdown or work stoppage) to a constant or predictable output. The typical system operates somewhere between these two extremes. The characteristics of reliability can be designed into the system by carefully selecting and arranging the operating components; the system is no more reliable than its weakest segment.
- *Economy.* An effective system is not necessarily an economical (efficient) system. It is often dysfunctional and, thus, expensive to develop much greater capacity for one segment of a system than for some other part. Building in redundancy or providing for every contingency usually neutralizes the operating efficiency of the system. When a system's objectives include achieving a particular task at the lowest possible cost, there must be some degree of trade-off between effectiveness and efficiency. When a system's objective is to perform a certain mission regardless of cost, there can be no trade-offs.
- *Acceptability.* Any system, no matter how well designed, will not function properly unless it is accepted by the people who operate it. If the participants do not believe it will benefit them, are opposed to it, are pressured into using it, or think it is not a good system, it will not work properly. If a system is not accepted, two things can happen: (1) the system will be modified gradually by the people who are using it, or (2) the system will be used ineffectively and ultimately fail. Unplanned alterations in an elaborate system can nullify advantages associated with using the system.

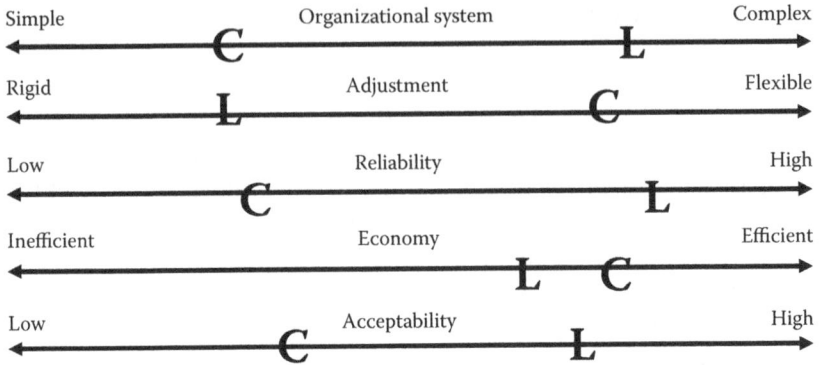

Figure 5.2 Organizational architecture parameters for criminal versus legal organizations (C: criminal, L: legal).

Organizational architecture parameters for criminal versus legal organizations are compared in Figure 5.2. For example, we suggest that criminals may be somewhat opposed to the system, but they are pressured into using it, causing the extent of acceptability to be lower than in legal business enterprises. Again, we may assume that the legal organization is a police investigation unit.

Organizations are constructed like any other kind of social system. An organization is observable through the actions and interactions of its members, both between themselves and with people in the organization's environment. To be observable, an organization must have a domain for its activity, and it must have a set of objectives and goals. The basic elements in organization structuring include division of labor, structuring of work, and coordination, as first suggested by Mintzberg (1979).

In the architecture of policing, Jones (2007) discussed three alternatives for compliance in terms of police use of force:

1. *Instrumental and prudential compliance,* where two alternatives are incentives and disincentives.
2. *Normative compliance,* where three alternatives are acceptance of (or belief in) norm, attachment leading to compliance, and legitimacy.
3. *Constrained-based compliance,* where three alternatives are physical restrictions or requirements on individual leading to compliance (natural or imposed), restrictions on access to target, and structural constraints.

The topic of police use of force is an important one, where the organization is constructed to encourage or discourage use of force. When the police officer is male, tall, and strong, the use of force may seem attractive. When the police officer is female, small, and not strong, she has to find other ways of solving problems. Maybe her solutions would be better even for the tall and strong policeman. Therefore, the use of physical constraints and architectures in policing are important (Jones, 2007).

Organization Building

Groth (1999) developed the idea of preconditions for organizing and suggested six areas where we quickly run into limits restricting organization building:

- *Capacity for work.* Both the need for organizations and their nature are strongly dependent on the nature and amount of work that has to be carried out.
- *Memory performance.* The brain has limitations in terms of storage capacity and retrieval capabilities.
- *Information processing.* The brain has limitations in terms of reasoning, problem solving, and decision making.
- *Communication.* The amount of information a person can absorb is limited by a communication bandwidth.
- *Interaction.* How fast a person can interact with other persons is limited.
- *Emotion.* Ambition, likes and dislikes, instincts, and preferences represent limitations.

According to Groth, it is difficult to ascertain which of these abilities or properties are most important, but they all represent limitations for organizational design. Because organizational design is about developing and implementing strategy (Bryan and Joyce, 2007), it is important to be aware of human limitations. Organizations can be designed to gain from strengths and compensate for weaknesses, and to avoid threats and to prosper from opportunities.

For example, hierarchy is efficient for setting aspirations, making decisions, assigning tasks, allocating resources, managing people who cannot direct themselves, and holding people accountable. Even in new times, hierarchy is needed to put boundaries around individuals and teams (Bryan and Joyce, 2007). All organizations are hierarchical, as compliance with authority is a universal feature of organizations. An authority structure is essential to decision making and its implementation (Andersen, 2002).

Furthermore, interdependencies among elements of organizational design might represent both barriers and enablers of strategy development and implementation. Because organizations are complex entities composed of tightly interdependent and mutually supportive elements, performance is determined by the degree of alignment among the major elements. The marginal costs and benefits associated with any design element depend on the configuration of others (Rivkin and Siggelkow, 2003).

Structure as Determinant of Strategy Implementation

According to Puonti (2007), the traditional mode of collaboration in police forces resembles a relay race. This *sequential collaboration* enables only the transmission of papers and information from one participant to another. In contrast, *parallel collaboration* enables working together and analyzing the information together. The intelligence work often requires shared word processes that involve interaction and open-minded exchange of different perspectives of crime.

Information technology has certainly enhanced the capacity of police to collect, retrieve, and analyze information. It has altered important aspects of the field of policing. It has redefined the value of communicative and technical resources, and institutionalized accountability through built-in formats and procedures of reporting. It has the potential of restructuring policing from *vertical information systems* to *horizontal information systems*. But, the impact of technology on the work processes of policing appears to be much less substantial, according to Chan (2003). The advantage brought about by technology—the capacity for a more responsive and problem-oriented approach to policing—has not been fully exploited.

In many police forces, there is a *command structure*, rather than a *knowledge structure* (Collier et al., 2004). In the command structure, the higher-ranking officer is always right. In the knowledge structure, the knowledge is always right. The command structure is a quasimilitary structure (Kelley, 2005).

The dependent variable in this conceptual research is the extent of strategy implementation, as illustrated in Figure 5.3. Implementation might be measured in four different ways: completion of tasks so far, tasks expected to be completed, completion of the overall strategy, and improved organizational performance from the strategy (Gottschalk, 1999).

Specifically, implementation might be measured using these alternative definitions (Gottschalk, 1999):

1. *Implementation rate to date*: Divide projects actually completed to date by projects scheduled to be implemented.
2. *Implementation rate to end*: Divide projects actually implemented to date by projects in the strategy and divide by percent of expired time horizon.

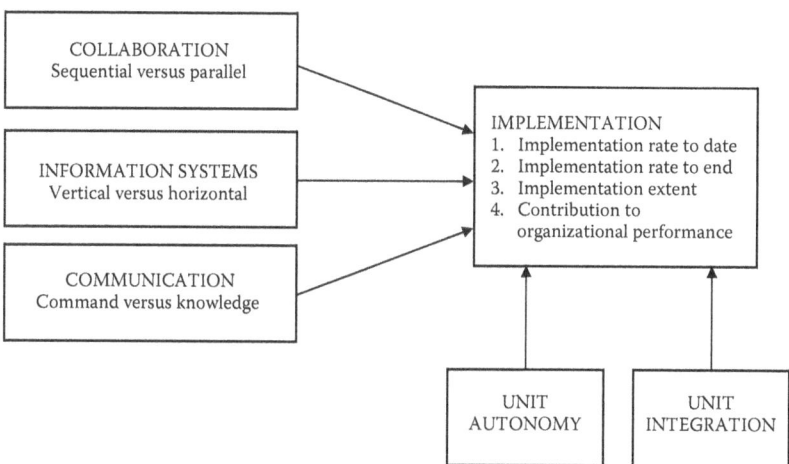

Figure 5.3 Research model to study the extent of strategy implementation from police structure.

3. *Implementation extent*: The extent to which the strategy has been completed on time, within budget, as expected, with desired results without deviations during implementation, and with satisfaction of stakeholders.
4. *Contribution to organizational performance*: Reduced crime, increased success rate, reduced resource consumption, and improved knowledge sharing.

In addition to collaboration, systems, and communication already presented as independent variables, two more are introduced. Autonomy of the unit is the extent to which the police unit is able to make strategic, tactical, as well as operational decisions without the involvement of central management. Interunit integration refers to the state of collaboration among units, and the techniques used to achieve this collaboration. These two dimensions represent differentiation and integration (Birkinshaw et al., 2002).

Organizational structure as a predictor of intelligence strategy implementation in policing might be conceptualized in terms of two alternative structures: bureaucratic and knowledge organization. The knowledge organization is very different from the bureaucratic organization. For example, the knowledge organization's focus on flexibility and public response is very different from the bureaucracy's focus on organizational stability and the accuracy and repetitiveness of internal processes. In the knowledge organization, current practices emphasize using the ideas and capabilities of police officers to improve decision making by senior leadership. In contrast, bureaucracies utilize autocratic decision making by senior leadership with unquestioned execution by the workforce.

In our perspective of strategy implementation, it is interesting and relevant to speculate whether a bureaucratic or a knowledge organization structure will lead to extended intelligence strategy implementation. It might be argued that a bureaucratic structure is better, as the autocratic leadership may implement the strategy by command. On the other side, it might be argued that a knowledge structure is better, as understanding and insight by police officers as knowledge workers will enable police intelligence. Only an empirical study based on the suggested research model will provide evidence for one or the other.

Case: An Empirical Study of Implementation and Structure

An empirical study was carried out in Norway in 2008 (Gudmundsen, 2009). In the survey research, implementation of national strategy for intelligence and analysis was measured in terms of three alternative constructs. First, there was a statement scale:

1. Not implemented
2. Implemented to a little extent
3. Partly implemented
4. Implemented to a great extent
5. Completely implemented

The average response was 2.59. This result implies that the strategy was implemented to some extent, as this average is between the statements "implemented to a little extent" and "partly implemented."

Next, there was a series of items to measure the extent of implementation:

We have implemented an intelligence and analysis unit.
We have implemented an operational analysis function.
We have implemented an operational intelligence function.
We have implemented a strategic analysis function.
We have implemented a strategic intelligence function.
We prioritize knowledge-based police work.
We have adapted the strategy to our own strategy.
We have created requirements to succeed with the strategy.
A change process according to the strategy is taking place.
We have planned when to evaluate our implementation.
Critical success factors for implementation are considered.
Goals for the implementation process are established.

We have deadlines for the implementation.
We have allocated resources for the implementation.
We have developed measurements according to the strategy.

These items were measured on a Likert scale from 1 (completely disagree) to 7 (completely agree). To determine whether all items could be included in a single scale, reliability analysis was carried out. The result was a Cronbach alpha coefficient of 0.948, which indicates a high reliability when all fifteen items are included. Thus, all items were included when the average score was computed. The average score was 3.34. This score is between 3 (somewhat disagree) and 4 (neither disagree nor agree).

The third and final measurement of implementation was carried out by asking the respondents to estimate the extent of implementation in terms of percentage. The average response was an implementation extent of 37 percent.

These three alternative measurements of implementation extent seem to be consistent. All of them indicate that the implementation extent is less than 50 percent by the average score of 2.59 (implemented to a little extent/partly implemented) and 3.34 (somewhat disagree/neither disagree nor agree).

The survey was carried out using police officers in Norway who work on intelligence and analysis. These experts have an annual meeting where they discuss police work in the area of intelligence and analysis. In May 2008, 305 police officers participated at this meeting. After the meeting, our survey questionnaire was e-mailed to all of them. We received 158 replies, which represents a response rate of 52 percent. Unfortunately, 17 responses were lacking most items, making them unfit for analysis. Thus, 141 usable responses were included in the analysis, reducing the response rate to 46 percent, which is still considered an acceptable response rate.

Organizational structure was measured on this multiple item scale in the questionnaire:

1. We work sequentially on a case at a time. (r)
2. We have freedom to choose how to do our job.
3. We have good routines for internal knowledge transfer.
4. We have good routines for external knowledge transfer.
5. We always follow institutional routines. (r)
6. We always have to follow hierarchical reporting. (r)
7. Program management is important in our organization.
8. We have a bureaucratic decision-making system. (r)
9. There is always consistency between responsibility and authority. (r)
10. We are always dependent on superiors' decisions. (r)
11. We change organizational structure according to new requirements.
12. Our organization is characterized by hierarchy. (r)

13. In our organization, formal authority is the only thing. (r)
14. Our organization is changing all the time.
15. We are a knowledge organization.
16. We have a flexible organizational structure.
17. We have an integrated collaboration in the organization.
18. We have an integrated collaboration with external partners.

These eighteen items were measured on a Likert scale from 1 (completely disagree) to 7 (completely agree). When testing reliability, the complete scale achieved a Cronbach alpha of .755, which is acceptable. However, given the very many items in the scale, it was decided to improve reliability by deleting items. First item to be deleted was number 5, thereby improving the alpha to .796. Further deletion of 9, 2, 1, and 6 improved the reliability to .885. Thirteen items remained. Calculation of average structure based on these items was 3.76. Because this number is between 3 (disagree somewhat) and 4 (neither agree nor disagree), this average score indicates a somewhat bureaucratic organizational structure on average. All items were interpreted on a scale from bureaucratic organization structure to knowledge organization structure. Those items formulated opposite were reversed (r) in the calculations.

Assuming that there is a causal relationship between organizational structure and the extent of implementation, we formulated the following hypothesis:

Hypothesis: The extent of implementation of national strategy for intelligence and analysis will be greater when the police unit is a knowledge organization rather than a bureaucratic organization.

This hypothesis can now be tested. Statistical analysis in terms of regression analysis was carried out, providing results that support the hypothesis. Statistical analysis showed that organizational structure might significantly predict the extent of implementation. Police units with a bureaucratic organization structure had implemented the strategy at a significantly lower extent than police units with a knowledge organization structure.

In Table 5.1, all three implementation constructs are applied. When implementation statements represent the dependent variable, then the

Table 5.1 Regression Analysis Linking Implementation Extent to Organization Structure

Model	Adjusted R Square	Significance Model	B Coefficient	Significance Coefficient
Implementation statements	.280	.000	.457	.000
Implementation items	.428	.000	.865	.000
Implementation percent	.328	.000	14.400	.000

independent variable organization structure predicts 28 percent (.280) of the variation in implementation extent. When implementation items represent the dependent variable, then the organization structure predicts 43 percent. Finally, the implementation percent model predicts 33 percent. All three models are significant, and organization structure as predictor is significant as coefficient in all three models as well.

References

Andersen, J.A. 2002 Organizational design: Two lessons to learn before reorganizing. *International Journal of Organization Theory and Behavior* 5 (3/4): 343–358.

Auteri, M. and Wagner, R. 2007. The organizational architecture of nonprofit governance: Economic calculation within an ecology of enterprises. *Public Organization Review* 7: 57–68.

Birkinshaw, J., Nobel, R., and Ridderstråle, J. 2002. Knowledge as a contingency variable: Do the characteristics of knowledge predict organization structure? *Organization Science* 13 (3): 274–289.

Bryan, L.L. and Joyce, C.I. 2007. Better strategy through organizational design. *McKinsey Quarterly*, 2: www.mckinseyquarterly.com.

Chan, J.B.L. 2003. Police and new technologies. In *Handbook of policing*, Ed. T. Newburn. Portland, OR: Willan Publishing.

Collier, P.M., Edwards, J.S., and Shaw, D. 2004. Communicating knowledge about police performance. *International Journal of Productivity and Performance Management* 53 (5): 458–467.

Ethiraj, S.K. and Levinthal, D. 2004. Bounded rationality and the search for organizational architecture: An evolutionary perspective on the design of organizations and their evolvability. *Administrative Science Quarterly* 49: 404–437.

Fiss, P.C. 2007. A set-theoretical approach to organizational configurations. *Academy of Management Review* 32 (4): 1180–1198.

Gottschalk, P. 1999. Strategic information systems planning: The IT strategy implementation matrix. *European Journal of Information Systems* 8: 107–118.

Groth, L. 1999. *Future organizational design*, Chichester, U.K.: John Wiley & Sons, Wiley Series in Information Systems.

Gudmundsen, Y.S. 2009. Implementering av strategi i politiet: En studie av nasjonal strategi for etterretning og analyse (Implementation of strategy in the police: A study of national strategy for intelligence and analysis), Mastergradsavhandling (Master's thesis), Norwegian Police University College, Oslo.

Jones, R. 2007. The architecture of policing: Towards a new theoretical model of the role of constraint-based compliance in policing. In *Transformations of policing*, Eds. A. Henry and D.J. Smith, 169–190. Oxford, U.K.: Ashgate Publishing.

Kelley, T.M. 2005. Mental health and prospective police professionals. *Policing: An International Journal of Police Strategies & Management* 28 (1): 6–29.

Ketchen, D.J., Combs, J.G., Russell, C.J., Shook, C., Dean, M.A., Runge, J., Lohrke, F.T., Naumann, S.E., Haptonstahl, D.W., Baker, R., Beckstein, B.A., Handler, C., Honig, H., and Lamoureux, S. 1997. Organizational configurations and performance: A meta-analysis. *Academy of Management Journal* 40 (1): 223–240.

Loveday, B. 2008. Workforce modernisation and future resilience within the police service in England and Wales. *The Police Journal* 81 (1): 62–81.

Markides, C.C. and Williamson, P. 1996. Corporate diversification and organizational structure: A resource-based view. *Academy of Management Journal* 39 (2): 340–367.

Mintzberg, H. 1979. *The structuring of organizations.* Englewood Cliffs, NJ: Prentice-Hall.

Moussavou, J. 2006. Organizational architecture and decision-making. *The Journal of Portfolio Management* (Fall) 103–111.

Puonti, A. 2007. Foreword. In *Knowledge management systems in law enforcement,* Ed. P. Gottschalk. Hershey, PA: IGI Global Publishing.

Rivkin, J.W. and Siggelkow, N. 2003. Balancing search and stability: Interdependencies among elements of organizational design. *Management Science* 49 (3): 290–311.

Sheptycki, J. 2007. Police ethnography in the house of serious and organized crime. In *Transformations of policing,* Eds. A. Henry and D.J. Smith, 51–77. Oxford, U.K.: Ashgate Publishing.

van Donk, D.P. and Molloy, E. 2008. From organizing as projects to projects as organizations. *International Journal of Project Management* 26: 129–137.

Zaitch, D. 2002. *Trafficking cocaine: Colombian drug entrepreneurs in the Netherlands,* Studies of Organized Crime. The Hague, Netherlands: Kluwer Law International.

Organizational Culture

6

There seems to be no such thing as one single police culture. Depending on organization, structure, and task, culture in police society varies. For example, Christensen and Crank (2001) found cultural differences between police officers in urban and nonurban areas, while Reuss-Ianni (1993) made a distinction between street cops and management cops. In this chapter, a research model is developed to study impacts of variation in police culture on the extent of intelligence strategy implementation. Our research question might be formulated: How does police culture influence the extent of intelligence strategy implementation?

Police Personnel Cultures

Police culture has been studied for many years (Fielding, 1984; Reuss-Ianni, 1993), and it has received increased attention in police organizations in recent years. For example, Christensen and Crank (2001) studied police work and culture in a nonurban setting in the United States. They found a police culture emphasizing secrecy, self-protection, violence, and the maintenance of respect.

At one point in the history of policing, domestic violence calls were thought to be the most dangerous situations handled by police officers. Of all police officers murdered in the line of duty in the United States in 1970, 22 percent were killed while handling family violence incidents. Family disturbances were the single most dangerous call police officers would handle. Domestic violence calls still pose great dangers for the safety of police officers in the United States as thousands of police officers are assaulted annually while handling domestic violence and domestic disturbance calls (Johnson, 2008).

In the literature, Lahneman (2004) studied knowledge-sharing in the international intelligence community after 9/11, while Granèr (2004) studied uniformed police officers' occupational culture. Barton (2004) found that the English and Welsh police epitomize organizations that are steeped in tradition, while Reuss-Ianni (1993) made a distinction between street cops and management cops.

According to Jaschke et al. (2007), the style of policing varies enormously from country to country and even within local police forces. In some countries, inhabitants tend to fear the police almost as much as they fear criminals. In such countries, the police force is perceived as corrupt, brutal, repressive, uneducated, and untrustworthy. In other countries, the police are the most trusted institution. The latter is the case in Norway, where police officers enjoy almost complete trust and confidence in the public. According to a global survey, confidence in the police among industrialized countries was highest in Norway (89 percent), Britain (87 percent), and Canada (79 percent).

An organizational culture is a set of shared norms, values, and perceptions that develop when the members of an organization interact with each other and the surroundings. It is holistic, historically determined, socially constructed, and difficult to change (Hofstede et al., 1990). Organizational culture might determine how the organization thinks, feels, and acts.

An occupational culture is a reduced, selective, and task-based version of culture that is shaped by the socially relevant worlds of the occupation (Christensen and Crank, 2001). Embedded in traditions and history, occupational cultures contain accepted practices, rules, and principles of conduct that are applied to a variety of situations, and generalized rationales and beliefs (Bailey, 1995).

For example, when one thinks about the investigation of a crime as a process of assembling knowledge, one begins to recognize that police officers are knowledge workers. The basic sets of raw material that police work with are information and interactions with people. How the police deal with these materials within their occupational culture is determined by a variety of factors, such as skills and education (Fraser, 2004).

Occupational culture plays an important role in organizational performance and change. Barton (2004) identified occupational culture and its perpetuation as key barriers that have substantially impeded the success of reform agendas. Similarly, Kiely and Peek (2002) studied the culture of the British police. Interviewed inspectors and sergeants felt that most members of the organization shared the established values of the police service. In another study, Glomseth et al. (2007) found that occupational culture is a determinant of knowledge sharing and performance in police investigations.

To some extent, occupational culture contains what is taken for granted by members, invisible yet powerful constraints, and thus it connects cognition and action, environment and organization, in an entangling and interwoven tapestry. They act as socially validated sources, one for the other (Bailey, 1995).

Occupational culture arises from a set of tasks that are repeated and encapsulated into routines in various degrees, and from a technology that is various and indirect in its effects (it is mediated by the organizational structure), producing a set of attitudes and an explanatory structure of belief (ideology). The tasks of policing are uncertain; they are various, unusual, and unpredictable in appearance, duration, content, and consequence. They are fraught with disorderly potential. The police officer is dependent on other officers for assistance, advice, training, working knowledge, protection in the case of threats from internal or external sources, and insulation against the public and periodic danger. The occupation emphasizes autonomy, both with respect to individual decision making or what lawyers term *discretion*, the public it serves and controls (officers will routinely experience adversarial relations with the public), and the rigid authority symbolized by the paramilitary structure of the organization. Finally, the occupational culture makes salient the displaying, creating, and maintaining of authority. The sources of the authority theme are multiple insofar as they draw on the state's authority, the public morality of the dominant classes, and the law (Bailey, 1995).

Organizational culture represents basic assumptions that are beliefs, values, ethical and moral codes, and ideologies that have become so ingrained that they tend to have dropped out of consciousness. These assumptions are unquestioned perceptions of truth, reality, ways of thinking and thinking about, and the feelings that develop through repeated successes in solving problems over extended periods of time. Important basic assumptions are passed on to new members, often unconsciously.

Beliefs and values are consciously held cognitive and affective patterns. They provide explicit directions and justifications for patterns of organizational behavior as well as the energy to enact them. Beliefs and values are also the birthplaces of basic assumptions.

While organizational culture describes joint perceptions and values among a group of persons, there will often be substantial individual variations in values and behaviors. For example, in a Norwegian survey of 766 police officers, Burke and Mikkelsen (2005) found significant variation in the use of violence by officers. The survey indicated that cynical police officers were more willing to use force, while pragmatic officers were more willing to use their social skills to solve problems. As long as police officers stay within laws and policies, they are free to choose the extent of violence applied to solve problems (Sims et al., 2005). Skolnick (2008, 36) finds this to be problematic:

> The capacity to use force is, of course, another necessary, enduring, and potentially troublesome feature of the police enterprise.

Police culture can be described as a confluence of themes (Christensen and Crank, 2001). Themes are areas of activity and sentiments associated with these activities, linked to each other by a dynamic affirmation, which is the idea that activities and dispositions are not easily separable ideas, but reciprocally causal. Activities confirm predispositions, and predispositions lead to the selection of activities. Themes are developed around particular contours of the day-to-day working environment of the police.

According to Jaschke et al. (2007), police culture is a shared system of ideas, values, and norms about behavior within the police force or particular segments of the police. Police culture consists of accepted practices, rules, and principles of conduct that are applied to a variety of situations. Police culture also consists of rationalities and beliefs. This culture becomes visible when expressed through patterns of police behavior in real situations.

Shared Occupational Values

Kiely and Peek (2002) studied the culture of the British police. The purpose of the study was to explore police culture and the perceived meanings of "quality" and "quality of service" in the police context. At the Police Staff College, the definition of culture suggested by police academic staff is that offered by Professor Edgar Schein of MIT (Kiely and Peek, 2002, 170):

> A pattern of basic assumptions invented, discovered or developed by a given group as it learns to cope with its problem of external adaptation and internal integration—that has worked well enough to be considered valid and, therefore, to be taught to new members in the correct way to perceive, think and feel in relation to those problems.

In this definition, the shared values perspective is used, rather than the shared practices perspective. They found several organizational values. For example, police inspectors viewed as important values such as honesty, morality, and integrity, providing a good service, value for money, and a desire to help. Others included commitment, self-discipline and restraint, courtesy, empathy and sympathy, fairness, and impartiality. Loyalty, consistency, trust, and sense of humor also were featured.

The degree to which police inspectors and sergeants espoused values that were felt to match those of the organization was explored by Kiely and Peek (2002). Some considered their values matched those, stated in some form or other, by chief officers. Others argued their values were reflected in published annual objectives.

Interviewed inspectors and sergeants felt that most members of the organization shared the values of the police service. The view was expressed that what could differ was the degree of emphasis on particular values or differences in priorities. The realities of police work were highlighted as "tarnishing" values, particularly those of young recruits. The greatest perceived influence was the "canteen culture." They learn their values eight hours a day, spending long periods of time sitting in cars watching how other policemen do their job, eating with them, socializing with them. Repeatedly alluded to were the dangers of canteen cultures with young officers being influenced by "old cynics" and picking up outdated values.

To those interviewed, quality of service signified "serving the community," "value for money," "just doing the best you can with the resources available," and "the public getting the service it funds us to supply." Half of those interviewed perceived quality of service to include internal quality, e.g., service to the people within the police force, in other words, the way they treat each other.

Corruption in the police represents the dark side of police culture. Almost every year in developed countries, such as the United Kingdom, there is a headline case of police corruption, which involves corrupt police officers working alone or with others (Caless, 2008, 4):

> Any investigation into criminality or corruption by the police is made much more difficult when insiders are involved. There is also the danger that the insiders themselves will be alerted by well-meaning friends or colleagues. Investigation techniques can be comprised and police intelligence passed to the very people the systems are designed to catch: the criminals.

Corruption occurs when a member of a police force illegally puts personal interests, or the interests of others, above those of the people he or she is pledged to serve. Some claim that corruption is not a cultural phenomenon, based on the bad apple theory. The argument in this theory is that a corrupt police officer or staff member is a single instance, isolated from the norm and by no means typical. Other theorists, however, look into the nature of policing itself as the reason that staff becomes corrupt. They argue that the law does not give the police sufficient powers and, therefore, the police themselves have to invent ways to get around the criminal justice system (Caless, 2008).

Culture as Determinant of Strategy Implementation

In analyzing the culture of a particular group or organization, Schein (1990) finds it desirable to distinguish three fundamental levels at which culture manifests itself: (1) observable artifacts, (2) values, and (3) basic underlying assumptions. When one enters an organization, one observes and feels its artifacts. This category includes everything from the physical layout, the dress code, the manner in which people address each other, the smell and feel of the place, its emotional intensity, and other phenomena, to the more permanent archival manifestations, such as company records, products, statements of philosophy, and annual reports.

Values as the second level can be studies through interviews and questionnaires in terms of norms, ideologies, charters, and philosophies. Basic underlying assumptions at the third and final level are concerned with perceptions, thought processes, feelings, and behavior. Once one understands some of these assumptions, it becomes easier to decipher the meanings implicit in the various behavioral and material phenomena one observes (Schein, 1990).

In their research, Hofstede et al. (1990) found that shared perceptions of daily practices are the core of an organization's culture, not shared values. The research measurements of employee values differed more according to the demographic criteria of nationality, age, and education than according to membership in the organization per se.

What by Hofstede et al. (1990) was labeled practices can be labeled conventions, customs, habits, mores, traditions, or usages. Culture is then that complex whole that includes knowledge, beliefs, art, morals, law, customs, and any other capabilities and habits acquired by man as a member of an organization.

Perceptions of daily practices can be measured in terms of shared practices. Practice differences can be found in terms of process-oriented versus results-oriented, employee-oriented versus job-oriented, parochial versus professional, open system versus closed system, loose control versus tight control, and normative versus pragmatic.

The main emphasis in this study is on the core element values because it is important in discussions of organization culture. Hofstede et al. (1990), for example, argue that values compose the core of any culture. Being relatively lasting, values are emotional perceptions of what is appreciated and preferred in an organization. In other words, values are essential for an organization's fundamental perception of what is right and what is wrong, and what is desirable and valuable in a work situation. Consequently, it is possible to claim that an organization's values dictate its behavior.

A total of eighteen police personnel values were applied in this research, all representing cultural dimensions of potential importance to law enforcement performance. We will now systematically and carefully introduce the research variables by drawing out characteristics of each of the eighteen factors that we examine.

1. *Time firm versus time floats.* Some police investigators value conscious use of time and punctuality. Time is regarded as an important factor, both in relation to ordinary policing and training, and especially when they are faced with aggravated and dangerous crime. The time factor is particularly decisive in armed responses.

2. *Legality versus effectiveness.* Legal protection and democracy versus efficiency and productivity is an important and interesting dimension for the entire public sector. The concept of public ethos might be linked to the question about the role of the police as an institution in society with the right to use coercive force, and the question that the police should serve. This dimension is of particular interest to the police, which act as society's machinery of power. Consequently,

the police's priorities in connection with the execution of power have great impact on our democracy. This dimension is also important because the police are action- and task-oriented.

3. *Direct versus indirect.* This factor is concerned with the style of communication. A direct style might be preferred, which has to be seen in relation to a context involving an open and relaxed tone between the officers and the absence of conflicts. In terms of subject matter and form, a unit's regular discussions might encourage a direct or indirect style.

4. *Open versus closed.* Closure, secrecy, loyalty, and no communication with the environment during investigations is suggested as a typical characteristic of police culture by Reuss-Ianni (1993).

5. *Informal versus formal.* This factor measures the extent to which police investigators are communicating informally or formally with each other.

6. *Equality versus hierarchy.* Equality is characterized by short distances between layers in the organization, minor differences in status, a relatively tight social environment, and a welcoming reception given to new members.

7. *Security versus challenge.* This dimension of security and safety versus challenge and suspense is perceived as very two-sided. On the one hand, it is a general feature of the police officers in the unit that they are drawn to suspense and seek challenges to test their ability to master difficult situations. On the other hand, we see that importance is given to planning, structure, situation analyses, and training. The significance of security is underlined by the priority given to health, environment, and safety regulations as well as the stress on personal safety in connection with different assignments.

8. *Change versus tradition.* On the one hand, the police officers are almost continually preoccupied with self-development, team development, and with developing their division. The management encourages them to frequent testing of new equipment, interview methods, evidence collection, competence building, and further development of police investigation methods. On the other hand, they also value experience and thoroughly tested routines and systems. It is also appreciated that routines are thoroughly tested and have proved to work. Most organizations (particularly police organizations) view tradition and history as important. Fielding (1984) shows that police officers, to a great extent, tend to trust their previous experiences and arrangements, which have proved to work in the past.

9. *Practical versus philosophical.* Detectives may have a clear practical and pragmatic orientation or a theoretical and philosophical orientation. They have a practical orientation when they are working

continuously with the purpose of finding simple and practical solutions. They have a theoretical orientation when they are testing new equipment, developing new plans, and combining evidence material in new ways. A similar distinction can be made between intellectually reflecting attitudes in contrast to an intuitive-, practical-, and action-oriented attitude among police officers.

10. *Liberty versus control.* Liberty and freedom is given to police investigators to be creative, follow the challenge of solving a crime, and applying each officer's skill. Control is needed so that detectives follow the book and they themselves do not break the law.

11. *Individual versus group.* Group orientation is often found in police work because a typical feature of policing is team cooperation or cooperation between two partners. This is a typical feature developed in newcomers when they go on car patrols together. Partnerships of this kind tend to last for many years, long after they have left the uniform in the closet. On the other hand, police officers are described as strong individuals with distinct leadership qualities. What is more, a detective is often completely responsible for his or her own actions, which leads to stronger emphasis on individualism.

12. *Privacy versus openness.* This factor is intended to capture how officers put into practice or how they value the social conditions in the unit. Which topics are being discussed, and to what extent do the police officers feel that the unit is characterized by openness and intimacy?

13. *Competition versus cooperation.* Cooperation is often appreciated among close colleagues. At the same time, detectives may be competitive in solving crimes. They have a strong desire to achieve results. This attitude can stimulate individual competition and competition among teams and divisions.

14. *Task versus relationship.* Task orientation versus relation orientation is a dimension that is frequently subjected to a variety of analyses of organizational culture. Members of police units often express a clear preference for task orientation. This tendency can be understood in the light of the officers' strong interest in professional matters and how much room they are given for self-development. The emphasis on action and result orientation are likely to reinforce this tendency.

15. *Firm leader versus individual creativity.* This factor measures management, where the investigation leader might be a strong manager. Traditionally, the police hierarchy encourages a culture of strong managers, where the senior investigation officer (SIO) makes decisions.

16. *Work versus balance.* This dimension of work being more important versus balance between work and spare time is an interesting culture factor among all kinds of professionals and managers. Detectives

might tend to be very enthusiastic about their job, their special field, and their work environment, causing an imbalance toward work. A prominent feature of the organizational culture in the police is to regard police work as more than just an ordinary job. Entering the police force might mean adopting a lifestyle. On the one hand, many police officers are also parents of small children (often many children), which is a factor that works contrary to the notion of police work as a lifestyle. In addition, a great number of police officers are actively taking part in sports, outdoor life, and organizational activities as well as taking on duties.

17. *Short term versus long term.* A police investigation can sometimes be described as guided by incidents and fragmented information. This indicates that extensive planning is not necessary, and that the focus is short term. Consequently, this might create a culture of short-term focus, fast solutions, and quick results. On the other hand, wherever possible, detectives value thorough analyses and decision-making processes characterized by a long-term perspective. For example, it might take several years of training leading up to approval or certification of a senior investigation officer in the United Kingdom.

18. *Act versus plan.* Also interesting is the dimension action orientation versus planning orientation. This is the only dimension where it is often possible to identify certain differences of some significance between managers and nonmanagers. Reuss-Ianni (1993) distinguishes between managers (management cops) and police officers on patrol (street cops) with widely different cultures of the two groups. Police officers who do not hold managerial positions display a general feeling of disdain for managers because they have lost the touch of everyday practical policing.

The dependent variable in this conceptual research is the extent of strategy implementation, as illustrated in Figure 6.1. Implementation might be measured in four different ways: completion of tasks so far, tasks expected to be completed, completion of the overall strategy, and improved organizational performance from the strategy (Gottschalk, 1999).

Specifically, implementation might be measured using these alternative definitions (Gottschalk, 1999):

1. *Implementation rate to date*: Divide projects actually completed to date by projects scheduled to be implemented.
2. *Implementation rate to end*: Divide projects actually implemented to date by projects in the strategy and divide by percent of expired time horizon.

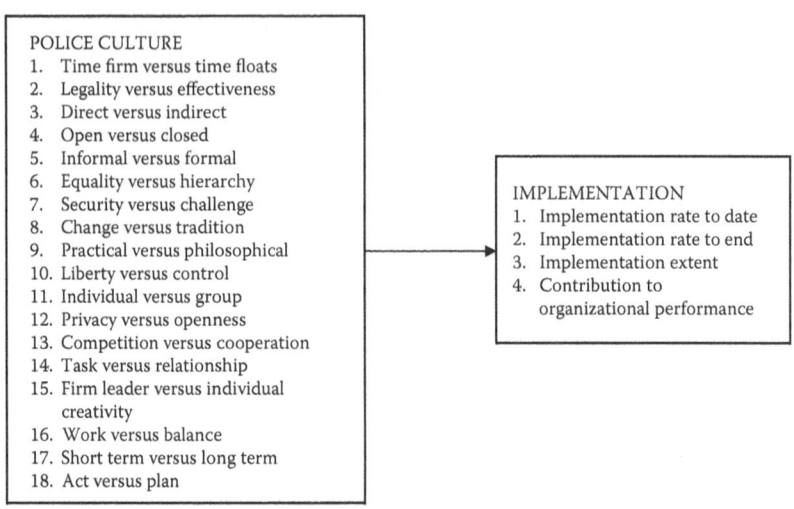

Figure 6.1 Police culture research model to study the extent of strategy implementation.

3. *Implementation extent*: The extent to which the strategy has been completed on time, within budget, as expected, with desired results, without deviations during implementation, and with satisfaction of stakeholders.
4. *Contribution to organizational performance*: Reduced crime, increased success rate, reduced resource consumption, and improved knowledge sharing.

As suggested in this conceptual research model, police culture might be a determinant of the extent of strategy implementation. The principal works of the police vary in method, in conceptual focus, in depth of analysis, and in the degree to which they are comparative. In a comparative study of Scottish and American police roles, peacekeeping and law enforcement were identified as two different police roles. Another comparative study of rural and urban English forces found higher dependency on other officers in the urban force where the public was seen as unsupportive. There, the radio and the police vehicle became primary tools. Rural forces were found less dependent on other officers (and more on the public) and less concerned with action, risk, excitement, and crime fighting (Bailey, 1995).

To implement such a model locally requires local strategy work, as indicated by the South Yorkshire strategy (SYPIS, 2007). To measure the extent of implementation, our research model suggests four alternative definitions (listed above). In empirical research, the situation will determine which ones are appropriate for implementation measurement.

There will be variation in the extent of implementation from police district to police district. This variation is explained in the research model by eighteen factors representing organizational values (listed above). The unit of analysis is the police district, implying that there will be variation in support from the national agency to different police districts.

As this research is conceptual, future research may empirically test the research model by testing the three research hypotheses (see Chapter 4, Section 4.6).

In conclusion, the need for improved implementation of strategies in law enforcement and policing has been emphasized by both scholars and practitioners. At the same time, strategy implementation suffers from a general lack of academic attention. Despite the importance of the strategy execution process, much more attention is paid to strategy formulation than strategy implementation.

This research model has made a contribution to the strategy implementation literature by developing a research model to study implementation of police intelligence strategy in the context of police culture. Future research might empirically test the suggested research model by developing research hypotheses for testing.

We may now combine organizational structure and organizational culture into one research model to study the extent of strategy implementation (Figure 6.2).

Again, we are studying cause-and-effect relationships, which can be formulated in terms of research hypotheses. A hypothesis is a theoretical claim about relationships in reality, which can only be verified empirically in terms of a survey, a case study, experiments, or other empirical methods. When structure and culture are the theoretical causes of variation in implementation extent, then these two hypotheses can be formulated:

Hypothesis 1: A knowledge organization structure will be associated with a greater extent of strategy implementation than a bureaucratic organization structure.

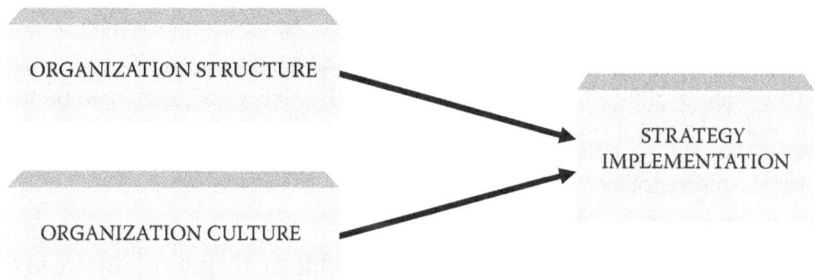

Figure 6.2 Structure and culture both affecting implementation.

Hypothesis 2: An open organization culture will be associated with a greater extent of strategy implementation than a closed organization culture.

These two hypotheses can be reasoned based on our discussion already presented on organizational structure and organizational culture. In terms of organizational structure, Toch (2008, 60) argues that change is extremely difficult in traditional police organizations:

> The organization of police departments along hierarchical, classic management lines makes it difficult for departmental leadership to tackle commonly experienced internal problems, so as to improve performance and enhance morale. The main reason for this fact is that top-down reform invites resistances from rank-and-file officers who feel that their views have been disregarded.

This quote can be found to be directly supporting our first hypothesis because implementation of strategy for intelligence and analysis implies an organizational change, which is more difficult to carry out in a hierarchical, traditional police organization. The same finding is confirmed by Sklansky and Marks (2008, 1):

> Police departments today are more attractive places than they used to be for experiments in participatory management and other forms of workforce empowerment, but experiments of this kind in law enforcement remain disappointingly rare ... The dominant mindset of police departments, police reformers, appellate judges, and criminal justice scholars—the dominant mindset, in short, of nearly everyone who thinks about policing and its problems—is, and always has been, that policing needs strong, top-down management. Good police officers are police officers that follow rules. Rank-and-file organizing is an obstacle to reform and an impediment to maintaining a "disciplined" work force.

Hierarchy and bureaucracy are often barriers to change. Similarly, support might be found for the second hypothesis about organizational culture from Skolnick (2008, 37), who writes about the consequences of a closed police culture:

> Skepticism, cynicism, mistrust of outsiders—all are traits observers of police apply to them and that they apply to themselves ... The feelings of loyalty and brotherhood sustaining a silence code unquestionably protect cops against genuine threats to safety and well-being ... However, of course, it is one thing to issue a directive, and another for it to be followed.

The first hypothesis implies that it is possible to distinguish between two types of organizational structure, where the knowledge organization is the opposite of the bureaucratic organization. The second hypothesis makes a distinction between open versus closed organizational culture. Both hypotheses are theoretical claims about causal relationships. But are they true? Only empirical studies can support such hypotheses.

Case: An Empirical Study of Implementation and Culture

In Chapter 5 on organizational structure, support for hypothesis 1 was discussed. Based on a survey, police officers working in the area of intelligence and analysis responded that implementation extent was greater in a knowledge organization than in a bureaucratic organization structure (Gudmundsen, 2009).

In the same empirical study, organizational culture was measured on this multiple item scale:

1. *Change*: Growth, development, change, new ways of doing things are appreciated.
2. *Tradition and continuity*: Stability, tradition, old and well-tested ways of doing things is appreciated. (r)
3. *Individualism*: Everyone is completely and fully responsible for his or her own actions and decisions; the individual is more important than the group.
4. *Group orientation*: The group's needs are more important than the individual's needs; the group is responsible for members' actions.
5. *Equality and influence*: Short distance between top and bottom in the hierarchy; a person is mainly valued based on results rather than position.
6. *Hierarchy and authority*: Long distance between top and bottom in the hierarchy; a person is mainly valued based on position rather than results. (r)
7. *Short-term focus*: Quick solutions and speedy results are valued; ability to quickly go into new relationships and also be able to quickly terminate them when necessary.
8. *Long-term focus*: Thorough and fundamental decision processes are valued; ability to sustain a relationship over a long period of time is valued. (r)
9. *Task orientation*: To complete all working tasks is perceived as most important; an officer's value is mainly measured in terms of performance. (r)
10. *Relational orientation*: To have a good relationship and work closely with colleagues is considered most important; an officer's value is mainly determined by the ability to create good relationships.

11. *Action orientation*: Actions leading to results are most important. (r)
12. *Planning orientation*: Thorough preparations and planning are valued.
13. *Practical and pragmatic orientation*: Setting goals and findings ways to achieve them are most important.
14. *Philosophical and theoretical orientation*: High-level principles, reflection, thinking, and reasoning are most important.
15. *Strong and visible management*: Management makes decisions about goals and how they are best accomplished; management control of personnel and their tasks is important. (r)
16. *Freedom, trust, initiative, and creativity*: Each officer may alone or with the team define the situation, determine goals, and relevant means.
17. *Closed organization culture*: No sharing of knowledge or flow of information. (r)
18. *Openness both internally and externally*: Sharing information and knowledge stimulates persons to act and take on responsibility.

Each item was measured on a scale from 1 (completely disagree) to 7 (completely agree). Some of the items were reversed (r), so that all scales represent the same direction from a bureaucratic kind of organizational culture to a knowledge-oriented kind of organizational culture. Reliability analysis in terms of Cronbach alpha indicated that some of the items did not match the scale. When all 18 items were included, the reliability coefficient was unacceptably low at .500. Because the number of items is very large, there is no problem involved in removing items from the scale.

The first item to be removed was 15, thereby improving the Cronbach alpha to .619. This improvement makes sense, as strong and visible management can be found in both bureaucratic knowledge-oriented cultures. The second item to be removed was 8, thereby achieving an improved alpha of .711. Again, it makes sense to argue that long-term focus is found in both bureaucratic as well as knowledge cultures. To further improve reliability, items 11, 9, 7, 2, and 3 were deleted. The final reliability with 7 deleted items and 11 remaining items was .865.

When computing average culture based on the remaining scale of 11 items, the average value based on 141 completed responses from intelligence officers was 4.14. Since the scale ran from 1 to 7, the average of 4.14 is slightly to the right of the middle, indicating that responding police officers find their organizations slightly more knowledge-oriented than bureaucracy-oriented.

While hypothesis 2 above was concerned with open versus closed culture, this empirical study was based on the following hypothesis:

Table 6.1 Regression Analysis Linking Implementation Extent to Organization Culture

Model	Adjusted R Square	Significance Model	B Coefficient	Significance Coefficient
Implementation statements	.234	.000	.431	.000
Implementation items	.382	.000	.825	.000
Implementation percent	.243	.000	12.501	.000

Hypothesis: The extent of implementation of national strategy for intelligence and analysis will be greater when the police unit has a knowledge culture rather than a bureaucratic culture.

This hypothesis can now be tested. Statistical analysis in terms of regression analysis was carried out, providing results that support the hypothesis. Statistical analysis showed that organizational culture might significantly predict the extent of implementation. Police units with a bureaucratic organization culture had implemented the strategy at a significantly lower extent than police units with a knowledge organization culture.

In Table 6.1, all three implementation constructs are applied. When implementation statements represent the dependent variable, then the independent variable organization culture predicts 23.4% (.234) of the variation in implementation extent. When implementation items represent the dependent variable, then organization culture predicts 38.2% (.382). Finally, the implementation precent model predicts 24.3% (.243). All three alternative models are significant, i.e. implementation statements, implementation items, as well as implementation percent. Thus, organization culture as a determinant of implementation is a significant predictor in all three models.

We have found that structure, as well as culture, are significant factors influencing implementation, when each of them is treated separately. Multiple regression analysis will now be applied where both structure and culture are to predict implementation simultaneously.

In Table 6.2, all three implementation constructs are applied again. While all three models are significant, culture is not anymore. When culture is to

Table 6.2 Regression Analysis Linking Implementation Extent to Both Structure and Culture

Model	Adjusted R Square	Factors	B Coefficient	Significance Coefficient
Implementation statements	.274	Structure	.358	.006
		Culture	.113	.386
Implementation items	.440	Structure	.625	.001
		Culture	.300	.097
Implementation percent	.309	Structure	12.161	.002
		Culture	2.138	.585

"compete" with structure as an explanation for variation in implementation, it "loses." Thus, only structure is a significant factor predicting implementation. When organizational structure moves from a bureaucratic structure to a knowledge structure, then the extent of implementation of national strategy for intelligence and analysis increases.

Case: Advanced Empirical Study of Implementation Predictors

> *Hypothesis 1*: The extent of implementation of national strategy for intelligence and analysis will be greater when the police unit is a knowledge organization rather than a bureaucratic organization.
>
> *Hypothesis 2*: The extent of implementation of national strategy for intelligence and analysis will be greater when the police unit has a knowledge culture rather than a bureaucratic culture.

To test the proposed research model, we adapted the survey method for data collection. Our hypotheses were examined by applying the partial least squares method to the collected data. The unit of analysis was the individual level.

Measurement and data collection implies an *evaluation of the measurement model*. Confirmatory factor analysis was approached using PLS-Graph* v. 3.0. While PLS (partial least squares) is typically used to model causal relationship among latent variables (factors), it is equally possible to use PLS to explore confirmatory factor analysis measurement models. The measurement model in this research was analyzed in three stages: (1) the individual item reliabilities, (2) the model's convergent validity, and (3) discriminant validity.

Individual item reliability was examined by looking at the loadings, or correlations, of each indicator on its respective construct. For reflective indicators, a generally recognized rule of thumb is that items with a loading of 0.707 or above demonstrate acceptable reliability (Barclay et al., 1995). This threshold implies that there is more variance shared between the measures and their constructs than there is error variance. The initial analysis indicated that elimination of some items would enhance the fit indices. Standardized residuals indicated significant cross loadings for several items, which were deleted. All factor loadings in the model have t-values that exceeded 2.0, as shown in Table 6.3.

---

* PLS-Graph, v. 3.0 is a copyright of Soft Modeling, Inc.

Table 6.3 Results from Confirmatory Factor
Analysis

Measures	Items	Composite Reliability	Average Variance Extracted
Implementation	15 (15)	0.956	0.591
Org. structure	9 (18)	0.920	0.562
Org. culture	8 (18)	0.895	0.517

The next step in analyzing the measurement model was to evaluate *convergent validity*. This indicates the indicators for a given construct should be at least moderately correlated among themselves. Poor convergent validity among the indicators for a factor may mean the model needs to have more factors. Convergent validity was evaluated by examining the composite reliability and average variance extracted from the measures. Reliability is a measure of the internal consistency of the construct indicators, depicting the degree to which they indicate the common latent (unobserved) construct. More reliable measures provide the researcher with greater confidence that the individual indicators are all consistent in their measurements. A commonly used threshold value for acceptable reliability is 0.70, although this is not an absolute standard, and values below that have been deemed acceptable if the research is exploratory in nature. Table 6.3 shows the composite reliability scores for each of the constructs are well above 0.70, ranging from 0.895 to 0.956, demonstrating an acceptable level of internal consistency of the construct indicators.

Another measure of reliability is the variance-extracted measure. This measure reflects the overall amount of variance in the indicators accounted for by the latent construct. Higher variance extracted values occur when the indicators are truly representative of the latent construct. Recommendations typically suggest that the variance-extracted value for a construct should exceed 0.50 (Fornell and Larcker, 1981). Table 6.3 shows that the average variance extracted by our measures ranges from 0.517 to 0.591, which are above the acceptability value. Bootstrap resampling procedure was used to assess the significance of PLS parameter estimates. The results of 500 resamples indicate that all measures are significant on their path loadings at the level of 0.01.

Discriminant validity indicates the extent to which a particular construct differs from other constructs. In PLS analysis, one criterion for adequate discriminant validity is that a construct should share more variance with its measure than it shares with other constructs in the model (Barclay et al., 1995). One method of assessing discriminant validity is to examine the average variance extracted (AVE) for the construct. This measure, developed by Fornell and Larcker (1981), is the average variance shared between a given construct and its indicators. The AVE of a given construct should be greater

Table 6.4   Means, Standard Deviations (SD), Correlation, and AVE of Variables

Variable	Mean	SD	1	2	3
1. Implementation	0.000	0.000	0.768		
2. Org. structure	0.000	0.000	0.713	0.749	
3. Org. culture	0.000	0.000	0.624	**0.765**	0.719

Note: The shared numbers in the diagonal row are squared roots of the average variance extracted, which is the square root of the variance shared between the constructs and their measure. Off diagonals are the correlations between constructs. The diagonal should be larger than any other corresponding row or column entry in order to support discriminant validity.

than the variance between that construct and other constructs. That is, the AVE should exceed the square of the correlation between any two constructs (or the square root of AVE should be greater than the correlation). This implies that more variance is shared between a particular construct and its indicators than between that construct and another construct. In addition, the AVE value should be greater than 0.50, indicating that more than 50 percent of the item's variance is captured by the construct (Chin, 1998).

Table 6.4 presents the AVE values (in bold type on the diagonal). The values shown for AVE are the square roots of the AVE; the other values are the correlations between constructs. An examination of the table shows that the AVE values meet the criteria. Values are greater than 0.50 for each construct, and they are greater than the correlations between their respective construct and all other constructs. The AVE values on the diagonal are greater than the off-diagonal values in the corresponding rows and columns; each construct shares larger variance with its own measures than with other measures.

Before testing for a significant relationship in the structural model, one must demonstrate that the measurement model has a satisfactory level of validity and reliability (Fornell and Larcker, 1981). The results from the confirmatory factor analysis indicate that the constructs are reliably measured and are adequate for hypothesis testing, as illustrated in Table 6.5.

With an adequate measurement model and an acceptable level of multicollinearity, the proposed hypotheses were tested with PLS to *evaluate the structural model*. The results of the analysis are depicted in Figure 6.3 and estimates of the relationships are shown in Table 6.6.

Antecedents of intelligence strategy implementation are the focus of hypotheses 1 and 2. We hypothesized in H1 that organizational structure would be positively related to implementation of national strategy for intelligence. Results indicate a significant positive relationship between these variables ($\beta = 0.568$, $t = 6.2994$, $p < 0.001$). In hypothesis H2, we suggested a

Table 6.5 Weights and Loadings of the Measures

Construct	Items	Weight	Loadings	Standard Errors	t-value
Implementation	IMP1	0.0787	0.7437	0.0060	13.0794
	IMP2	0.0690	0.6402	0.0086	8.0393
	IMP3	0.0914	0.7135	0.0075	12.2537
	IMP4	0.0683	0.6813	0.0075	9.0830
	IMP5	0.0966	0.7626	0.0066	14.5908
	IMP6	0.0965	0.7582	0.0092	10.4632
	IMP7	0.1079	0.8450	0.0068	15.7871
	IMP8	0.1145	0.8939	0.0072	15.8693
	IMP9	0.1033	0.8057	0.0082	12.6636
	IMP10	0.0582	0.6723	0.0086	6.7458
	IMP11	0.0876	0.8049	0.0066	13.2982
	IMP12	0.0918	0.8357	0.0051	18.0050
	IMP13	0.0738	0.7759	0.0069	10.7609
	IMP14	0.0807	0.7980	0.0054	14.9148
	IMP15	0.0715	0.7546	0.0093	7.6731
Organizational structure	STR3	0.1403	0.7410	0.0132	10.6396
	STR4	0.1442	0.7185	0.0140	10.3291
	STR7	0.1239	0.5747	0.0213	5.8118
	STR11	0.1728	0.7538	0.0162	10.6988
	STR14	0.1345	0.7232	0.0155	8.7030
	STR15	0.1733	0.8108	0.0130	13.3276
	STR16	0.1582	0.8160	0.0143	11.0541
	STR17	0.1461	0.8151	0.0125	11.7286
	STR18	0.1373	0.7650	0.0150	9.1471
Organizational culture	CUL1	0.2361	0.8358	0.0235	10.0643
	CUL4	0.1759	0.6352	0.0265	6.6325
	CUL5	0.1662	0.7541	0.0206	8.0531
	CUL10	0.1477	0.6456	0.0241	6.1410
	CUL12	0.1798	0.7567	0.0211	8.5279
	CUL13	0.1704	0.7656	0.0233	7.3177
	CUL14	0.1766	0.6615	0.0300	5.8843
	CUL16	0.1293	0.6717	0.0256	5.0596

Note: Both standard errors and t-values are for loading, not weights.

positive relationship between organizational culture and implementation of national strategy for intelligence. A significant, positive relationship between these two variables was found ($\beta = 0.190$, $t = 2.1589$, $p < 0.01$). Explained variance for intelligence strategy implementation was found to be 52.3 percent, as shown in Table 6.6.

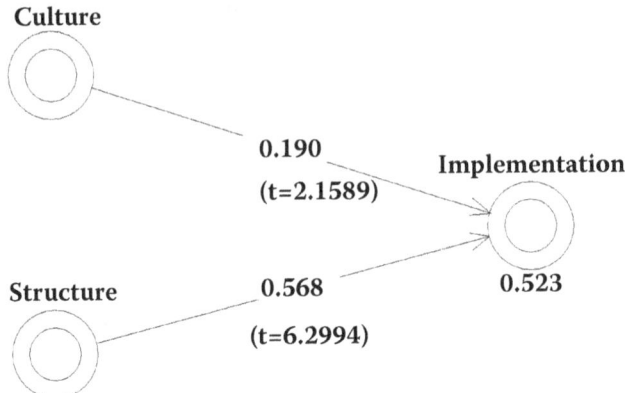

Figure 6.3 Results of PLS (partial least squares) analysis.

Table 6.6   Results of Hypotheses Testing

Dependent Variable	Predictor Variable	Hypothesized Sign	Path Coefficients	t	Significance Level	R^2
Implementation	Org. structure	+ +	0.568	6.2994	$p < 0.001$	0.523
	Org. culture		0.190	2.1589	$p < 0.01$	

Note: If the absolute value of the test statistic is greater than the upper critical value, then we reject the null hypothesis.

Strong correlation was found between organizational culture and organizational structure, as indicated in the following two alternative models. We see in Figure 6.4 and Figure 6.5 that structure has a very strong influence on culture, as well as structure having a very strong influence on culture, thereby limiting the validity of statistical results.

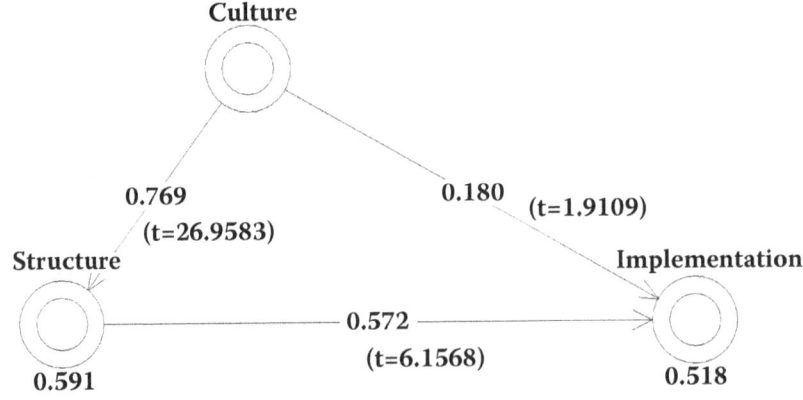

Figure 6.4 Alternative 1 PLS (partial least squares) analysis: Culture on structure.

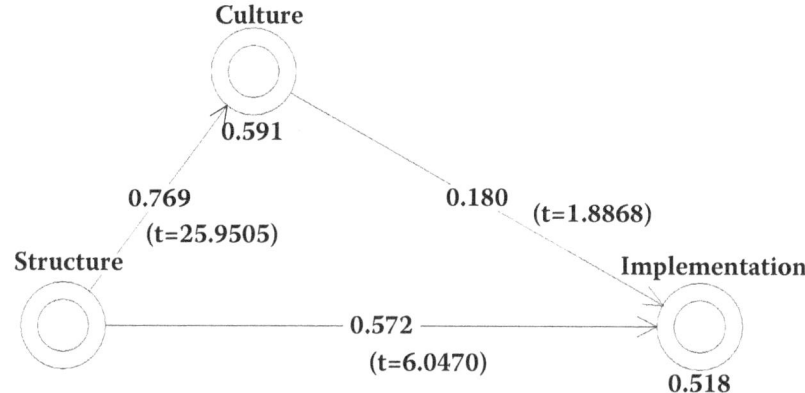

Figure 6.5 Alternative 2 PLS (partial least squares) analysis: Structure on culture.

References

Bailey, W.G., Ed. 1995. *The encyclopedia of police science*, 2nd ed. New York: Garland Publishing.

Barclay, D., Higgins, C.A., and Thompson, R. 1995. The partial least squares (PLS) approach to causal modeling: Personal computer adoption and use as an illustration. *Technology Studies* 2 (2): 285–324.

Barton, H. 2004. Cultural reformation: A case for intervention within the police service. *International Journal of Human Resources Development and Management* 4 (2): 191–199.

Burke, R.J. and Mikkelsen, A. 2005. Burnout, job stress and attitudes towards the use of force by Norwegian police officers. *Policing: An International Journal of Police Strategies & Management* 28 (2): 269–278.

Caless, B. 2008. Corruption in the police: the reality of the "dark side." *The Police Journal*, 81 (1): 3–24.

Chin, W.W. 1998. Issues and opinion on structural equation modeling. *MIS Quarterly* 22 (1): vii–xvi.

Christensen, W. and Crank, J.P. 2001. Police work and culture in a nonurban setting: An ethnographical analysis. *Police Quarterly* 4 (1): 69–98.

Fielding, N. 1984. Police socialization and police competence. *The British Journal of Sociology* 35 (4): 568–590.

Fornell, C. and Larcker, D.F. 1981. Evaluating structural equation models with unobservable variables and measurement error. *Journal of Marketing Research* 18 (2): 39–50.

Fraser, C. 2004. *Strategic information systems for policing*. Washington, D.C.: Police Executive Research Forum.

Glomseth, R., Gottschalk, P., and Solli-Sæther, H. 2007. Occupational culture as determinant of knowledge sharing and performance in police investigations. *International Journal of the Sociology of Law* 35: 96–107.

Gottschalk, P. 1999. Strategic information systems planning: The IT strategy implementation matrix. *European Journal of Information Systems* 8: 107–118.

Granèr, R. 2004. Patruljerande polisers yrkeskultur (Patrolling police officers' occupational culture), Lund Dissertations in Social Work, University of Lund, Sweden.

Gudmundsen, Y.S. 2009. Implementering av strategi i politiet: En studie av nasjonal strategi for etterretning og analyse (Implementation of strategy in the police: A study of national strategy for intelligence and analysis), Mastergradsavhandling (Master's thesis), Politihøgskolen (Norwegian Police University College), Oslo.

Hofstede, G., Neuijen, B., Ohayv, D.D., and Sanders, G. 1990. Measuring organizational cultures: A qualitative and quantitative study across twenty cases. *Administrative Science Quarterly* 35 (2): 286–316.

Jaschke, H.G., Bjørgo, T., Romero, F.del B., Kwanten, C., Mawby, R., and Pogan, M. 2007. *Perspectives of police science in Europe*, Final Report. Hampshire, U.K.: European Police College, CEPOL, Collège Européen de Police.

Johnson, R.R. 2008. Officer firearms assaults at domestic violence calls: A descriptive analysis. *The Police Journal* 81 (1): 25–45.

Kiely, J.A. and Peek, G.S. 2002. The culture of the British police: Views of police officers. *The Service Industries Journal* 22 (1): 167–183.

Lahneman, W.J. 2004. Knowledge-sharing in the intelligence community after 9/11. *International Journal of Intelligence and Counterintelligence* 17: 614–633.

Reuss-Ianni, E. 1993. *Two cultures of policing: Street cops and management cops.* New Brunswick, NJ: Transaction Publishers.

Schein, E.H. 1990. Organizational culture. *American Psychologist* 45 (2): 109–119.

Sims, B., Ruiz, J., Weaver, G., and Harvey, W.L. 2005. Police perceptions of their working environment: Surveying the small department. *International Journal of Police Science & Management* nr. 7 (4): s. 245–263.

Sklansky, D. and Marks, M. 2008. The role of the rank and file in police reform. *Policing & Society* 18 (1): 1–6.

Skolnick, J.H. 2008. Enduring issues of police culture and demographics. *Policing & Society* 18 (1): 35–45.

SYPIS. 2007. *South Yorkshire Police Intelligence Strategy 2007—Breaking the chain*, South Yorkshire Police, U.K.: www.policereform.gov.uk.

Toch, H. 2008. Police officers as change agents in police reform. *Policing & Society* 18 (1): 60–71.

Intelligence Sources

7

While unanalyzed data are numbers and letters without meaning, information is data in a context that makes sense. Information combined with interpretation and reflection is knowledge, while knowledge accumulated over time, as learning, is wisdom. In this hierarchical structure, we find intelligence as more than information and less than knowledge. Intelligence is analyzed information, as illustrated in Figure 7.1.

Data is considered the raw material out of which information develops. As noted, information is data endowed with relevance and purpose. The same can be said about intelligence in that it is a form of insight to which some relevance has been attached through an attempt to offer an organized analysis of the information received by a crime analyst and/or intelligence officer. Hence, this is why intelligence is placed between information and knowledge in the above continuum, as ideally, intelligence represents, as argued, a form of validated information.

A core process of policing and law enforcement is investigation. It is a policing truism that information is the lifeblood of an investigation. An investigation goes nowhere if information is not forthcoming about an incident. Information is the raw data that supplies the oxygen that breathes life into an investigation. Information is collected by ordinary rank and file police officers either working on the street, patrolling and talking to the public, or sitting at a computer doing searches, background checks, or more sophisticated crime mapping and intelligence analysis reports.

Information and, to a similar extent, intelligence then consists of facts and other data that is organized to characterize or profile a particular situation, incident, or crime and the individual or group of individuals presumed to be involved. This organizing of the data to meaningful, necessary information involves some level of interpretation of the facts as presented. However, the role of interpretation in information is relatively minor in comparison to its role in terms of knowledge construction. In this regard, the role of interpretation in intelligence is greater and more explicit than in information, but not as full blown as in the creation of knowledge.

Knowledge helps develop relevant meaning to information in police intelligence (Innes and Sheptycki, 2004, 6):

> The distinction between information and intelligence is well established, but can be difficult to grasp. Information consists of bits of data that, when combined and viewed together with relevant background knowledge, may be used to produce intelligence, which informs the actions and decisions of policing organizations.

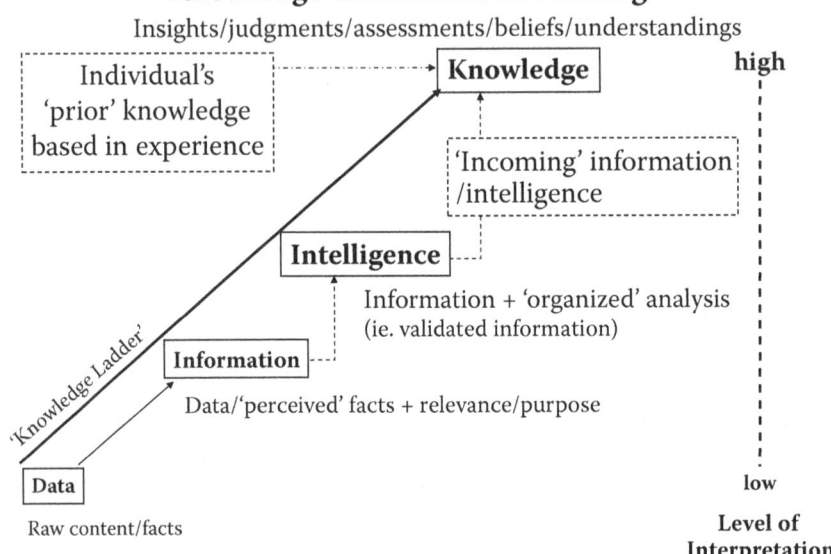

Figure 7.1 Hierarchy of police insight expressed as a continuum.

Knowledge as implied operates at a higher level of abstraction and consists of judgments and assessments based in personal beliefs, truths, and expectations about the information received and how it is should be analyzed, evaluated, and synthesized, in short, interpreted, so that it can be used and implemented into some form of action.

Classification of Information Sources

In intelligence work for policing criminal business enterprises, a variety of information sources are available. Sheptycki (2007) lists these sources: victim reports, witness reports, police reports, crime scene examinations, historical data held by police agencies (such as criminal records), prisoner debriefings, technical or human surveillance products, suspicious financial transactions reporting, and reports emanating from undercover police operations. Intelligence analysis may also refer to records of other governmental departments and agencies, and other more open sources of information may be used in elaborate intelligence assessment.

However, Sheptycki found that most crime analysis is organized around existing police sector data. Intelligence analysis is typically framed by already existing institutional ways of thinking. He argues that organized crime notification, classification, and measurement schemes tend to reify preexisting notions of traditional police practice.

In this perspective, it is important for strategic criminal analysts to be aware of the variety of information sources available. We choose to classify information sources into these categories in this chapter:

1. *Interview.* By means of *interrogation* of witnesses, suspects, reference persons and experts, information is collected on crimes, criminals, times and places, organizations, criminal projects, activities, roles, etc.
2. *Network.* By means of *informants* in the criminal underworld as well as in legal businesses, information is collected on actors, plans, competitors, markets, customers, etc. Informants often have connections with persons that a police officer would not be able to approach formally.
3. *Location.* By analyzing potential and actual *crime scenes*, information is collected on criminal procedures, preferences, crime evolution, etc. Hot spots and traces are found. Secret ransacking of suspicious area is part of this information source. Crime scene photographs are important information elements.
4. *Documents.* Studying documents from *confiscations* may provide information on ownership, transactions, accounts, etc.
5. *Observation.* By means of *anonymous police presence,* both persons and activities can be observed. In the physical as well as the virtual world, observation is important in police intelligence. An example is digital forensics where successful cyber crime intelligence requires computer skills and modern systems in policing. Digital forensics is the art and science of applying computer science to aid the legal process. It is more than the technological, systematic inspection of electronic systems and their contents for evidence or supportive evidence of a criminal act. Digital forensics requires specialized expertise and tools when applied to intelligence in important areas, such as online victimization of children (Davidson and Gottschalk, 2008).
6. *Action.* For example, *provocation* is an action by the police to cause reactions that represents intelligence information. In the case of online victimization of children, online grooming offenders (persons who set up others to be victims of sexual abuse) in a pedophile ring are identified and their reaction to provocations leads intelligence officers into new nodes (persons, computers) and new actual and potential victims. While the individual pedophile is mainly concerned with combining indecent image impression and personal fantasy to achieve personal satisfaction, online organizers of sexual abuse of children are doing it for profit. By claiming on the Internet to be a boy or girl of 9 years, police initiate contact with criminal business enterprises making money on pedophile customers (Davidson and

Gottschalk, 2008). Undercover operations by police officers, as well, belong to the action category of information sources.

7. *Surveillance.* Surveillance of places by means of *video cameras* as well as microphones for viewing and listening belong to this information source. Police officers listen in on what is discussed in a room without the participants knowing. For example, police in one country identified which room in a resort was being used by the local Hells Angels members for crime planning and the police installed listening devices in that room. Harfield (2008, 64) argues that when surveillance is employed to produce evidence, such product is often considered incontrovertible (hence, defense lawyers' focus on process rather than product when cross-examining surveillance officers): "An essentially covert activity, by definition surveillance, lacks transparency and, therefore, is vulnerable to abuse by over-zealous investigators."

8. *Communication control.* Wire tapping in terms of *interception* belongs to this information source. Police listen in on what is discussed on a telephone or data line without the participants knowing. In the United Kingdom, the interception of communications (telephone calls, emails, letters, etc.), while generating intelligence to identify more conventional evidential opportunities, is excluded from trial evidence by law, to the evident incredulity of foreign law enforcement colleagues (Harfield, 2008).

9. *Physical material.* Investigation of material to identify, e.g., *fingerprints* on doors or bags, or material to identify blood type from blood splatters. Another example is legal visitation, which is an approach to identify illegal material. DNA is emerging as an important information source, where DNA is derived from physical material, such as hair or saliva from a person. Police search is one approach to physical material collection.

10. *Internet.* As an *open source*, the Internet is as important for general information and specific happenings to police intelligence as to everyone else.

11. *Policing systems.* Readily available in most police agencies are *police records*. For example, DNA records may prove helpful when there is DNA material from new suspects.

12. *Citizens.* Information from the *local community* is often supplied as tips to local police using law enforcement tip lines.

13. *Accusations.* Victimized persons and goods file a *claim* with the police.

14. *Exchange.* International *police cooperation* includes exchange of intelligence information. International partners for national police include national police in other countries as well as multinational organizations, such as Europol and Interpol.

15. *Media.* By reading newspapers and watching TV, intelligence officers have access to *news*.
16. *Control authorities.* Cartel agencies, stock exchanges, tax authorities, and other control authorities are *suppliers of information* to the police in case of suspicious transactions.
17. *External data storage.* A number of business and government organizations store information that may be useful in police intelligence. For example, telecom firms store data about traffic, where both sender and receiver are registered with date and time of communication.

All these information sources have different characteristics. In Figure 7.2, information sources are distinguished in terms of the extent of trustworthiness and the extent of accessibility.

Prisons and other correctional environments are potential places for several information sources and production of intelligence useful to law enforcement. The total prison environment, including the physical plant, the schedule regimens of both staff and inmates, and all points of ingress and egress can be legitimately tapped for intelligence purposes in countries such as the United States (Maghan, 1994). Because organized criminals often are sophisticated in using the correction environment to their advantage, police and correction personnel need to be

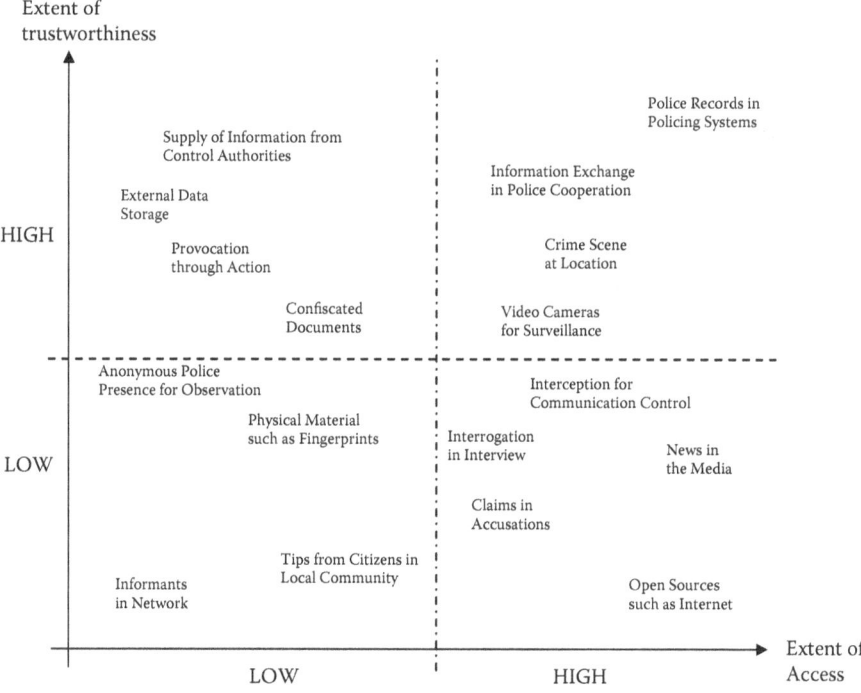

Figure 7.2 Trust in and access to information sources.

immersed in the intelligence operations and strategies of their respective agencies. Legal visitation and escape attempts are sources of information. Prisoners are reluctant to testify and their credibility is easily attacked. Communication control is derived from inmate use of phones, visits, mail, and other contacts.

The seventeen information sources can be classified into two main categories. The first category includes all person-oriented information sources where the challenge in police intelligence is to communicate with individuals. The second category includes all media-oriented information sources where the challenge in police intelligence is to manage and use different technological and other media. This distinction into two main categories leads to this classification of seventeen information sources.

Person-oriented information sources
1. Interrogation in interview
2. Informants in network
5. Anonymous police presence undercover for observation
6. Provocation through action
12. Tips from citizens in local community
13. Claims in accusations
14. Information exchange in police cooperation

Media-oriented information sources
3. Crime scenes at location
4. Confiscated documents
7. Video cameras for surveillance
8. Interception for communication control
9. Physical materials, such as fingerprints
10. Open sources, such as the Internet
11. Police records in police systems
15. News in the media
16. Supply of information from control authorities
17. External data storage

Crime Intelligence Analysis

For Innes et al. (2005, 41), crime analysis is concerned with insight and understanding:

> There has been a move away from an ad hoc, intuitive and largely unstructured mode of analytic work, to a more ordered, rationalized approach, based upon specific methodologies, on the basis that this provides a more "objective" perspective on patterns of crime and offending. This has raised the profile and status

of intelligence analysis within policing, and seen new techniques and technologies introduced, which should, at least in theory, allow police a better understanding of how, when and why crimes are occurring.

Crime analysis is described by the Council of Europe (2002) as a law enforcement function whereby data relating to crime are collected, collated, analyzed, and disseminated. Crime analysis is the study of crime patterns and trends in an attempt to solve crimes or prevent their repeat occurrence.

A distinction can be made between operational/tactical and strategic analyses. Operational analysis is directed toward a short-term law enforcement goal with an immediate impact in mind, e.g., arrest, seizure, and forfeiture. The goal of strategic crime analysis is to develop a policy, to implement that policy, or to evaluate the policy based on insights into the nature of a type of crime or criminal; the scope and projections of growth in types of criminal activities. But strategic analysis need not be restricted to crime; methods of strategic analysis can be used principally for all kinds of security and safety problems. Strategic analysis can deal with crime as well as with other security issues like traffic problems and public order maintenance. According to the Council of Europe (2002), it starts with the question of which information is needed, which data is lacking. A structured plan has to be developed and discussed. The next step is the detection of a problem, the consideration of a new phenomenon, and the gathering of information.

Examples of strategic crime analysis include:

- *Crime pattern analysis*: Examination of the nature and distribution of crime within an area, in order to identify emerging and current trends and patterns, linked crimes or incidents, hot spots of activity. Includes crime trend identification, crime series identification, general profile analysis, and hot spot analysis. Examination of the nature and scale of crime within an area and within a time frame.
- *Crime control methods analysis*: Evaluation of investigative or preventive methods and techniques with the aim of establishing their future usefulness.
- *General profile analysis*: Identification of the typical characteristics of perpetrators of certain crimes.
- *Results analysis*: Evaluation of the effectiveness of law enforcement activities.
- *Demographic/social trends analysis*: Examination of the nature of demographic changes and their impact on criminality, as well as the analysis of social factors (e.g., unemployment), which might underlie changes in trends in offending patterns. Also to describe statistically the constitution of the population of a given area and the associated economic indicators with reference to law enforcement requirements.

- *Criminal business analysis/profile*: Examination in detail of how illegal operations/businesses and techniques work.
- *Market profile*: A survey of the criminal market around a given commodity (e.g., illicit drugs, stolen vehicles). It can include crime pattern analysis and network analysis.
- *Strategic analysis*: Category of types of crime analysis designed to aid the formation or the evaluation of crime policy. Aims to provide information that can represent a picture of a phenomenon, and which can identify trends in criminality where management can base their decisions.

Examples of tactical/operational crime analysis include:

- *Specific profile analysis*: Identification of the specific characteristics of perpetrators of certain crimes. This includes the construction of a hypothetical picture of the perpetrator of a serious crime or series of offenses on the basis of crime scene data, witness statements, and other available information.
- *Offender group analysis*: Examination of the structure of a group of suspects, the significance of each member, and their involvement with criminal activities.
- *Investigations/operations analysis*: Evaluation of the effectiveness of activities that are undertaken within the context of an investigation.
- *Case analysis*: Establishment of the course of events immediately before, during, and after a serious offense.
- *Comparative case analysis*: Identification of series of crimes with common offenders by seeking similarities between offenses.
- *Operational crime analysis*: Category of types of crime analyses designed to support the investigation of one particular crime or one specific series of crimes with common offenders. Aims to provide an understanding of the information collected during a specific investigation.
- *Network analysis*: Provision of a detailed picture of the roles played by individuals, the nature and significance of the links between people, and the strengths and weaknesses of the criminal network.

United Kingdom police forces are required to report every three months on the crime analysis of organized crime. The regional offices deal with the various law enforcement organizations and some nongovernmental organizations. Organized criminal groups are mainly investigated by the regional police forces, sometimes assisted by national agencies. In complex cases, which include most of the investigations of organized crime, analysts are involved. They apply various analysis techniques, including a large variety of charting techniques, e.g., to visualize associations between entities (link charts), flows of money or other commodities (flow charts), or sequences of events in time (event charts).

In intelligence analysis, the raw material for analysis is information (based on information sources) and knowledge (based on experience). We have argued that intelligence is located on a continuum somewhere between information and knowledge. Ratcliffe (2008, 99) has presented an alternative view by arguing that intelligence is at a higher level on the continuum than knowledge, and he uses the acronym DIKI (data, information, knowledge, and intelligence) to illustrate his point:

> To place the DIKI continuum in context, consider this example. At a local police station, a computer database records and retains the location of residential burglary incidents. These computer records are *data*. When a crime analyst accesses the data and recognizes an emerging pattern of new burglaries in an area not normally plagued with a break-and-enter problem, then this becomes *information*. In essence, raw data have been enhanced with sufficient meaning to recognize a pattern. If the analyst subsequently talks to a detective and shares this information, and the detective remembers that a new pawnshop has just opened in the area and that known burglars have been seen entering the pawnshop, this collective wisdom becomes *knowledge*. Various information strands have coalesced to enable the detective and the analyst to build a picture of the criminal environment in their minds, a picture that undoubtedly has gaps, but that also has enough substance to support hypotheses and contain implications. This is the structure of knowledge. Finally, when the crime analyst and the detective take their knowledge to a senior officer who agrees to investigate the pawnshop and mount a surveillance operation to target burglars and gather further information, then this knowledge becomes *intelligence*. In other words, somebody uses it explicitly to try to reduce crime.

While this definition is certainly fascinating, it is neither mainstream nor feasible when our basic assumption is that intelligence is input to analysis. Furthermore, the definition of information also does seem a little bit strange, as information here seems to imply input from knowledge. Therefore, we continue using our stage approach in terms of data, information, intelligence, knowledge, and wisdom (DIKI).

Market Intelligence Analysis

For a long time, it was assumed that organized criminals had monopoly in their markets (Chang et al., 2005) because competition and competitors seemed invisible in their criminal activities. Therefore, theories of monopoly were frequently used in the study of organized crime.

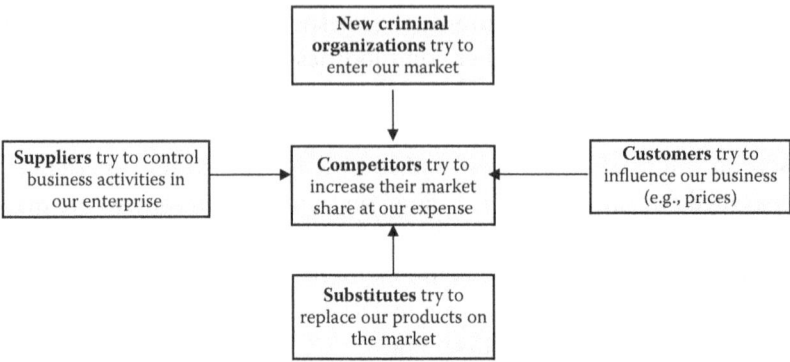

Figure 7.3 Competitive forces in criminal markets.

However, more recent studies have concluded that competitive markets exist for most criminal business enterprises. A market is characterized by five different kinds of actors: the criminal business enterprise, competing criminal enterprises, customers, suppliers, and substitute product business enterprises, as illustrated in Figure 7.3. Market share of the criminal business enterprise will only increase if the market shares of competing criminal enterprises decrease. If the market is growing and sales are stable for a criminal business enterprise, then it means that the market share for the enterprise is decreasing.

Competitive forces can be influenced by law enforcement actions. For example, after police shot and killed Ramon Arellano Felix, who headed the Tijuana cartel in Mexico in 2002, the position of Ismael Zambada-Garcia's Sinaloa cartel was strengthened by increasing market share in the drug trade (Small and Taylor, 2006).

One of the studies showing that there are competing market forces was conducted by Paoli (2001, 31), who studied drug trade in Italy, Germany, and Russia.

> The drug markets of the three environments we have investigated are open markets; the relationships between drug dealing enterprises usually more nearly resemble competition than collusion. There are virtually no barriers to entry. Although some suppliers (such as Italian [M]afia groups) may occasionally enjoy considerable monopolistic power over local (usually small) markets, in most European and Russian cities drug enterprises seem to be price-takers rather than price-givers. This means that none of them are able to influence the commodity's price appreciably by varying the quantity of the output sold.

When there are many customers and suppliers in a market, no single supplier or customer can determine the price. The price is determined in the market by what is called "the invisible hand of the market." Paoli (2001, 37) states that, because of the invisible hand of the market, it is so difficult for law enforcement to find evidence on what is actually going on.

> Law enforcement agencies often resort to the specter of large-scale criminal organizations to back their requests for extra funding. As a matter of fact, it is the "invisible hand of the market" that reduces the effects of their repressive actions near to zero. At the retail level, the "industrial reserve army" willing to sell drugs seems to have no end. As a Milanese drug user noted, "For every five Moroccans who are arrested, there are at least fifty ready to do the same job even at less."

While there are few criminal organizations that completely dominate a market and have a monopoly situation, there are also few criminals who enter a market on their own. Most criminals will join forces with others in a network or hierarchy to gain strength in a competitive market. By joining forces with other criminals, there will be added value that is shared among participants (Pérez, 2007).

Another study, showing that there are competing market forces, was conducted by Kenney (2007, 235), who studied Colombia's drug trade.

> Contrary to [perceived] wisdom, Colombia's drug trade has never been dominated by a price-fixing association. Even during the respective heydays of the Medellin and Cali "cartels," cocaine production and exportation in Colombia was highly competitive, as independent trafficking groups in more than a dozen cities smuggled substantial amounts of cocaine to American and European drug markets. While some of these enterprises transacted with Pablo Escobar, the Orchoa brothers, and other prominent traffickers, their business relations more closely resembled informal producer–export syndicates than public or private cartels that controlled prices and monopolized markets. Although different groups occasionally pooled their resources to complete large-scale drug shipments, while reducing their exposure to government authorities, they steadfastly maintained their own sources of supply, financing, and clientele.

These kinds of competitive forces in criminal markets are illustrated in Figure 7.3.

The invisible hand of the market causes a price to be fixed in a market based on supply and demand. Suppliers will be willing to sell more products if the price is higher. Customers will be willing to buy more products if the price is lower. Hence, an increasing product price leads to rising supply and falling demand, as illustrated in Figure 7.4.

The term *elasticity* in economics refers to the elasticity of demand and supply when price changes occur. For example, if supply changes drastically by a minor price change, then we say that price elasticity in demand is high. Price elasticity of demand is an elasticity that measures the nature

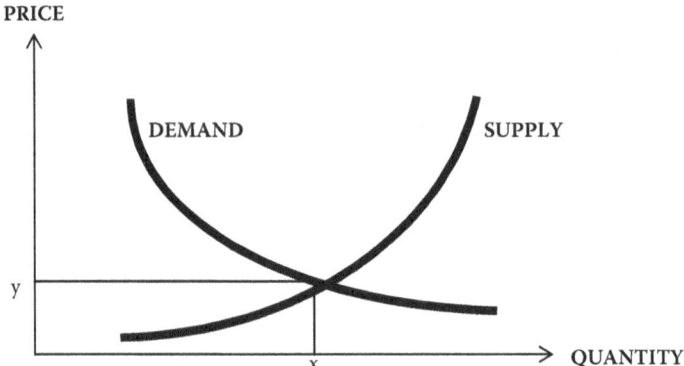

Figure 7.4 Market price determined by supply and demand curves.

and degree of relationship between changes in quantity demanded of goods and changes in the price. A price elasticity of 1.0 means that the demand will drop with the same percentage as that of the price increase. If, in response to a 10 percent decline in the price of a product, the quantity demanded increases by 20 percent, then the price elasticity of demand would be 2.0 (Dijck, 2007).

The invisible hand of the market determines the market price at *y* with a quantity of *x*. This is where the demand curve meets the supply curve in Figure 7.4.

Both demand and supply curves will change over time causing change in price and quantity. For example, when law enforcement is successful in getting a criminal group into prison, some of the supply disappears from the market. This will move the supply curve to the left in the figure causing price increase and quantity decrease, as illustrated in Figure 7.5. The price increases from *y* to *y′*, while the quantity decreases from *x* to *x′*.

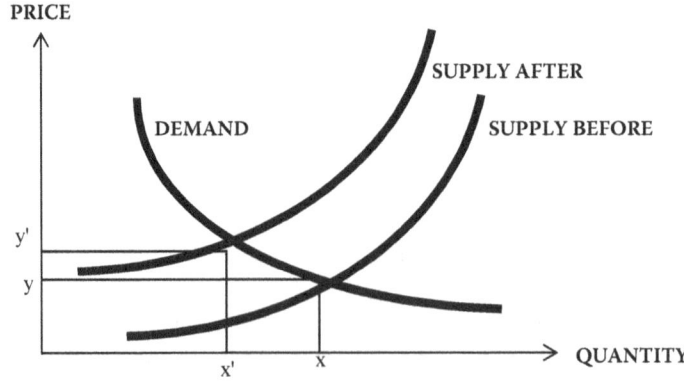

Figure 7.5 Market price determined by changing supply curve.

With a higher market price than before, new criminal groups may be interested in entering this market. If they do so, the market price will drop in direction from y' back toward y.

Both in legal and illegal markets, the practice of market economics varies. For example, when trying to introduce the American way of business to the legal economy in Russia, it failed (Buss, 2001, 95):

> Much of the failure probably resulted because American approaches to economic development—highly successful in other contexts—could not work during Russia's transition from a command economy to its current state. Such things as promoting entrepreneurship, developing public–private partnerships, creating a market economy, accessing start-up capital, attracting foreign investment, overcoming bureaucratic corruption and high taxation, working within the rule of law, and negating organized crime either should not have been done, or could not have been done, leaving many of our programs ineffective.

Similarly, Tanev (2001) found that the Western-style market economy did not work in Bulgaria. The central government was not willing to lose power in favor of local democracy and market forces.

Demand on criminal markets is determined by a number of factors. Consumers may be dependent on the goods supplied on the market, which is the case for many drugs. Consumers may be willing to explore, which is the case for many sex buyers. Europol (2006, 25) made the following finding concerning criminal markets in Europe:

> With regard to the facilitating factors in the discussion of criminal markets, a general evolution toward increasingly complex setups for criminal endeavors can be witnessed. Increasingly, horizontal facilitating factors such as document forgery and identity theft, technology, the transport sector, the financial sector and the presence or absence of borders are employed for criminal gain. The latter mainly refers to opportunities provided by decreased border controls whilst administrative and legal borders remain.

Criminal markets expand across national borders because demand is present in several countries, while nations may have different law enforcement practices. When Europol (2006, 26) divides Europe into regions for organized crime, Norway was described as a country with heavily taxed goods and services that stimulate organized crime.

- Northeast Europe with regard to highly taxed products aimed at the Nordic countries and beyond
- Southwest Europe in particular with regard to illegal immigration, cocaine, and cannabis trafficking for further distribution in the European Union (EU)

- Southeast Europe specifically with regard to heroin trafficking, illegal immigration, and trafficking in human beings, aimed at the whole of the EU

The price elasticity in both demand and supply will vary from market to market. For example, in a heavily dependent drug market, where consumers are completely dependent on their daily dose, elasticity may be very low, as indicated in Figure 7.6. Whatever the price, a low-varying quantity is in demand to satisfy needs.

Market share is the percentage or proportion of the total available market or market segment that is being serviced by an organization. It can be expressed as on organization's sales revenue (from that market) divided by the total sales revenue available in that market. It can also be expressed as an organization's unit sales volume (in a market) divided by the total volume of units sold in that market.

An interesting example of market size and market share is the sex market in Norway, since this country was criminalizing sex customers in 2008. This is similar to Sweden, where prostitute clients were criminalized some years earlier. While selling sex remains legal, both organizers and customers are illegal actors. The criminal organization trafficking women to the sex market in Norway is illegal. How does the market change? First, the demand curve will change. Next, market shares will change. While the prostitution market has been shared among criminal organizations offering Nigerian, East European, and Asian women, it might be expected that there may be some pull out of the market, enabling the others to increase their market share. While the total market size is expected to decline, some may increase their market share, thereby sustaining their sales volume.

Increasing market share is one of the most important objectives used in legal business. Market share has the potential to increase profits given positive

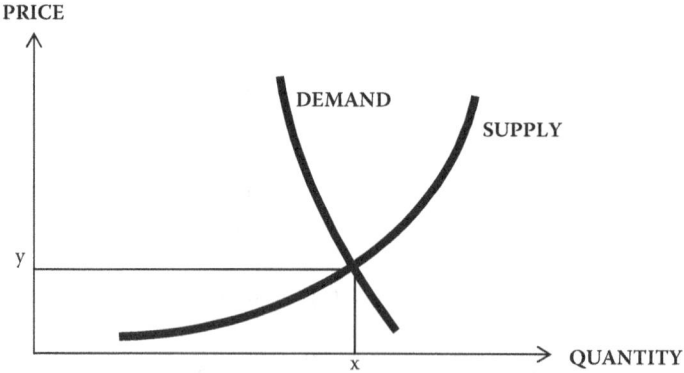

Figure 7.6 Market price when demand elasticity is low.

or no change in market size. Increasing market share enables a criminal business enterprise to change the power structure in the competitive forces game. If the CBE significantly increases its market share, then it might be able to reduce the (negative) influence from substitutes, rivals, customers, clients and new entrants.

Increasing market share is part of marketing management, which is a business discipline focused on the practical application of marketing techniques and the management of an organization's marketing resources and activities. Marketing managers are often responsible for influencing the level, timing, and composition of customer demand in a manner that will achieve the organization's objectives. Typical marketing techniques used by criminal business enterprises include threats, violence, and corruption.

In order to increase market share, businesses develop a marketing strategy based on an objective understanding of their own business and the market in which they operate. Traditionally, marketing analysis was structured into three areas: customer analysis, company analysis, and competitor analysis. More recently, collaborator analysis and industry context analysis have been added.

The focus of customer analysis is to develop a scheme for market segmentation, breaking down the market into various constituent groups of customers, which are called customer segments or market segments. Marketing managers work to develop detailed profiles of each segment, focusing on any number of variables that may differ among segments; demographic, psychographic, geographic, behavioral, needs benefit, and other factors all may be examined.

In order to increase market share, competitor analysis is the most important. In competitor analysis, marketers build detailed profiles of each competitor in the market, focusing especially on their relative competitive strengths and weaknesses, opportunities, and threats. Marketing managers will examine each competitor's cost structure, sources of profits, resources and competencies, competitive positioning and product differentiation, degree of vertical integration, historical responses to industry developments, alliances, and relationships.

While our main focus here is organized crime on criminal markets, it is also interesting to look at legal markets where organized crime occurs. The *theory of occupational crime* suggests that illegal business activities are forced on market actors because of market pressures. Leonard and Weber (1970) argued that insufficient attention had been focused by sociologists and others on the extent to which market structure, i.e., the economic power available to certain corporations in concentrated industries, may generate criminal conduct.

Leonard and Weber present an example of occupational crime caused by manufacturer–dealer relationships in the 1970s. While there were only four domestic manufacturers of cars, their products were distributed through 30,000 dealers with facilities scattered throughout the United States. Technically, the dealer is an independent businessman. Rarely, however, does he have the capital to acquire more than a fraction of the value of property involved in the dealership. The manufacturer supplies the rest and, although the dealer may increase his ownership, rising costs of real estate, equipment, and facilities, plus expansion of the dealership, may keep him dependent on the manufacturer for some time. Further, he operates under restrictive agreements, terms of which are set by the manufacturer.

Dealers were pressured to accept the manufacturer's low margin on car sales. To compensate for these low margins, many dealers introduced illegal practices to survive in the business. Typical practices included (Leonard and Weber, 1970, 415):

- *Forcing accessories.* For example, new cars arrive with accessories, which the buyer did not order, but must pay for in order to get delivery.
- *Used car markups.* Since dealers made little per unit on new car sales, they endeavored to compensate for this by large markups on used cars.
- *Service gouging.* Dealers also made up for their low returns in the sale of new cars by overcharging for service. This can be managed in may ways: by putting down more labor time than that actually consumed in repairs, by charging for repairs not actually made, by finding things wrong with the car that did not actually need repair, and by replacing parts unnecessarily.
- *High finance.* Dealers would often finance cars themselves, borrowing money from a bank or credit agency and lending at a higher rate of interest.
- *Parts pushing.* This involves overcharging for parts, or use of a rebuilt part while charging for a new one.

According to the theory of occupational crime, such practices were introduced by dealers because of the market structure under which they were operating. The only way to survive as a car dealer was to be criminal. It is argued that what appears to the public as unethical or criminal behavior on the part of dealers and mechanics represents "conditioned" crime, or crime stimulated by conditions over which the dealer or mechanic has little control. Dealers and mechanics operate within systems controlled by outsiders, specifically by a few large automobile manufacturers.

Dijck (2007) studied the illicit cigarette market in The Netherlands. He found the market to be relatively open in the sense of a low threshold to enter this market. Newcomers can easily set up a cigarette trafficking scheme. The Netherlands, being a nation of transit and transport, provides a setting for untaxed cigarettes. The market share of untaxed tobacco was estimated to be 3 percent in 2003 and 5 percent in 2005, while the total consumption of tobacco in The Netherlands was declining.

Traffickers of smuggled cigarettes may experience difficulties in linking supply and demand at any given time (Dijck, 2007, 165):

> In one case, for example, offenders discussed over the phone the question whether they would accept a substitute shipment of counterfeit Marlboro cigarettes instead of the original brand cigarettes they bought at previous occasions. The supplier of the original brand cigarettes could not continue his delivery because the police had raided one of the main warehouses and confiscated all cigarettes. Though there is a market for counterfeit cigarettes in The Netherlands as well, these offenders were afraid that their customers particularly favored brand cigarettes, more precisely Marlboro, and that they would not be able to get rid of other brands than Marlboro cigarettes.

Dijck (2007) found that cigarette traffickers rely on limited networks, consisting of one or two suppliers and a dozen customers. The cigarette black market provides ample opportunity to make a good profit. The profit opportunities exceed the low risk involved.

Markina (2007) conducted a similar study of the cigarette black market in Estonia. The market share of untaxed tobacco in Estonia is estimated to be much higher than in The Netherlands. This is not because legal tobacco prices are higher in Estonia. It is because neighboring countries, such as Russia, have much cheaper tobacco and because tobacco prices have risen much faster in Estonia compared to The Netherlands.

To join the European Union, Estonia had to harmonize taxes on cigarettes and other tobacco goods quite quickly. For an ordinary smoker, the harmonization of taxes meant nothing else than a shocking increase in cigarette prices within a relatively short period of time. As a consequence, many smokers looked for alternative supplies of tobacco and they found it on the black market. A survey in Estonia found that 60 percent of the respondents were ready to purchase illegal cigarettes as a reaction to the price increase.

While a package of legal cigarettes had the price of 2.05 euro in 2007, an illegal package only cost 0.57 euro. The places where illegal cigarettes are sold are quite well known to the public in Estonia. Customers buy illegal cigarettes either directly from retailers on the street (53 percent) or at the trader's home (35 percent). Most of the illegal cigarettes come from bootlegging (Markina, 2007, 204):

> This particular type of smuggling, called bootlegging, involves the purchase of cigarettes in a country where cigarettes are low-priced and transporting them either for personal consumption or resale to the high-priced country in quantities exceeding limits set by custom regulation.

Bootlegging involves transporting cigarettes over relatively short distances, usually between neighboring countries. Shipments of inexpensive Russian brands, such as Prima, Prima Nevo, North Star, or Arktika, end up in Estonia.

Intelligence Knowledge Work

Policing is generally viewed as a highly stressful and demanding profession. Considerable research has examined stress in policing. According to Richardsen et al. (2006), most of this work has focused on the effects of the distress of police officers, the impact of police work on their spouses and families, suicide, alcoholism, mortality, fatigue, posttraumatic stress disorder, and the effects of shift work schedules on police performance and health. Although it is not clear whether police work is inherently more demanding than other professions, police officers experience work events that are frequently associated with psychological distress.

Richardsen et al. (2006) studied the mediating role of both negative (cynicism) and positive (work engagement) work attitudes in the relationship between work events and work and health outcomes. The cynicism theory proposes that police officers come into the occupation with idealistic notions, but quickly come to realize the hard realities of the world and of police work. Over time, they become increasingly intolerant of faults and mistakes in others and may lose a sense of purpose. Cynicism may be a way to cope with what is perceived to be an unfriendly, unstable, and insecure world, providing a convenient explanation for constant disillusionment and a way of acting out anger and resentment in the work place.

Richardsen et al. found that cynicism and engagement were highly correlated with both work and health outcomes in the expected direction, i.e., cynicism was associated with increased health complaints and reduced commitment and efficacy, and engagement was associated with reduced health complaints and increased commitment and efficacy.

To understand knowledge, the notion of practice and the individual as a social participant in applying knowledge is important. Knowing and learning are integrated, continuous processes for detectives in police investigations. Knowledge always undergoes construction and transformation in use. It is not simply a matter for taking in knowledge. It is an act of construction and creation where knowledge is neither universal nor abstract, but dependent on context (Chiva and Alegre, 2005).

It is relevant here to touch on the role of women in policing. While we find significant variance on a global basis, more and more countries have female officers working with male officers on a regular basis. It is not rare anymore to find a woman police officer heading a policing unit. In fact, in the present day, it isn't surprising to see a woman heading an entire police organization. For example, in Norway, the managing director of the entire police force is a woman.

While significant barriers still confront women in policing in many parts of the world, a number of legal and cultural obstacles to women in policing have recently been removed. Some gender differences enable female and male officers to complement each other. For example, studies show that female police officers rely on a policing style that uses less physical force and are less confrontational than male officers.

Detective Knowledge Work

According to Tong (2007), the secretive nature of the detective world has attracted little attention from researchers. However, competing perspectives about detective work can be discerned from available literature. Detective work has been characterized as an art, a craft, a science, and a combination of all three. The old regime of the seasoned detective highlighted the notion of detective work as a craft. An alternative perspective highlights the scientific nature of detective work, which focuses on the skills needed for crime scene management, the use of physical evidence, investigative interviewing, informant handling, offender profiling, management of the investigative process, and knowledge management.

It is important for detectives to be effective in their work, as new public management is focusing closely on the effective use of resources. However, measuring effectiveness is no easy task. Measurement, in an investigative context, has focused upon the outcome of cases, often at the expense of evaluating the process of the investigation and quality of its outputs. Tong (2007) argues that not only have the police been subject to inadequate measurement criteria, such as clear-up rates, there has also been a lack of recognition of good quality police work. The task of recognizing good detective work involves more than providing an appropriate method of measurement, it also implies an awareness of the impact of practice as well as an awareness of the knowledge accumulation, sharing, and reuse.

It follows that the most useful approach to measuring detective effectiveness will not necessarily be the measurement of specific outcomes, although such measures will be useful for resource management. Tong argues that effectiveness in the context of detective work is best measured by focusing on the key processes and decisions in which detectives engage to encourage a professional working culture based on how detectives come to decisions. In the context of the so-called value shop for knowledge work, decisions are made in all five primary activities of the value shop: understanding the problem, identifying problem solutions, prioritizing actions, implementing investigation, and evaluating and controlling detective work.

Tong (2007) constructed this profile of an effective detective after analyzing the academic literature relating to detective skills and abilities:

1. *Personal qualities*: Intelligence, common sense, initiative, inquisitiveness, independence of thought, commitment, persistence, ability to talk to people, flexibility, ability to learn, reflexivity, lateral thinking, creative thinking, patience, empathy, tolerance and interpreting uncertain and conflicting information, ability to work away from family and home, interpreting feelings, ideas and facts, honesty, and integrity.

2. *Legal knowledge*: Knowledge of the law referring to police powers, procedure, criminal justice process, a good grounding in criminal law, awareness of changes to legislation, courtroom protocol, rules of disclosure, use of evidence, format of case file, and awareness of defense arguments.

3. *Practical knowledge*: Technology available to detectives and used by criminals, understanding the context in which crime is committed, and awareness of investigative roles of different functions of the police organization and specialist advisors. Recognition that crime changes with time and place and may require police responses that are tailored to specific context. Forensic awareness and practical expertise (e.g., crime scene preservation and packaging of evidence).

4. *Generic knowledge*: Recognition that knowledge changes, awareness of developments in practice will allow the detective to remain up to date.

5. *Theoretical knowledge*: Understanding of theoretical approaches to investigative reasoning and theories of crime.

6. *Management skills*: The management and control of case information, implementing investigative action, formulating investigative strategies, verifying expert advice, prioritizing lines of enquiry, formulating media strategies, awareness of resource availability, and knowledge of roles of personnel available to the investigation. Manage knowledge and learning through the use of research skills to enable the detective to remain up to date.

7. *Investigative skills*: Interview technique, presenting evidence, cultivating informants, extracting core information (from files, reports, victims, and witnesses), file construction, appraising and evaluating information, ability to absorb and manage large volumes of information, statement taking, problem solving, formulating lines of enquiry, create slow time, assimilate information from crime scene, continually review lines of enquiry, and question and challenge legal parties.

8. *Interpersonal skills*: Ability to communicate and establish a rapport with a range of people, remain open minded, be aware of consequences of actions, and avoid speculation.

Stelfox and Pease (2005) argue that there has been surprisingly little empirical research into the way in which individual officers approach the task of investigating crime. In their own research, they found that investigators are practical people. Assuming that the cognitive abilities of the average investigator are no more or less than the population as a whole, it can be anticipated that he or she will remain liable to make the same cognitive errors as the rest of us. Assuming also that the decision-making environment the detective works in is unlikely to change much, it can be anticipated that errors will recur.

Intelligence has emerged as an important component of contemporary policing strategies. However, Innes et al. (2005) argue that crime intelligence analysis is used in line with traditional modes of policing, is a way of claiming "scientific objectivity" for police actions, and is largely shaped by police perspectives on data. They argue that the sense of enhanced objectivity often attributed to the products of "intelligence work" is frequently overstated. Therefore, the products of crime analysis might better be understood as an artifact of the data and methods used in their construction, rather than providing an accurate representation of any crime problems.

Added to which, Innes et al. found that there has been increasing frustration within certain sections of the police organization, with the perceived failure of community-policing programs to facilitate the routine supply of high-quality information to the police from members of the community. Any such concerns with low policing have been reinforced and amplified by recent developments at the "high policing" level where there is a well documented shift toward trying to effect enhanced national security from threats posed by terrorist groups, drug cartels, and organized crime networks.

The presence of criminal markets and networks implies a degree of organization to the conduct of crime. In turn, this serves to recursively justify the investment in technologies of analysis. It signals to the police that simply arresting isolated individuals will have only a temporary effect on crime levels before the adaptive qualities and replacement mechanisms of the surrounding networks and markets cause them to reform. Therefore, they need to conduct analysis so as to improve their awareness of the shape and makeup of the supporting networks and markets in which motivated criminals are located, so that any interventions taken against these criminals will have more impact (Innes et al., 2005).

One of the bottlenecks in international police cooperation is the targeting of the proceeds of crime. International agencies, such as Interpol and Europol, are sometimes involved in the interaction between the authorities and enforcement organizations of the countries concerned. Borgers and Moors (2007) studied bottlenecks in international cooperation for The Netherlands in targeting the proceeds of crime. While no bottlenecks were found in cooperation with countries such as Belgium and the United Kingdom, bottlenecks were found in relation with countries such as Spain and Turkey. In relation to Turkey, The Netherlands acts mainly as the requesting state and not the requested state (Borgers and Moors, 2007, 8).

> Regarding the cooperative relations with Turkey, Turkish respondents state that the framing of Dutch mutual assistance requests is inadequate. On the part of the Netherlands, there are different opinions on the depth of the investigation conducted at the request of the Netherlands. As far as the way in which people address one another is concerned, it is striking that the Turkish respondents sometimes consider the Dutch manner of operation as haughty and impatient. According to Dutch respondents, communication difficulties also occur if Dutch police officials directly contact the Turkish judges involved.

To fight organized crime, law enforcement in the United Kingdom reorganized. The United Kingdom's Serious Organized Crime Agency (SOCA) commenced operations in 2006 with an annual budget of £400 million. SOCA consists of the National Crime Squad, the National Criminal Intelligence Service (NCIS), and investigators from Customs and the Home Office's Immigration Service (Segell, 2007).

Case: Lawyers as Information Sources

Sometimes, lawyers and notaries are potentially excellent information sources about organized crime. The case of Evert Hingst, although exceptional in many ways, reflects the fact that people who render financial and legal services may play a vital role within and between criminal networks (Nelen and Lankhorst, 2008, 127):

> On Monday, 31 October 2005, 36-year-old Dutch lawyer Evert Hingst was murdered in front of his house in Amsterdam. Among Hingst's clients were many noted and alleged criminals, including John Mieremet, who was once shot in front of Hingst's office. After this assault, Mieremet claimed that Hingst had tried to set him up. Mieremet was murdered three days after the liquidation of Hingst, on 2 November, in Thailand. Hingst, a fiscal specialist, had been accused of assisting criminals to launder their money abroad. He was imprisoned for several weeks after police discovered three firearms and a large sum of cash during a raid of his office in 2005. A suspect of money laundering, membership of a criminal organization and possession of firearms, Hingst gave up his profession as a lawyer in July 2005. He had previously been arrested on charges of forgery of documents in 2005.

The lawyer Evert Hingst could be linked to Hells Angels Holland through John Mieremet and Willem Holleeder. Willem "The Nose" Holleeder is a Dutch criminal born May 29, 1958, in Amsterdam. He was one of the perpetrators of the kidnapping of brewery president Freddy Heineken, in 1983, for which Holleeder received a jail sentence of eleven years. He is assumed to be responsible for extortion of various real estate magnates, including Willem Endstra, who was murdered in 2004. A total of twenty-four people are suspected of being part of a crime ring controlled by Holleeder. The nickname of "The Nose" is because of the size of Holleeder's nose (www.wikipedia.org).

With companions Sam Klepper, John Mieremet, and his later brother-in-law Cor van Hout, Holleeder was already, in the 1970s, a member of an opportunity-based criminal organization. They carried out armed robberies more or less at random. At the age of eighteen, they had already enough money to drive around in expensive cars. The kidnapping of Heineken in 1983 garnered them a ransom of €16 million (www.wikipedia.org).

In 2002, Holleeder came in the news when the monthly magazine *Quote* printed a photo of Holleeder alongside Willem Endstra. Endstra was regarded as "the banker" of the Dutch underworld. Endstra laundered drug money and invested it in real estate. Holleeder ordered the extortion of Endstra in 2004 after Endstra started to give information to the Dutch national police. Hells Angels carried out the extortion because Holleeder enjoyed significant influence in the criminal motorcycle club (www.wikipedia.org).

Nelen and Lankhorst (2008) argue that lawyers and notaries sometimes are facilitators of organized crime. Culpable involvement of lawyers and notaries in organized crime tends to come from occasional cases in which they are involved. Culpable involvement of lawyers tends to be in systematic mortgage frauds and huge sums of money transferred through law firms. Culpable involvement of notaries tends to be in transactions on the property market, the establishment of legal entities to shield criminal activities, and drafting fraudulent deeds to enable money laundering.

References

Borgers, M.J. and Moors, J.A. 2007. Targeting the proceeds of crime: Bottlenecks in international cooperation. *European Journal of Crime, Criminal Law and Criminal Justice*, 1–22.

Buss, T.F. 2001. Exporting American economic development practice to Russia. *Policy Studies Review* 18 (3): 94–108.

Chang, J.J., Lu, H.C., and Chen, M. 2005. Organized crime or individual crime? Endogenous size of a criminal organization and the optimal law enforcement. *Economic Inquiry* 43 (3): 661–675.

Chiva, R. and Alegre, J. 2005. Organizational learning and organizational knowledge. *Journal of Management Learning* 36 (1): 49–68.

Council of Europe. 2002. *Crime analysis: Organized crime—Best practice survey no. 4*, Economic Crime Division, Department of Crime Problems, Directorate General I–Legal Affairs, Council of Europe, Strasbourg, France.

Davidson, J. and Gottschalk, P. 2008. Digital forensics in law enforcement: The case of online victimization of children. *Electronic Government—An International Journal* 5 (4): 445–451.

Europol. 2006. OCTA: *EU organized crime threat assessment 2006*. European Police Office, The Hague, The Netherlands.

Harfield, C. 2008. Paradigms, pathologies, and practicalities: Policing organized crime in England and Wales. *Policing* 2 (1): 63–73.

Innes, M., Fielding, N., and Cope, N. 2005. The appliance of science: The theory and practice of crime intelligence analysis. *British Journal of Criminology* 45: 39–57.

Innes, M. and Sheptycki, J.W.E. 2004. From detection to disruption: Intelligence and the changing logic of police crime control in the United Kingdom. *International Criminal Justice Review* 14: 1–24.

Kenney, M. 2007. The architecture of drug trafficking: Network forms of organization in the Colombian cocaine trade. *Global Crime* 8 (3): 233–259.

Leonard, W.N. and Weber, M.G. 1970. Automakers and dealers: A study of criminogenic market forces. *Law & Society Review* 4 (3): 407–424.

Maghan, J. 1994. Intelligence gathering approaches in prisons. *Low Intensity Conflict & Law Enforcement* 3 (3): 548–557.

Markina, A. 2007. Cigarette black market in Estonia. In *Crime business and crime money in Europe: The dirty linen of illegal enterprise*, Eds. P.C. van Duyne, A. Maljevic, M. van Dijck, K. von Lampe, and J. Harvey, 195–208. Nijmegen, The Netherlands: Wolf Legal Publishers.

Nelen, H. and Lankhorst, F. 2008. Facilitating organized crime: The role of lawyers and notaries. In *Organized crime: Culture, markets and policies*, Eds. D. Siegel and H. Nelen, 127–142. New York: Springer-Verlag.

Paoli, L. 2001. The "invisible hand of the market": The illegal drugs trade in Germany, Italy and Russia. Third Colloquium on Cross-border Crime, Police Academy Bratislava, Slovak Republic, October 19–38.

Pérez, N. 2007. *Crime networks*, Job Market Paper, University of Maryland, College Park.

Ratcliffe, J.H. 2008. *Intelligence-led policing*, Devon, U.K.: Willan Publishing.

Richardsen, A.M., Burke, R.J., and Martinussen, M. 2006. Work and health outcomes among police officers: The mediating role of police cynicism and engagement. *International Journal of Stress Management* 13 (4): 555–574.

Segell, G.M. 2007. Reform and transformation: The UK's serious organized crime agency. *International Journal of Intelligence and Counterintelligence* 20: 217–239.

Sheptycki, J. 2007. Police ethnography in the house of serious and organized crime. In *Transformations of policing*, Eds. A. Henry and D.J. Smith. 51–77, Oxford, U.K.: Ashgate Publishing.

Small, K. and Taylor, B. 2006. State and local law enforcement response to transnational crime. *Trends in Organized Crime* 10 (2): 5–17.

Stelfox, P. and Pease, K. 2005. Cognition and detection: Reluctant bedfellows? In *Crime science: New approaches to preventing and detecting crime*, Eds. M. Smith and N. Tilley. Devon, U.K.: Willan Publishing.

Tanev, T.A. 2001. Emerging from post-communism chaos: The case of Bulgaria. *International Journal of Public Administration* 24 (2): 235–248.

Tong, S. 2007. *Training the effective detective: Report of recommendations*, Cambridge, U.K.: University of Cambridge.

van Dijck, M. 2007. Cigarette shuffle: Organising tobacco tax evasion in the Netherlands. In *Crime business and crime money in Europe: The dirty linen of illicit enterprise*, Eds. P.C. van Duyne, A. Maljevic, van Dijck, M., K. von Lampe, and J. Harvey, 157–194. Nijmegen, The Netherlands: Wolf Legal Publishers.

Enforcing Law on Criminal Business

8

An important reason for enforcing law on criminal business is for the prevention of organized crime. van den Bunt and van der School (2003) define organized crime prevention as all measures (laws and regulations) that have been established for fighting organized crime, except for measures pertaining to criminal law. The death penalty does not fall under this definition, but all administrative measures and all measures undertaken by financial institutions do.

When the U.S. Federal Bureau of Investigation (FBI, 2008) launched its law enforcement strategy to combat international organized crime, it emphasized four priority areas of action to be taken against international organized crime:

1. *Marshal information and intelligence.* Collect, synthesize, and timely disseminate the best available information and intelligence from multiple sources—including law enforcement, the intelligence community, foreign partners, and the private sector—to optimize law enforcement's ability to identify, assess, and draw connections among nationally-significant international organized crime threats.
2. *Prioritize and target the most significant international organized crime threats.* Select and target for high-impact law enforcement action the international organized crime figures and organizations that pose the greatest threat to the United States, and ensure the national coordination of investigations and prosecutions involving these targets.
3. *Attack from all angles.* Employ all available law enforcement and non-law enforcement tools—including drawing upon the unique expertise of every participating U.S. law enforcement agency in domestic operations, partnering with foreign counterparts to pursue cases at home and abroad, and employing U.S. government sanctions and advisories—all in a crosscutting effort to disrupt international organized crime activity.
4. *Enterprise theory.* Develop aggressive strategies for dismantling entire criminal organizations, especially their leadership, by using proactive investigative techniques and multilayered prosecutions.

The senior investigating officer (SIO) is in charge of a criminal investigation in the law enforcement area. As the leader of a crime-solving project, it has been argued that the SIO needs investigative ability and crime knowledge as well as management skills. An empirical study in Norway was conducted, which indicated that management skills are more important than crime knowledge and investigative ability. Furthermore, among management roles, the motivating role of personnel leader was found to be most important for effective SIOs.

Administrative Approach to Organized Crime

The concept of an administrative approach to organized crime was developed in New York City two decades ago. Complementing a very intensive criminal policy, administrative measures enabled the authorities to break the positions of power of the five big Mafia families in the city. The administrative approach consists of a number of instruments, ranging from the integrity testing of civil servants, the purchasing of strategically positioned buildings, and the refusal or withdrawal of permits to the screening of companies who compete for major contracts (Nelen and Huisman, 2008).

One decade later, the administrative approach to organized crime was introduced in the city of Amsterdam. The Amsterdam administrative approach had a somewhat different background (Nelen and Huisman, 2008, 208):

> Because of the specific problems in the red-light district, Amsterdam city council emphasized that additional administrative attention should be devoted to this part of the city centre and called for the appointment of a so-called red-light district manager.

According to Nelen and Huisman, the administrative approach to organized crime is in line with recent developments in the context of situational crime prevention. Administrative intervention strategies aim at criminal organization deterioration, organized crime decline, crime profit collapse, and reduction in criminal business enterprises. In Amsterdam, the city authorities acquired more than fifty-six buildings from criminal business enterprises. Four illegal casinos and several establishments in the hotel and restaurant industries were closed down. More than twenty licenses for bars and restaurants were refused or withdrawn, and eight permits in the catering industry were withdrawn. The licenses of the key players in the sex industry in the red-light district were withdrawn until the entrepreneurs concerned were able to submit a transparent accounting result (Nelen and Huisman, 2008).

According to van den Bunt and van der Schoot (2003), case studies of organized crime show that illegitimate and legitimate environments intermingle. Although these criminal interfaces are a threat to the legitimate world, they also offer opportunities for prevention. The message in their research is that, if criminal organizations are able to easily acquire or access resources, then the number of these resources should be reduced or made more difficult to acquire or access. Their study identified opportunities that facilitate organized crime and presented measures to prevent them.

van der Schoot (2006) asked: What is the effectiveness of organized crime prevention? His research examined the possible effectiveness of three preventive measures taken against organized crime in The Netherlands: the antimoney laundering intervention, the screening and auditing approach, and the administrative approach of the City of Amsterdam. By assessing the program theory, process, and impacts, van der Schoot determined plausible outcomes and observed outputs. Together these outcomes and outputs determine the possible effectiveness of the preventive measures.

Investigation Value Shop

Police investigations have the value configuration of a value shop (Gottschalk, 2007). As can be seen in Figure 8.1, the five activities of a value shop are interlocking and while they follow a logical sequence, much like the management of any project, the difference from a knowledge management perspective is the way in which knowledge is used as a resource to create value in terms of results for the organization. Hence, the logic of the five interlocking value shop activities in this example is of a police organization and how it engages in its core business of conducting reactive and proactive investigations.

The sequence of activities starts with problem understanding, moves into alternative investigation approaches, investigation decision, and

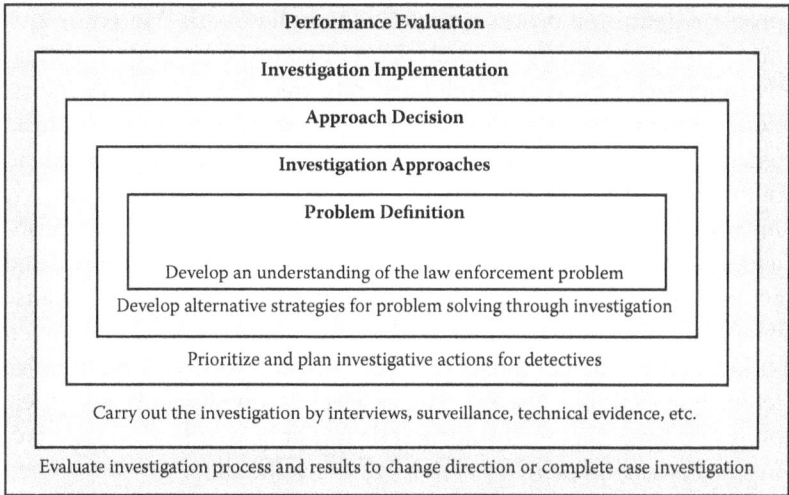

Figure 8.1 The knowledge organization of police investigations as value shop activities.

investigation implementation, and ends up with criminal investigation eval-uation. However, these five sequential activities tend to overlap and link back to earlier activities, especially in relation to activity 5 (control and evaluation) in police organizations when the need for control and command structures is a daily necessity because of the legal obligations that police authority entails. Hence, the diagram is meant to illustrate the reiterative and cyclical nature of these five primary activities for managing the knowledge collected during and applied to a specific police investigation in a value shop manner. Furthermore, Figure 8.1 illustrates the expanding domain of the knowledge work performed in police investigations, starting in the center with problem understanding and ending at the edge with evaluation of all parts of the investigation process.

These five primary activities of the value shop in relation to a police investigation unit can be outlined as (Gottschalk, 2007):

1. *Problem definition.* This involves working with parties to determine the exact nature of the crime and, thus, how it will be defined. For example, a physical assault in a domestic violence situation, depending on how the responding officers choose and/or perceive to define it, can be either upgraded to the status of grievous bodily harm to the spouse victim (usually female) or it may be downgraded to a less serious assault where a bit of rough handing took place toward the spouse. This concept of making crime, a term used on how detectives choose to make incidents into a crime or not, is highly relevant here and is why this first activity has been changed from the original problem-finding term used in the business management realm to a problem definition process in relation to police work. Moreover, this first investigative activity involves deciding on the overall investigative approach for the case, not only in terms of information acquisition, but also, as indicated on Figure 8.1, in undertaking the key task, usually by a senior investigative officer in a serious or major incident, of forming an appropriate investigative team to handle the case.

2. *Investigation approaches.* This second activity of identifying problem-solving approaches involves the actual generation of ideas and action plans for the investigation. As such, it is a key process because it sets the direction and tone of the investigation and is very much influenced by the composition of the members of the investigative team. For example, the experience level of investigators and their preferred investigative thinking style might be a critical success factor in this second primary activity of the value shop.

3. *Approach decision.* This solution choice activity represents the decision of choosing between alternatives generated in the second activity. While the least important primary activity of the value shop in

terms of time and effort, it might be the most important in terms of value. In this case, trying to ensure, as far as is possible, that what is decided on is the best option to follow to get an effective investigative result. A successful solution choice is dependent on two requirements. First, alternative investigation steps were identified in the problem-solving approaches activity. It is important to think in terms of alternatives. Otherwise, no choices can be made. Next, criteria for decision making have to be known and applied to the specific investigation.

4. *Investigation implementation.* As the name implies, solution execution represents communicating, organizing, investigating, and implementing decisions. This is an equally important process or phase in an investigation, as it involves sorting out the mass of information coming into the incident room about a case and directing the lines of enquiry as well as establishing the criteria used to eliminate a possible suspect from further scrutiny in the investigation. A miscalculation here can stall or even ruin the entire investigation. Most of the resources spent on an investigation are used here in this fourth activity of the value shop.

5. *Performance evaluation.* Control and evaluation involves monitoring activities and the measurement of how well the solution solved the original problem or met the original need. This is where the command and control chain of authority comes into play for police organizations and where the determination of the quality and quantity of the evidence is made as to whether or not to charge and prosecute an identified offender in a court of law.

Senior Investigating Officer

The performance of the police in the area of investigation is continually under scrutiny by the government, the criminal justice system, and the media. There is widespread recognition within the police service for a need to improve the professionalism of the investigative response. In the United Kingdom, the professionalizing investigation program was introduced in 2005. The purpose is to significantly improve the personal, functional, and organizational ability of the service to investigate crime of any category. In performance terms, the aim of the program is to deliver (Home Office, 2005b):

- Improved rates of crime detection
- Improvement in the quality of case files
- A reduction in the number of failed trails

- Improved levels of judicial disposal
- Increased public confidence in the police service

The long-term outcomes of the program shall deliver the professional development of staff against robust national occupational standards by developing police staff that is better qualified and thereby better skilled in investigation, more focused training for investigation, and minimal accreditation bureaucracy.

In all complex or serious cases on which a team of investigators is deployed, the senior investigating officer sets out what the main lines of enquiry are and records his or her decisions on those lines of enquiry as the investigation progresses. For example, the SIO directs which policy decisions are recorded in the HOLMES (Home Office large major enquiry system) in the United Kingdom. The Major Incident Policy Document is maintained whenever a Major Incident Room using HOLMES is in operation (Home Office, 2005a).

The SIO plays a pivotal role within all serious crime investigations. Concerns have been expressed, however, that there is a shortage of investigators with the appropriate qualities to perform this role effectively. The consequences of such a shortage could be severe. Not only might it threaten the effective workings of the judicial process, it can also waste resources, undermine integrity, and reduce public confidence in the police service. The principal aim of research conducted by Smith and Flanagan (2000) was to establish what skills, abilities, and personal characteristics an SIO ought to possess to be effective in the investigation of low-volume serious crimes (stranger rape, murder, and abduction). Interviews were conducted with forty officers from ten forces in the United Kingdom. These were selected to reflect a range of roles and experience with Criminal Investigation Departments (CID). Ten of these officers were nominated by their peers as examples of particularly effective SIOs.

Although the debate around SIO competencies has often polarized into arguments for and against specialist or generalist skills, the research highlighted the fact that the role of an SIO is extremely complex and the skills required wide-ranging. By applying a variety of analytical techniques, a total of twenty-two core skills were identified for an SIO to perform effectively in the role. The twenty-two skills were organized into three clusters:

1. *Investigative ability.* This includes the skills associated with the assimilation and assessment of incoming information into an enquiry and the process by which lines of enquiry are generated and prioritized.
2. *Knowledge levels.* This relates to the different types of underpinning knowledge an SIO should possess.

3. *Management skills.* These encompass a broad range of skill types that were further subdivided between people management, general management, and investigative management.

The research revealed that the effective SIO is dependent upon a combination of management skills, investigative ability, and relevant knowledge across the entire investigative process, from initial crime scene assessment through to post-charge case management.

Ideally, an SIO should possess a high level of competency across each of the three clusters. In reality, this is not always possible and, when one or more is lacking, there is an increased risk that the investigation will be inefficient or, in the worst case, will fail.

For example, an SIO from a predominantly non-CID background will have little experience within an investigative context. Hence, there is an increased risk that an investigation will fail due to suboptimal investigative decisions being made. Similarly, an SIO from a predominantly CID background may have less general management experience. Therefore, there may be an increased risk of failure from suboptimal management decisions.

The research suggested that some—but not all—deficiencies in an SIO's skill portfolio may be compensated for by drawing on the skills and abilities of more junior officers within his/her investigative team. However, it was recognized that this was still a high-risk and short-term strategy.

In police investigations, the manager of an investigative unit is generally referred to as an SIO. This is a middle management-type position in the command and control hierarchy of a police organization. Such a middle-ranking position carries a good deal of responsibility for making sure an investigation stays on track, within budget, and produces good results in terms of evidence and prosecution. Such responsibility places strong leadership demands on the SIO. Hence, Mintzberg's (1994) research on management roles is relevant and provides a firm basis on which to appreciate and understand the interrelated activities of a manager.

A manager's job consists of several parallel roles. At a certain point in time, the manager may perceive one role as more important than the others. Mintzberg found that it is a peculiarity of the management literature that its best-known writers all seem to emphasize one particular part of the manager's job to the exclusion of the others. Together they cover all the parts, but even that may not describe the complete task of managing.

Mintzberg's role typology is frequently used in studies of managerial work. When such role terminology is applied to a police investigation context, some modification is required as the SIO will not necessarily be responsible for all aspects of each role. Furthermore, business management terminology does not fit so well in a policing and law enforcement domain. Hence, some of the role labels have been changed to provide a more accurate fit with police terminology.

These six police manager roles, adapted from Gottschalk (2007), are briefly described along with the police-specific role label noted in parentheses.

1. *Personnel leader* (motivating role). As a leader, the manager is responsible for supervising, hiring, training, organizing, coordinating, and motivating a cadre of personnel to achieve the goals of the organization. This role is mainly internal to the police investigation unit. As stated previously, an SIO generally would not be responsible for hiring a particular individual in a business sense, but would have a say in which particular police investigator might join his/her team for a particular investigation. However, the main thrust of this role for the SIO is that of motivating his/her staff and keeping such motivation up, especially in a difficult and protracted investigation.
2. *Resource allocator* (resourcing role). The manager must decide how to allocate human, financial, and information resources to the different tasks of the investigation. This role emphasizes planning, organizing, coordinating, and controlling tasks, and is mainly internal to the police investigation unit. Often, the SIO has to be an advocate in this regard to get the necessary resources for his/her team to be able to conduct the investigation efficiently and effectively.
3. *Spokesperson* (networking role). As a spokesperson, the manager extends organizational contacts to areas outside his or her own jurisdiction. This role emphasizes promoting acceptance of the unit and the unit's work within the organization of which they are part. For the manager it means contact with the rest of the organization. Frequently, he or she must move across traditional departmental boundaries and become involved in personnel, organizational, and financial matters. Thus, with regard to the SIO, this key role is one of networking within the police organization. We distinguish between the following roles, as illustrated in Figure 8.2:
4. *Entrepreneur* (problem-solving role). The manager identifies the police needs and develops solutions that change situations. A major responsibility of the manager is to ensure that rapidly evolving investigation methods are understood, planned, implemented, and strategically utilized in the organization. Such a role is more akin to being a problem solver than an entrepreneur in a police setting.
5. *Liaison* (liaising role). In this role, the manager communicates with the external environment, and it includes exchanging information with government agencies, private businesses, and the media. This is an active, external role. This is a very similar role description for an SIO who has to liaise with a wide range of people throughout an investigation who are external to the police service, such as the public

Police Management: Role Activities in Investigation Process

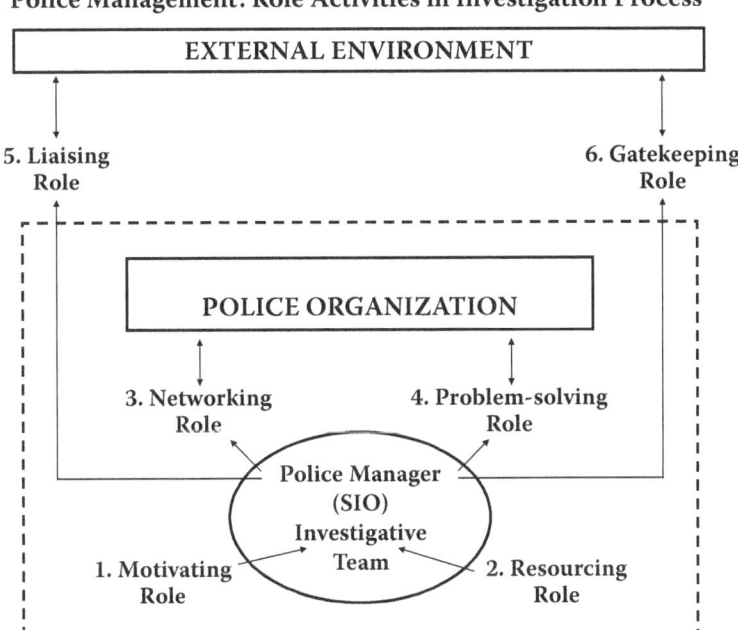

Figure 8.2 Police manager roles in investigations.

prosecutor's office, but who are part of the overall criminal justice system.

6. *Monitor* (gatekeeping role). This role emphasizes scanning of the external environment to keep up with relevant changes, such as politics and economics. The manager identifies new ideas from sources outside his or her organization. To accomplish this task, the manager uses many resources, including vendor contacts, professional relationships, and a network of personal contacts. While the SIO clearly monitors the progress of an investigation, the role description here is more like a gatekeeping role, in that it is not so much external politics or economics, which an SIO has to contend with, but rather making sure the media and other outside forces do not disrupt the progress on an investigation. Therefore, in that sense, this is a gatekeeping role to protect the investigative team from undue external pressure.

These six police manager roles are illustrated in Figure 8.3. As can be seen, the motivating and resourcing roles are internal to the investigation team for the SIO. The networking and problem-solving roles are directed toward the police organization, and the liaising and gatekeeping roles are linked to the external environment for the SIO.

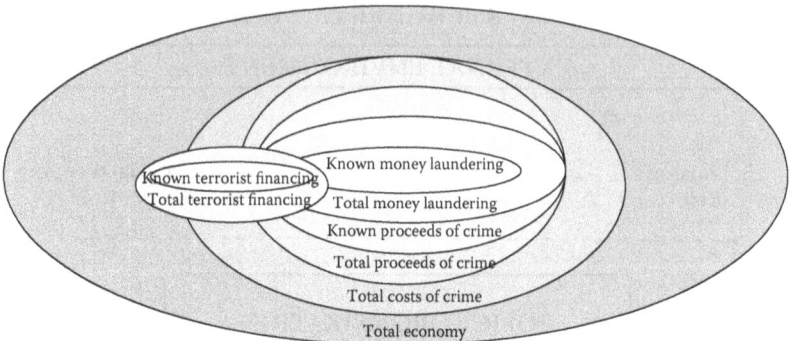

Figure 8.3 Conceptual model of the economic relationships between crime, money laundering, and terrorist financing. (Adapted from Stamp and Walker. 2007.*Trends and issues in crime and criminal justice.* Canberra: Australian Government's Institute of Criminology.)

We would expect that these roles are not equally important for an SIO in relation to creating investigative success. Moreover, some roles may be more influential in terms of stimulating knowledge sharing. For example, adopting a motivating role may be more important for the SIO to engage in within the investigative team, but not as important in relation to the wider police organization. There is some research that suggests that the networking role (or spokesperson) is the most important for dealing with the larger organization when knowledge is communicated to stakeholders (Lahneman, 2004).

A survey instrument was applied in this research, where respondents filled in a space. In the open electronic space, respondents could write five characteristics in their own wording. To classify these responses, content analysis was needed. According to Riffe and Freitag (1997), seven features of content analysis distinguish poor studies from excellent studies. First, an explicit theoretical framework is needed. In this research, the theoretical framework of management roles as developed by Mintzberg (1994) is applied. Second, hypotheses or research questions are needed. In this research, the research question "what" is concerned with descriptions of characteristics. Third, other research methods should also be applied. In this research, a survey is supplemented with content analysis. Forth, extramedia data should be incorporated. In this research, results from another investigation survey were incorporated (Glomseth et al., 2007). Fifth, intercoder reliability should be reported. In this research, two researchers independently coded the characteristics content construct. Sixth, reliability based on a random sample of coded content was not relevant in this research, as there is a complete set of responses. Finally, presentations of only descriptive statistics should be avoided. In this research, two independent researchers coded characteristics by respondents, and interpretations are presented in the paper.

The questionnaire was sent to 325 detectives by e-mail. With 110 responses returned, this gave a response rate of 34 percent. However, only 71 detectives filled in the open space for characteristics of effective detectives, thereby reducing the response rate to 22 percent. Since each detective wrote five characteristics each, a total of 355 characteristics were collected, as listed in Table 8.1.

Two raters were involved in the classification of responses. There was no need to develop key words in this research (Gottschalk, 2001), as respondents provided responses in terms of key words. Acceptable interrater judgment reliability (IJR) of 0.94 was achieved. Reliability is an assessment of the degree of consistency between multiple raters of a variable (Hair et al., 2006).

As can be seen in the table, most respondents provided five characteristics of effective SIOs as requested. Only three respondents provided four characteristics. A total of 352 characteristics represent our data in this research. Respondents were not asked to prioritize their five characteristics. Therefore, all 352 characteristics are treated as equally important in this research.

Our first analysis was simply to look for words, which were mentioned by several respondents. We find words such as "creativity," "communication," and "cooperation," indicating that the manager of the investigation should contribute with new ideas (creativity), should talk to people (communication), and should work with people (cooperation).

Our second analysis was concerned with person focus versus task focus. It was assumed that SIOs tend to be task focused, while investigators would like them to be more person focused. When classifying all responses in Table 8.1 along these two categories, we found that 54 percent of the statements are person focused, while 46 percent are task focused.

Our third analysis was classification of items in the table according to management areas. We make distinctions between four management areas:

- *Task management.* Managing the tasks of the investigation.
- *Person management.* Managing the officers involved in the investigation.
- *Administration management.* Managing the systems supporting the investigation.
- *Strategy management.* Managing the direction of the investigation.

When independent raters applied this classification scheme to the 352 items in Table 8.1, this distribution emerged:

- 40 percent of the characteristics were assigned to *person management.*
- 30 percent of the characteristics were assigned to *task management.*

Table 8.1   Characteristics of Effective SIOs According to Respondents (5 characteristics by 71 respondents)

Objectivity	Cooperative Skills	Authority When Needed	Keeping Overview	Organizational Skills
Creative	Investigative knowledge	Cooperative skills	Organizational skills	Motivational skills
Creative	Motivational skills	Listening skills	Participating in work	Managing the case
Curious	Detailed	Knowledge of law	Not giving up	Human knowledge
Motivational skills	Inspirational	Professional	Patient	
Open mind	Communicative skills	Empowering skills	Exploring personnel	Analytic skills
Communicative skills	Feedback skills	Identifying connections	Investigative knowledge	Resisting pressure
Experience	Broad competence	Action oriented	Understanding the case	
Communicator	Good listener	Ability to motivate	Avoiding details	Creating ideas
Investigative insights	Integrity	Ability to listen	Judgment	Decision maker
Analytic skills	Creative	Systematic	Showing empathy	Good leader
Objective	Sensitive	Analytic	Structured	Creative
Listening to others	Experienced in the field	Motivational	Good mood	Make decisions
Ability to lead	Find good solutions	Value employees	Cooperation	Good mood every day
Clever at organizing	Clear speech	Cooperative	Creative	Lots of experience
Good organized	Speed	Knowledgeable	Good memory	Divide work
Good overview	Delegation skills	Analytic ability	Team leadership	Motivational skills
Stimulate officers	Delegate	Humor	Structured	
Ability to communicate	Positive attitude	Flexibility	Investigative knowledge	Involvement
Structure	Goal oriented	Self confidence	Engaged	Creative
Motivational	Engaged	Analytic	Professional skills	Systematic
Seeing the whole picture	Motivator	Good at delegating	Good feedback	Does care
Ability to supervise	Knowledge of the cases	Ability to delegate	Investigative knowledge	Open minded
Openness	Organized	Motivating	Results oriented	Fair

Table 8.1   Characteristics of Effective SIOs According to Respondents (5 characteristics by 71 respondents) (Continued)

Objectivity	Cooperative Skills	Authority When Needed	Keeping Overview	Organizational Skills
Systematic	Thorough	Honest	Calm	Empathetic
Objectivity	Good at listening	Good mood	Ability to prioritize	Having good overview
Motivational	Systematic	Good communication	Human	Balanced
Concrete	Caring	Thorough	Open to proposals	Experience
Patient	Seeking options	Listening	Motivational	Giving feedback
Results oriented	Not afraid	Communicative skills	Stimulate employees	Action oriented
Leadership skills	Offensive	Active	Curious	Fair
Cooperative skills	Structured	Creative	Listening	Engaged
Investigative insights	Ability to receive	Ability to systematize	Ability to delegate	Ability to motivate
Structured	Investigative knowledge	Fair	Positive attitude	Ability to have oversight
Understanding people	Honesty	Offensive	High moral	Objective
Creative	Encouraging	Open	Knowledgeable	Overview
Cooperative skills	Sees a person's potential	Ability to listen	Tactical	Open to new ideas
Knowledgeable of law	Delegating	Being creative	Make decisions	Motivate officers
Ability to see all	Ability to inspire	Ability to listen	Ability to implement	Ability to correct
Professional	Decision oriented	Engaged	Motivational	Team leader
Human	Professional	Openness	Honesty	Energy
Investigative insights	Motivational	Including	Ability to delegate	Goal oriented
Broad experience	Ability to cooperate	Listen to others' opinions	Being explicit	Ability to delegate
Open mind	Good at communicating	Decision minded	Investigative knowledge	Present
Distribute tasks	Thinking creatively	Good monitoring	Good consulting	Thinking new
Having good overview	Give credit and criticism	Good at encouraging	Suggesting solutions	Ability to cut the crap
Mature soul	Investigative level	Good organizer	Communicative skills	Contribute to openness

Table 8.1   Characteristics of Effective SIOs According to Respondents (5 characteristics by 71 respondents) (Continued)

Objectivity	Cooperative Skills	Authority When Needed	Keeping Overview	Organizational Skills
Communication	Humility	Authority	Self insight	Humor and good mood
Open to proposals	Let others lead	Give feedback	Push progress	Make decisions
Systematic	Analytic	Creative	Determined	Knowledgeable
Good team leader	Stimulating creativity	Having overview	Open minded	Patient
Motivator	Keeping calm	Decision power	Creative	Listening
Objectivity	Listen	Leading	Think new	Cooperation
Professional skills	Thorough	Create team feeling	Ability to motivate	Analytic ability
Motivational	Ability to stimulate	Communicative skills	Including personnel	Systematic
Leadership skills	Investigative skills	Organizational skills	Creative	Supervising skills
Stimulating team	Full of initiatives	Knowledgeable	Involving officers	Clear messages
Listening	Relevant attitude	Objective	Humble	Person oriented
Open	Creative	Innovative	Inspirational	Integrity
Knowing how to motivate	Able to cooperate	Thinking creatively	Being structured	Being effective
Creative	Motivational	Listening	Social	Investigative competent
Integrity	Objective	Cooperative skills	Reliable	Experience
Objective	Motivational	Structured	Competent	Thinking systematically
Investigative strengths	Ability to lead	Having good overview	Being creative	Good to communicate
Knowledge	Experience	Attitude	Patience	Overview
Ability to motivate	Ability to listen	Investigative competence	Identifying limitations	Creativity
Good to communicate	Ability to delegate	Ability to prioritize	Decision power	Ability to cooperate
Ability to motivate	Ability to be critical	Decision making ability	Ability to delegate	Ability to evaluate
Ability to motivate	Having patience	Relevant experience	Being team oriented	Listen to others
Motivator	Listening	Supervising	Create good environment	Let all into the team act
Focus	Cooperative skills	Knowledge	Creativity	Humility

- 18 percent of the characteristics were assigned to *strategic management.*
- 12 percent of the characteristics were assigned to *administrative management.*

The fourth analysis was concerned with our adoption of Mintzberg's (1994) management roles into motivating role, resourcing role, networking role, problem-solving role, liaising role, and gatekeeping role. Although not explicitly asked for, characteristics of effective detectives can be interpreted in terms of their importance to the management roles. Each characteristic might be assigned to one of the roles according to importance of the characteristic in that specific role. This was done in the research, which resulted in this distribution:

- 38 percent of the characteristics were assigned to the motivating role of *personnel leader.*
- 23 percent of the characteristics were assigned to the resourcing role of *resource allocator.*
- 11 percent of the characteristics were assigned to the networking role of *spokesperson.*
- 19 percent of the characteristics were assigned to the problem-solving role of *entrepreneur.*
- 5 percent of the characteristics were assigned to the liaising role of *liaison.*
- 4 percent of the characteristics were assigned to the gatekeeping role of *monitor.*

The fifth and final analysis was concerned with the distinction between investigative ability, knowledge levels, and management skills, as suggested by Smith and Flanagan (2000). When these three categories were applied to Table 8.1, we found 38 percent investigative ability, 9 percent knowledge, and 53 percent management skills as characteristics of effective SIOs as defined by investigators.

Survey results indicate that the most important leadership role for SIOs is the motivating role of the personnel leader. In this role, the SIO is responsible for supervising, hiring, training, organizing, coordinating, and motivating a cadre of personnel to achieve the goals of the organization. This role is mainly internal to the police investigation unit. As stated previously, an SIO generally would not be responsible for hiring a particular individual in a business sense, but would have a say in which particular police investigator might join his/her team for a particular investigation. However, the main thrust of this role for an SIO is that of motivating his/her staff and keeping such motivation stimulated, especially in a difficult and protracted investigation.

Table 8.2   Measurement of Management Roles

Management Roles in Police Investigations	Mean
Motivating role—responsible for guiding and follow-up personnel who participate in the investigation	4.7
Resourcing role—making decisions about allocation of resources in the investigation	4.8
Networking role—informing other involved units in the police about the investigation	4.4
Problem-solving role—identifying opportunities and initiatives in the investigation	5.0
Liaising role—managing information and knowledge about external matters that might be relevant for the investigation	4.6
Gatekeeping role—communicating with the external environment about the progress in the investigation	4.4

Note: 1 = not important to 7 = very important.

In different study, Glomseth et al. (2007) asked SIOs how they would rate the importance of each leadership role. Their results are listed in Table 8.2. SIOs themselves find the problem-solving role most important (5.0), followed by the resourcing role (4.8).

When compared to the current responses from detectives, we find some interesting results. While the SIOs do not find the motivating role particularly important, detectives that are supervised by SIOs find this role most important. On the other hand, while SIOs find the problem-solving role most important, detectives do not find this role particularly important.

Two important limitations in the current study have to be addressed. First, the response rate of 22 percent is low. As there were no follow-ups in the survey administration and responding to each open-ended question was voluntary, the response rate as such is as expected. However, a bias in responses is not unlikely, limiting the possibility of generalized findings. For example, only detectives with strong opinions about leadership and management may have articulated their views in the survey. Future research designs should strive for higher response rates and include contacting some random nonrespondents.

Second, the construct "effective" SIOs is problematic. Implicitly, we argue that there is a significant, positive relationship between detectives' opinions and actual effectiveness, since we only measured what detectives consider to be effective. Also, because effectiveness was not defined in the questionnaire, responding detectives might have emphasized very different interpretations of this construct. Future questionnaire designs should strive to solve such research design problems.

Effective SIOs as evaluated by their subordinates are characterized by being person-oriented rather than case-oriented. Important skills are motivational skills, communicative skills, listening skills, and orga-nizational skills. According to this study, the least important for SIOs is investigation knowledge, when compared to investigative ability and man-agement skills.

Organized Crime Economics

The Home Office in the United Kingdom announced a new report on orga-nized crime in 2007, but on the Internet (www.homeoffice.gov.uk/rds/whatsnew1.html), this message was presented:

> The Online Report "Organized crime: revenues, economic and social costs, and criminal assets available for seizure" has been withdrawn.

Reversing decisions and secrecy is questionable, as knowledge workers always should know more than there is information in a report. Knowledge is always ahead of its capture in documents. Police leadership is needed to fight organized crime. Development leadership has three characteristics: the leader acts as an exemplary model, shows individualized consideration, and demonstrates inspiration and motivation (Larsson et al., 2003).

The economic side of organized crime is important, and it manifests itself in money laundering and other ways of spending proceeds from criminal activity. In Australia, Stamp and Walker (2007) developed a conceptual pic-ture of economic relationships, as illustrated in Figure 8.3.

The costs of crime are part of the Australian economy. The proceeds of crime are a subset of the costs. Some of the proceeds of crime in Australia are laundered, but some laundered money also comes from outside the Australian economy. Terrorist finance may not have criminal origins and is not necessarily laundered. The "known" components are very small subsets of their respective estimated totals. Figure 8.3 is not drawn to scale (Stamp and Walker, 2007).

Case: Hawala Bankers Transferring Criminal Proceeds

In the summer of 2008, a Nigerian prostitute went to an official bank in Oslo, Norway, to transfer money to Nigeria. This seemed to be a legal transaction as proceeds from prostitution are legal income. What the bank did not know was that the money was not from prostitution. The money was proceeds from drug trafficking rather than human trafficking, which is illegal income. When the bank discovered the prostitutes were lying about their income, money transfers were stopped.

Therefore, the Nigerian drug dealers went to hawala bankers instead. Hawala bankers are financial service providers who carry out financial transactions without a license and, therefore, without law enforcement control. They accept cash at one location and pay a corresponding sum in cash or other renumeration at another location. This service is similar to services provided by official banks, but hawala bankers disregard all legal obligations concerning the identification of clients, record keeping, and the disclosure of unusual transactions, to which official financial institutions are subject (van den Brunt, 2008).

Hawala banking has a long history (van den Brunt, 2008, 113):

> Primarily entrenched in the monetary facilitation of trade between distant regions, these bankers still provide a useful service especially to migrants who wish to transfer money to their country of origin. The informal system has long existed, but only recently gained prominence in conflict torn regions, such as Afghanistan and Somalia. After years of conflict, confidence in the formal banking system is absent and the remaining banks neither accept deposits nor extend loans. Significantly, these formal banks do not have the capacity to provide international or domestic remittance services.

Both official and hawala banks often transfer money without actually moving it. They are remitted without being physically moved elsewhere. It is also not a distinguishing feature of hawala banking that funds or value are transferred without leaving trails of the completed transactions. Rather, the essence of hawala banking is simply that financial transactions occur in the absence of, or parallel to, official banking sector channels (van den Brunt, 2008, 115):

> Hawala banking is not certified and supervised by any government. There are international differences in regulation and supervision of financial transactions by Central Banks, but hawala banking has been legally banned in almost all countries of the world, even those, which are strongly Islamic, such as Pakistan and Iran.

Transactions between hawala bankers are based on trust. Banker A receives money paid out by hawalader B, making A indebted to B. Next time the roles will be reversed: B receives money from a remitter to be paid out by A to the recipient. Conflicts and misunderstandings about settlements seem likely to arise; yet in practice, relations between hawaladers appear to run smoothly (van den Brunt, 2008).

References

FBI. 2008. Department of Justice launches new law enforcement strategy to combat increasing threat of international organized crime, press release (April 23), *Overview of the law enforcement strategy to combat international organized crime*. Washington, D.C.: U.S. Department of Justice, Federal Bureau of Investigation.

Glomseth, R., Gottschalk, P., and Solli-Sæther, H. 2007. Occupational culture as determinant of knowledge sharing and performance in police investigations. *International Journal of the Sociology of Law* 35: 96–107.

Gottschalk, P. 2001. Descriptions of responsibility for implementation: A content analysis of strategic information systems/technology planning documents. *Technological Forecasting and Social Change* 68: 207–221.

Gottschalk, P. 2007. *Knowledge management in law enforcement: Technologies and techniques.* Hershey, PA: Idea Group Publishing.

Hair, J.F., Black, W.C., Babin, B.J., Anderson, R.E., and Tatham, R.L. 2006. *Multivariate data analysis*, 6th ed. Upper Saddle River, NJ: Prentice Hall.

Home Office. 2005a. Guidance on statutory performance indicators for policing 2005/2006. Police Standards Unite Home Office of the UK Government, www.policeform.gov.uk.

Home Office. 2005b. Senior investigating officer development programme. Police Standards Unit, Home Office of the UK Government, www.policeform.gov.uk.

Lahneman, W.J. 2004. Knowledge-sharing in the intelligence community after 9/11. *International Journal of Intelligence and Counterintelligence* 17: 614–633.

Larsson, G., Carlstedt, L., Andersson, J., Andersson, L., Danielsson, E., Johansson, A., Johansson, E., Robertsson, I., and Michel, P.O. 2003. A comprehensive system for leader evaluation and development. *Leadership & Organization* 24 (1): 16–25.

Mintzberg, H. 1994. Rounding on the managers' job. *Sloan Management Review* 36 (1): 11–26.

Nelen, H. and Huisman, W. 2008. Breaking the power of organized crime? The administrative approach in Amsterdam. In *Organized crime: Culture, markets and policies*, Eds. D. Siegel and H. Nelen, 207–218. New York: Springer-Verlag.

Riffe, D. and Freitag, A. 1997. A content analysis of content analyses, twenty-five years of journalism quarterly. *Journalism Mass Communication Quarterly* 74: 873–882.

Smith, N. and Flanagan, C. 2000. *The effective detective: Identifying the skills of an effective SIO.* Police Research Series Paper 122, Policing and Reducing Crime Unit, London.

Stamp, J. and Walker, J. 2007. Money laundering in and through Australia. In *Trends and issues in crime and criminal justice.* Canberra: Australian Government's Institute of Criminology.

van den Brunt, H. 2008. The role of hawala bankers in the transfer of proceeds from organized crime. In *Organized crime: Culture, markets and policies*, Eds. D. Siegel and H. Nelen, 113–126. New York: Springer-Verlag.

van den Bunt, H.G. and van der Schoot, C.R.A. 2003. *Prevention of organized crime: A situational approach.* Devon, U.K.: Willan Publishing.

van der Schoot, C.R.A. 2006. *Organized crime prevention in the Netherlands: Exposing the effectiveness of preventive measures.* Devon, U.K.: Willan Publishing.

Policing Motorcycle Club Organized Crime 9

A distinction must be made between noncriminalized and criminalized bikers. The latter outlaw bikers are typically motorcycle club members referring to themselves as "1 percenters." Among the criminal biker clubs, we find Hells Angels, Outlaws, Bandidos, Pagans, and Coffin Cheaters. The most well known is Hells Angels Motorcycle Club (HAMC), which is in charge of many criminal business enterprises all over the world.

Lavigne (1996: 1) described criminal bikers in this way:

> The darkness of crime lies not in its villainy or horror, but in the souls of those who choose to live their lives in the abyss. A man who toils from youth to old age to violate the line that divides civilization from wilderness; who proclaims he is not of society, but an outsider sworn to break its laws and rules, yet who readily seeks refuge in its lenient legal system, embraces its judicial paternalism and gains substance from its moral weakness; whose very existence as an outlaw is defined by society's being, is but a shadow of the real world, bereft of freedom and doomed to tag along in society's wake.

An important aspect of intelligence for policing criminalized bikers is to understand outlaw economics in terms of the financing of a subculture. For example, Wolf (1991, 247–268) studied a brotherhood of outlaw bikers in Canada called the Rebels:

> It costs money to run an outlaw club, more money than the average citizen might think. The Rebels need cash continually to meet expenditures that are characteristic of all outlaw motorcycle clubs.
>
> The most expensive item is the clubhouse, since members have to rent or buy and furnish a building. ... The Rebels always maintain enough money in their savings accounts in the event that one of their members requires bail or the services of a lawyer. ... Outlaw clubs are well aware that the police are usually more reasonable in their surveillance procedures if they know that a club has the money to employ a sound legal defense and does not hesitate to bring up charges of police harassment. ... The Rebel reserve fund is also available to patch holders who simply find themselves short of cash. ... The Rebels replenish their club treasury with money from five major sources: membership dues and club fines, the sale of various commodities to members, the brokerage of club shares, sponsoring "boogies," and holding "field days." ... Outlaw motorcycle clubs vary in the extent to which they may engage in criminal activities for profit. Some clubs hold aloof from what could be classified as recurring organized crime. Clubs such as the Satan's Choice, Outlaws, pagans, Bandidos, and Hells Angels, who have run the full gamut of crime, remain in distinct minority. Yet, even among these outlaw federations, the amount and nature of criminal activity vary from chapter to chapter and from year to year.

In this chapter, we will assume that the Norwegian police is in the process of establishing a national intelligence project to fight the criminal MC organizations, such as the Hells Angels Motorcycle Club in Norway.

Hells Angels Motorcycle Club

In the case of Criminal Intelligence Service Alberta's annual report in Canada (von Rassel and Komarnicki, 2007), Hells Angels were gathering outside Calgary to celebrate the group's tenth anniversary in Alberta. Hells Angels were identified as having been involved in the street-level drug trade. The worldwide biker gang arrived in Alberta ten years ago when it took over locally based independent gangs, such as the Grim Reapers in Calgary. Despite that history and three HAMC chapters in Alberta—Calgary, Edmonton, and a "Nomad" chapter based in Red Deer—Criminal Intelligence Service Alberta said the gang had failed to make significant inroads in the province's criminal underworld (von Rassel and Komarnicki, 2007).

"Without making light of their propensity for extreme violence—augmented by loyalty to the club's name—members of the Hells Angels continue to lack in criminal business savvy," the report said. "They have proven themselves to be an available source of 'muscle' either for their own endeavors or for other criminal organizations. They are preoccupied with the supremacy of their name within the criminal biker subculture" (Rassel and Komarnicki, 2007).

The Hells Angels' Calgary chapter has suffered some highly publicized setbacks, notably having to abandon a fortified clubhouse under construction in Bowness because it violated building codes. The chapter's then president, Ken Szczerba, was jailed in 2001 for trying to arrange a plot to bomb the homes of Alderman Dale Hodges and a community activist involved in getting the construction halted. Nevertheless, police agencies underestimate the Hells Angels in this province at their peril, said the author of several books on the gang, as reported to von Rassel and Komarnicki (2007).

In the province of Quebec, the situation is very different. Police claim that Hells Angels control most of the organized crime in the province. Criminologists who argue that the government is to blame for the situation support this view. This is because of the policy of fighting the Mafia, which resulted in Hells Angels getting the opportunity to grow dominantly in the vacuum that emerged. Until then, Hells Angels were viewed as the street boys for the Mafia. In the years after 1994, wars between street gangs in the province have caused more than one hundred killings (including a person randomly passing who was killed by a car bomb). More than eighty-four bomb attacks have occurred, one hundred thirty cases of fires, and nine missing persons.

In Amsterdam in The Netherlands, Hells Angels are running much of the operations in the red light district. The motorcycle club owns restaurants and gambling casinos, and they run the prostitution and drug business. Because Hells Angels have full control of the situation, there is not much public crime in the district. Therefore, Dutch police seem satisfied with the situation, although they know it is wrong. Dutch police know that many of the major drug deals for Europe are settled in the red light district where Hells Angels are in charge.

Also, spectacular killings are linked to Hells Angels MC Holland. For example, the Dutch lawyer Evert Hingst was murdered in front of his house in Amsterdam. Among Hingst's clients were many noted and alleged criminals, including John Mieremet, who was once shot in front of Hingst's office. After the assault, Mieremet claimed that Hingst had tried to set him up. Mieremet was murdered three days after the liquidation of Hingst, who could be linked to Hells Angels MC Holland through John Mieremet and Willem Holleeder. Willem "The Nose" Holleeder is a Dutch criminal born in 1958 in Amsterdam. He was one of the perpetrators of the kidnapping of brewery president Alfred "Freddy" Heineken in 1983 (Nelen and Lankhorst, 2008).

Holleeder came in the news when the monthly magazine *Quote* printed a photo of Holleeder accompanied by Willem Endstra, who was regarded as the banker of the Dutch underworld. Endstra laundered drug money and invested it in real estate. Holleeder ordered the extortion of Endstra in 2004 after Endstra started to give information to the Dutch national police. Hells Angels carried out the extortion because Holleeder enjoyed significant influence in the criminal motorcycle club.

When Dutch police were informed where to find the meeting room where criminal activities were planned, they installed listening devices and interception for communication control on the Hells Angels MC Holland premises. However, the police informant in the club was soon severely punished by the club, and meetings were moved to another HA resort.

When looking back at history, it all started in 1948 (www.wikipedia.org — search Hells Angels):

The Hells Angels club was formed in 1948 in Fontana, California. The name "Hells Angels" was believed to have been inspired by the common historical use, in both World War I and II, to name squadrons or other fighting groups by fierce, death-defying names, such as Hells Angels and Flying Tigers. The Howard Hughes film *Hell's Angels* was a major film of 1930 displaying extraordinary and dangerous feats of aviation. Several military units used the name Hells Angels prior to the founding of the motorcycle club of the same name. [...]

The Hells Angels are shrouded in a cloud of mystery and controversy, thanks to a very strict code of secrecy and what can be construed as a practice of deliberate mythologizing by some members of the club. Members don't use last names, even with one another. They just use a first name and, more often than not, a nickname. Due to its colorful history and the confirmed links of some of its members to organized crime, speculation and rumor about the club's activities is rife.

It is assumed that HAMC has more than 2,000 members and trial members (prospects) in 189 local departments (chapters) in 22 countries all over the world. HAMC was the symbol of an outlaw biker anticulture in the 1960s. The U.S. Federal Bureau of Investigation (FBI) estimates that Hells Angels make more than $1 billion a year on their global trafficking in drugs and women. This is denied by spokespersons of the club, who also argue that crimes committed by members are not the responsibility of the organization. Spokespersons of the club claim that they are only a motorcycle club, and that the majority of members are regular citizens who are misrepresented in the media. Nevertheless, HAMC presents itself as a 1 percent club, a phrase that was introduced because the American Motorcyclist Association claimed that 99 percent of all MC drivers are regular citizens.

When analyzing a Hells Angels motorcycle club, it should be understood that it most likely is a criminal organization. As a criminal organization, it is both similar to and different from other organized crime groups. When policing ethic street gangs, it is sometimes compared to fighting local Hells Angels chapters. Nothing could be farther from the truth. While street gangs should be understood in a context of temporary and dynamically changing relationships and finances, MC groups should be understood as more permanent structures and with permanent finances. Understanding both similarities and differences between criminal business enterprises is critical in successful policing of organized crime. As illustrated in the law enforcement road map, it would not be considered a success if a closed down Hells Angels chapter in one city is revitalized in another.

Hells Angels can be identified both by the Harley Davidson motorcycles they ride and in the trafficking, drugs, extortions, money laundering, and other criminal activities. Hells Angels carried out the extortion of Endstra because Holleeder enjoyed significant influence in the criminal motorcycle club.

In analyzing the culture of a particular group or organization, Schein (1990) finds it desirable to distinguish three fundamental levels at which culture manifests itself: (1) observable artifacts, (2) values, and (3) basic underlying assumptions. When one enters an organization, one observes and feels its artifacts. This category includes everything from the physical layout, the dress code, the manner in which people address each other to the more permanent archival manifestations, such as company records, products, statements of philosophy, and remains at crime scenes. These are all observable artifacts in the organization. A typical example is artifacts found on jackets and tattoos found on bodies, such as A.F.F.A. (Angel. Forever. Forever. Angel.), which are manifestations of Hells Angels MC members.

Motorcycle clubs, such as HAMC, are fairly consistent in their modal organization, consisting of national, regional/state, and local tiers, which emerged after a formative period. Individual bikers, cliques, and chapters answer to the national leadership, which controls their right to claim membership, but they also have sufficient autonomy to accommodate their extremely independent and rebellious personalities and wide-ranging local circumstances (Quinn and Koch, 2003).

This tension between intense loyalty and hierarchical control on the one hand and autonomous masculinity on the other is perplexing to many outsiders. Loyalty to a singular national hierarchy reinforces deeply felt tribal solidarity and power. Autonomy permits local flexibility in promoting growth and hegemony and avoids instigating rebellion among individuals. It also functions to make their actions difficult to directly link to the group's formal leadership and keeps the relationship between the club and the actions of its members distant from each other (Quinn and Koch, 2003).

Values at the second level of Schein's (1990) research can be studied in terms of norms, ideologies, charters, and philosophies. Strong values in Hells Angels MC include respect of other members. Basic underlying assumptions at the third and final level of organizational culture are concerned with perceptions, thought processes, feelings, and behavior.

While studies have shown that people within the same legal organization have very different values, often measured in terms of deviation from the mean, we might expect members of illegal organizations to have very similar values. Their values will not only be typical for criminal organizations, they will also have much smaller deviations between members than in criminal gangs and networks that are not so well established.

A criminal business organization is an enterprise where all people in all parts of the organization are involved in criminal activity. Hells Angels MC is a legal motorcycle club in most countries (not in Canada), where the members are involved in criminal activity based on emerging internal networks. For example, when a local Hells Angels MC organization runs a chain of legal tattoo shops, members are at the same time involved in drug smuggling, human trafficking, and other criminal activities. Thus, the chairman and entrepreneur in Hells Angels MC Holland, Willem van Boxtel, needs to express an overall strategy for the entire criminal business organization.

Hells Angels MC tends to have a matrix organization where the legal motorcycle club is along the vertical axis, while the criminal activities of HAMC are along the horizontal axis. The criminal activities are not initiated and organized from the top. Instead, one core entrepreneurial member initiates a criminal project by identifying an opportunity and recruiting fellow members to the project. Top management is informed, but not necessarily involved.

Sometimes, HAMC gets into rivalry with similar clubs. For example, tough competition characterized MC organizations in Scandinavia a decade ago, where Bandidos, Hells Angels, and Outlaws were the main competitors. Among other business areas, they were competing in the amphetamine market. This competition was labeled the "MC war," as a variety of competitive weapons were used by the parties, including bombs.

One of the violent occasions in the history of HAMC occurred during a Rolling Stones concert in Altamont, California, in 1969. HAMC members were hired as guards for a compensation, which is claimed to include beer with a value of $500. During the song "Under My Thumb" (and not "Sympathy for the Devil" as many believe), Alan Passaro knifed to death Meredith Hunter, who had drawn a gun. Passaro was later released because the murder was defined as self-defense. Both Hunter and Passaro were members of HAMC.

In the 1960s, during the Vietnam War, HAMC offered its services to American troops abroad. Although they were not allowed, this offer from the HAMC was perceived as a traitor's act by all those who idolized the biker anticulture. The critics of HAMC argued that the biker club tried to make an alliance with the U.S. authorities. Six members of The John Brown Brethren group, a small but violent antiwar activist group, attacked a HAMC in San Francisco and killed four members.

Criminal Motorcycle Clubs in Norway

In Norway, we find three known criminal MC organizations—Hells Angels, Bandidos, and Outlaws—with different organizational structure and culture. Hells Angels seems to separate most systematically between the legal motorcycle club and criminal activity. The criminal HAMC activity is often based on private and personal initiative, where one member asks another member: "Would you like to take part in this?" Organized crime is then carried out by several HAMC members, but the criminal group is set up by initiative and contact directly among members. HAMC management is seldom directly involved. The organized crime is typically in areas such as narcotics, trafficking, and torpedo activities. If crime fails and members get prosecuted, then they may be expelled from HAMC as failures.

Let us start with the beginning of Hells Angels in Norway, which was founded in 1992 (www.hells-angels.com):

> In August 1992, Norway got its first Hells Angels chapter, Hells Angels MC Trondheim ... In January 1995, the Club moved into a new clubhouse outside the city, the same as today.

While HAMC has recruited mainly motorcycle club-interested men, the Outlaws, on the other hand, has primarily recruited criminals as members. Therefore, there is a more visible link between motorcycle activities and criminal activities. Bandidos seems to be somewhere in the middle between

Table 9.1 Matrix Organization of Hells Angels

Legal/Illegal	Hells Angels MC Norway	Hells Angels MC Sweden	Hells Angels MC Holland	Hells Angels MC Germany
Criminal project A	Members	Members	Members	Members
	Prospects	Prospects	Prospects	Prospects
	Hangarounds	Hangarounds	Hangarounds	Hangarounds
Criminal project B	Members	Members	Members	Members
	Prospects	Prospects	Prospects	Prospects
	Hangarounds	Hangarounds	Hangarounds	Hangarounds
Criminal project C	Members	Members	Members	Members
	Prospects	Prospects	Prospects	Prospects
	Hangarounds	Hangarounds	Hangarounds	Hangarounds

Hells Angels and Outlaws. Some of the proceeds from organized crime in Norway is laundered and invested in Thailand by HAMC.

HAMC applies a matrix organization, where the motorcycle club is along the vertical axis while the organized crime is along the horizontal axis, as illustrated in Table 9.1. Hells Angels members, prospects, and hangarounds are potentially included in criminal projects A, B, and C. Project participants are recruited from national chapters as well as chapters in other countries. For example, when cocaine is to be smuggled from Holland to Norway, members of HAMC Norway and HAMC Holland plan the operation. Next, prospects and hangarounds are recruited to carry out the smuggling. In the matrix organization, each chapter emerges as a legal activity, while each project emerges as an illegal activity.

In the last decade, the number of criminal MC clubs have increased three-fold in Norway. Hells Angels is still the largest, but is challenged by Bandidos, Outlaws, and also the Coffin Cheaters club is on its way (*Aftenposten*, 2007). In 1997, Bandidos and Hells Angels shared geographical areas and criminal markets among themselves. This mutual agreement was achieved after the bloody Scandinavian MC war, which culminated with a 1997 bomb attack by Hells Angels on Bandidos headquarters in Drammen, Norway, west of Oslo. Now this mutual understanding is challenged and threatened by new gangs over the entire country.

HAMC Norway President Leif Kristiansen

Leif Ivar Kristiansen is head of HAMC in Norway. He is located at the Hells Angels' clubhouse and headquarters in Trondheim, north of Oslo. He was interviewed in the Norwegian newspaper *Adresseavisen* (2005) when a power fight was going on in the Hells Angels organization. Hells Angels MC Norway has chapters in Hamar, Stavanger, Skien, Oslo, Drammen,

Tromsø, and Trondheim (www.hells-angels.no), as shown on their Web page in Figure 9.1. When Hells Angels decides to present itself as clean from criminality, such as bomb attacks, women trafficking, or cocaine smuggling, then typically a person without a criminal record from HA management is presented.

Two-thirds of all MC members in Hells Angels, Bandidos, and Outlaws have a criminal record in Norway. Some in management do as well. For example, Torkjel "The Rat" Alsaker was sentenced to several years in prison because of a shooting as well as participating in the bomb attack on Bandidos in Drammen in 1997. Leif Ivar Kristiansen, however, has no serious criminal record so far.

The headquarters building of HAMC Norway is at Trolla in Trondheim. The "chief executive officer" Leif Ivar Kristiansen has tried to become rich by establishing tattoo shops for money laundering. In 2001, he opened another outlet of his business chain called Tattoo World in the town of Lillehammer. According to *Aftenposten* (2001), police considered Hells Angels to be established in Lillehammer by the presence of Kristiansen's Tattoo World.

In an interview when confronted with the question whether he was the president of Hells Angels MC Norway and, hence, top executive in Norway, Kristiansen replied in *Aftenposten* (2001): "I don't answer such questions. This is my secret. All my business activity occurs within my personal enterprise.

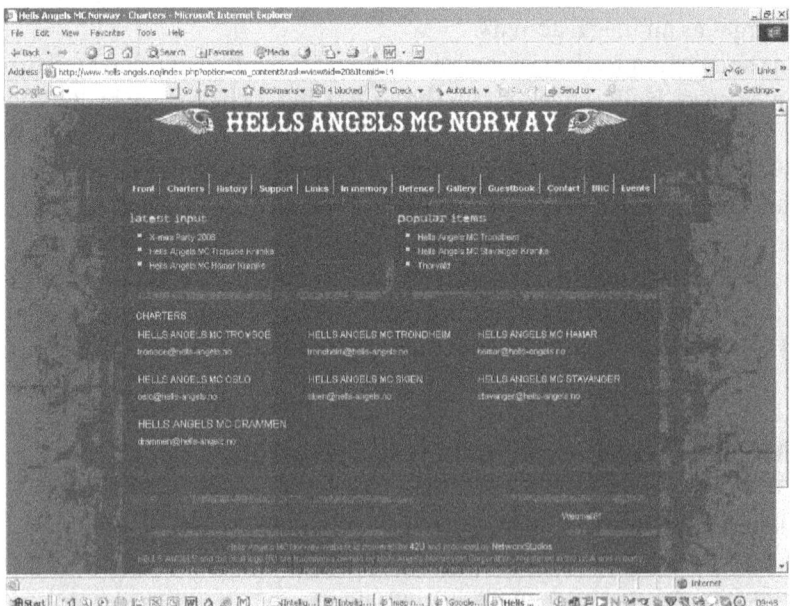

Figure 9.1 Home page for Hells Angels Motorcycle Club Norway.

It has nothing to do with HA. Such allegations build on stupidity, but it does not provoke me."

The author contacted Hells Angels MC Norway in November 2008. The idea was to create another information source to triangulate information from police and open sources. The author decided to approach HAMC using a survey research. A questionnaire was developed with the contents listed in Table 9.2.

An e-mail was sent to all seven chapters in Norway at: tromsoe@ hells-angels.no, oslo@hells-angels.no, drammen@hells-angels.no, trond-heim@hells-angels.no, skien@hells-angels.no, hamar@hells-angels.no, and stavanger@hells-angels.no. These locations are shown in Figure 9.2, including the prospect location of Bergen.

Our e-mail contained this text:

Survey research among members of HAMC

To member of HAMC
I am carrying out survey research among members of HAMC. The purpose of the survey is to contribute to research about HAMC. I hope you are willing to participate in the survey. I ask you to fill in the attached questionnaire and return it to me.
Best wishes,
Petter Gottschalk
Professor at the Norwegian School of Management
Lecturer at the Norwegian Police University College

This e-mail was sent to all seven chapters at 5 p.m. When logging on the next morning, there was this e-mail in the inbox from the previous night at 11:30 p.m.:

Hi you, I urge you to contact me immediately about this inquiry LEIF HAMC TEL 900 81 666.

When calling this number in the same morning, Leif answered the phone. We had a conversation for about forty minutes. His first response was that nobody within HAMC Norway would fill in the questionnaire. We asked why, and he answered that issues related to money (income and wealth) as well as crime (smuggling and narcotics) were irrelevant and impossible to respond to.

At this early point in the conversation, it was interesting to reflect what might have happened the previous night. While we had e-mailed directly to all seven chapters in Norway as illustrated on the map in Figure 9.2, they had all immediately reported to President Leif about this incident, causing him

Table 9.2   Attempted Survey Research Form for the Hells Angels MC Norway in 2008

Questionnaire for Members of HAMC

I am _____ years old

I have been member of HAMC for _____ years

I am educated as _____ (profession)

I went to school for _____ years

I have been in prison for _____ years

I have _____ children

Your Reaction to Statements about Hells Angels MC Norway	Completely Disagree		Completely Agree
I enjoy being member of HAMC		1 2 3 4 5 6 7	
Interests of the club are more important than my personal interests		1 2 3 4 5 6 7	
I am proud of our work attitude		1 2 3 4 5 6 7	
I am proud of our clubhouse		1 2 3 4 5 6 7	
Our chapter is one of the best within HAMC		1 2 3 4 5 6 7	
Our chapter has good profitability		1 2 3 4 5 6 7	
HAMC is a popular club locally		1 2 3 4 5 6 7	
Police is not problem for us in HAMC		1 2 3 4 5 6 7	
Local authorities are no problem for us in HAMC		1 2 3 4 5 6 7	
I am happy with my motorcycle		1 2 3 4 5 6 7	
I make sufficient money		1 2 3 4 5 6 7	
HAMC is a criminal organization		1 2 3 4 5 6 7	
I have participated in smuggling		1 2 3 4 5 6 7	
I have participated in money retrieval		1 2 3 4 5 6 7	
I have participated in narcotics trade		1 2 3 4 5 6 7	
I have participated in organized crime		1 2 3 4 5 6 7	
I believe there will be more HAMC chapters in Norway		1 2 3 4 5 6 7	
I think Knut Storberget is a clever minister of justice		1 2 3 4 5 6 7	
I think Jens Stoltenberg is a clever prime minister		1 2 3 4 5 6 7	
I think Ingelin Killengreen is a clever chief of police		1 2 3 4 5 6 7	
Our chapter is well organized		1 2 3 4 5 6 7	
We perceive no competition from Outlaws		1 2 3 4 5 6 7	
We perceive no competition from Bandidos		1 2 3 4 5 6 7	
We perceive no competition from Coffin Cheaters		1 2 3 4 5 6 7	

as president to send us an e-mail six hours later. Leif had ordered all seven chapters not to respond to our questionnaire.

On the phone, Leif furiously denied that HAMC was a criminal organization. He said, "Police ha[ve] never been able to prove it." And, "Ever since we started up in Norway in 1992, police ha[ve] tried to make a serious case against me. But they will never succeed."

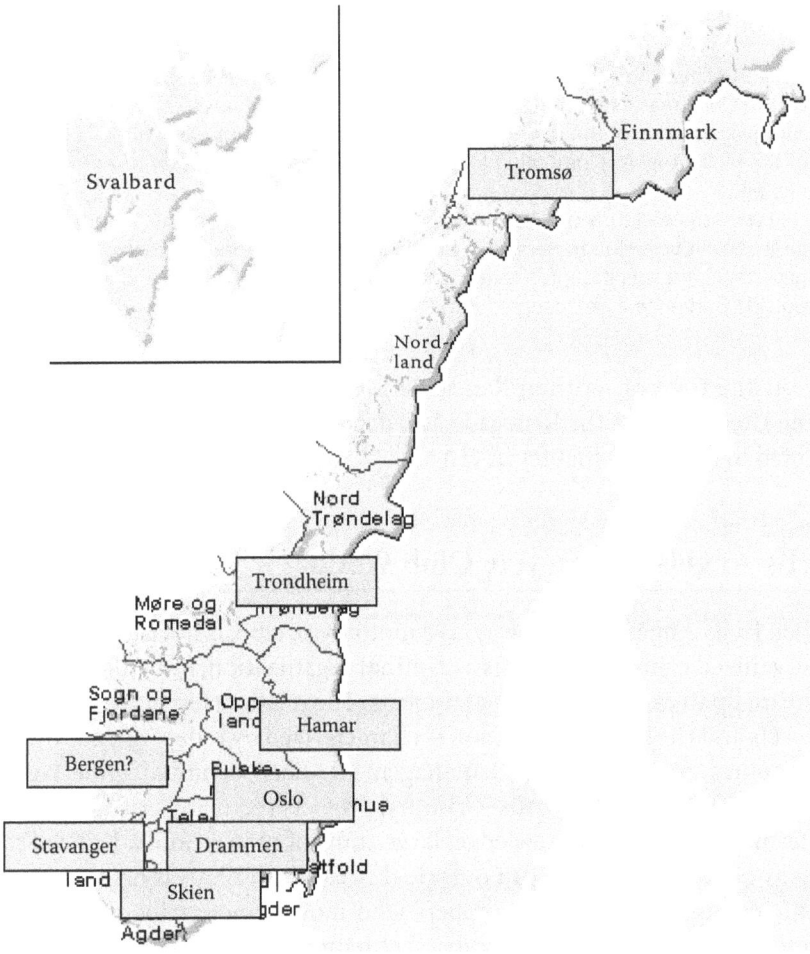

Figure 9.2 Seven chapters and one potential chapter of HAMC Norway.

We told him that our students at the Norwegian School of Management this year had an assignment concerning police knowledge management related to organized MC crime. He asked if students at the Drammen campus had this assignment as well, since his daughter is one of the students there. We replied in the negative, as the assignment was only for the Oslo campus. Leif seemed obviously proud of his daughter being a student at our school.

When asked whether there would be a new chapter in Bergen (see Figure 9.2), Leif replied, "You may ask what you want, but I do not always respond." We told him about newspaper stories speculating on an eighth Norwegian chapter in Bergen (Schmidt, 2008):

Fears that the Hells Angels will establish in Bergen

Police believe the Hells Angels want to establish themselves in Bergen already before Christmas. Now they are warning local municipalities to allow the criminal MC gang to get a foothold. Bergen is the only big city in Norway without a chapter of the Hells Angels. Competing Bandidos and Outlaws are not represented in the city either.

We know a club is on its way. Indications suggest that we will soon have one large motorcycle club in Bergen, said police executive Norvald Visnes. The police have received specific information about the Bergen club Renegade MC in Fana outside Bergen will be accepted into the Hells Angels.

At the time of writing, Renegade MC had the status of prospect club. Rune Hans Tvedt in the Renegade MC denied to the newspaper that the club wanted to become a chapter in HAMC.

Hells Angels Motorcycle Club World

When Hells Angels MC Norway, as a motorcycle club, is not directly involved in organized crime, though it is a criminal organization, individual members do team up to carry out criminal projects. The relationship between criminal projects and the base organization is characterized by independence in terms of resource mobilization and management. Each criminal project enjoys freedom as long as it succeeds. Criminal projects requiring critical resources in terms of innovative knowledge, large sums of money, and advanced technology are organized and run outside the base Hells Angels organization by participating criminal HA members who move temporarily out of chapter homes. Such criminal projects represent temporary organizations with their own goals, resources, and deadlines.

However, HAMC management decides the policy and rules to be followed both in the legal motorcycle club operations as well as in criminal activities. Global, European, Norwegian, and chapter management represent levels of authority reporting and taking orders. It is an obvious hierarchy. Global executives visit local management, and local management visits global executives. Informal communication among managers takes place during "motorcycle parties" where hundreds of executives and members from a number of countries around the world may join to drink and talk.

Similar to the situation in Canada, where Hells Angels expanded their criminal activities into areas where the Mafia had been active because law enforcement was concerned with the Mafia, Norwegian police for a while ignored Hells Angels and other MC clubs to fight gangs that had established themselves in the capital city of Oslo. The gangs had shot at each other in a well-known restaurant district, causing public attention and politicians' concern. High priority was put on policing Pakistani and other gangs, while Hells Angels, Bandidos, and Outlaws could develop their criminal organizations with little police attention.

In Norway, HAMC and the others are perceived by the press, politicians, and public to be criminal clubs, although the clubs, as such, are not defined as criminal organizations. Canada seems still to be the only country that has officially labeled HAMC a criminal organization. Therefore, being a member in Canada is being a criminal, while this is not the case in Norway.

It seems that new recruits among Hells Angels in Norway carry out most of the criminal activities. They qualify for higher positions in the organization by successfully completing human trafficking, cocaine smuggling, debt collection, and money laundering.

In September 2007, the earlier MC club Norsmen in the town of Øvre Eiker became a full and complete member of HAMC. Hells Angels MC Drammen became the new name of Norsmen and became the seventh HA chapter in Norway. It came as quite a surprise to many Norwegians, a surprise that indicates that Hells Angels MC Norway is still making progress in the country. The mayor of Øvre Eiker, Anders B. Werp, expressed in an interview by *NRK News* (2007) that he very much disliked having HA in his town.

Shortly after, he received the following letter from Drammen Mayor T. O. Hansen. Drammen is close to the town of Øvre Eiker.

The threat from the MC clubs are of concern to the whole region

Open letter to the Mayor of Øvre Eiker, Anders B Werp.

In recent days, people in the Drammen Region did get confirmed what they all have feared, MC Norway Drammen has become full worthy member of Hells Angels.

Many, not at least Drammen people, do still remember the bomb in Konnerud street ten years ago very well. While it has been quite [*sic*] on the surface for some years now, the fact that Hells Angels establish themselves so strongly in our region now is of great concern to all of us.

An opportunity has lead to the establishment of Hells Angels in Øvre Eiker. But this does not imply that the challenge involved is only of concern to Øvre Eiker. The MC clubs are not restricted by municipality boarders. The criminality that we can assume these people bring with them, will also be felt in neighboring municipalities, not at least in Drammen as the regional center.

Therefore, it seems so important in law enforcement to prevent births of criminal organizations and pull all roots of established criminal organizations out of the earth.

Hells Angels MC Norway had chapters in Trondheim, Hamar, Oslo, Skien, Stavanger, and Drammen in 2008. Other MC clubs in Norway are Bandidos, Outlaws, and also Coffin Cheaters.

Bandidos and Outlaws

The Bandidos Motorcycle Club was founded in 1966 in Texas. The membership in this MC club is estimated to 2,400 members in fourteen countries. In Norway, Bandidos has approximately forty members in five departments: Oslo, Fredrikstad, Drammen, Kristiansand, and Stavanger. Bandidos is involved in organized crime (www.wikipedia.org, search Bandidos):

> In October 2006, George Wegers, then Bandidos' international president, pleaded guilty and received a two-year sentence for conspiracy to engage in racketeering. Also, in November 2006, Glenn Merrit of the Bellingham, Washington, chapter was sentenced to four years in prison for drug possession and trafficking in stolen property. A total of 32 members were indicted in the associated investigation, on charges including conspiracy, witness tampering, and various drug and gun violations. Eighteen of those plead guilty.

Outlaws was founded in McCook, Illinois, in 1935. The club consists of two hundred local clubs in the United States, Canada, Australia, Asia, and Europe. In Norway, Outlaws has four departments in Oslo, Drammen, Fredrikstad, and Romerike. Outlaws involvement in organized crime includes (www.wikipedia.org, search Outlaws):

- On June 10, 1997, U.S. attorneys indicted seventeen members of the Outlaws motorcycle club for racketeering, murder, narcotics trafficking, and bombing. Members were from Wisconsin, Illinois, and Indiana chapters. The Bureau of Alcohol, Tobacco, and Firearms (ATF) completed a 2½-year investigation sparked by a war between the Outlaws and Hells Angels for control over areas of Chicago and Milwaukee.
- On December 19, 2000, Kevin O'Neill, president of the Wisconsin/Stateline Outlaws chapter, received a sentence of life in prison after being convicted on racketeering charges.
- On May 31, 2001, Edward Anastas, one-time president of the Milwaukee chapter of the Outlaws motorcycle club, was arrested after being named in a sealed indictment charging him with racketeering conspiracy, cocaine conspiracy, and participating in a bombing.
- On March 14, 2003, Thomas Sienkowski, president of the Milwaukee chapter of the Outlaws motorcycle club, was sentenced to ten years in prison for racketeering.
- On August 8, 2006, four Outlaws members were wounded, three seriously, in an ambush in Custer State Park, South Dakota, among bikers gathered for the Sturgis Motorcycle Rally. A woman acquaintance was also wounded. Two men arrested and charged with attempted murder were said to be Canadian members of the Hells Angels. A

statement posted on the Outlaws' Web site had announced Outlaws members would attend Sturgis, but not make any "display of power," and claimed that they had given prior notice to federal law enforcement of their intention to sightsee and enjoy the rally.

- Frank Rego Vital of Roberta, Georgia, an Outlaws MC member, was shot and killed in an early morning gunfight June 24, 2007, in the parking lot of The Crazy Horse Saloon strip club in Forest Park, Georgia, by two members of the Renegades MC in what has been described as a self-defense shooting after Vital and other Outlaws members followed the men from the club. Both Renegade members were shot several times, but survived.
- On June 27, 2006, Christopher Legere of Raymond, New Hampshire, an Outlaws member, was arrested in the murder of a man who was wearing a Hells Angels shirt. The victim, John Denoncourt, 32, of Manchester, New Hampshire, was shot and killed outside the 3-Cousins Pizza and Lounge in Manchester on Sunday, June 25, 2006, after he was spotted hugging the bartender, who was Legere's girlfriend. Denoncourt, according to friends and family, was not a Hells Angel member himself, but had friends who were. Legere had been involved in another incident in Connecticut in early 2006 when he was charged with illegal possession of body armor by a convicted felon, telling police that "tensions were high" between the Hells Angels and the Outlaws at the time and that members from outside of the state were brought in to protect Marty Warren, who claimed to be the East Coast representative for the Outlaws.
- On July 31, 2007, the FBI raided Brockton, Massachusetts, Outlaws. The Taunton, Massachusetts, clubhouse was raided, but due to immunity of the Brockton clubhouse nothing happened. Many people were arrested, including Joseph Noe, from the former Taunton chapter of the Outlaws.
- On the morning of August 16, 2007, federal agents, along with the Daytona Beach SWAT (Special Weapons and Tactics) team, raided the Outlaws biker club's hangout on Beach Street in Daytona Beach, Florida. Federal agents also raided a site in Ormond Beach and two others around the state. The search of the Jacksonville clubhouses netted federal agents sixty weapons. U.S. Attorney General Alberto Gonzales announced a Detroit grand jury indictment of sixteen of the Outlaws National Club's members. The Detroit grand jury indictment included various charges, including assault and drug distribution. Eleven Outlaws leaders and high-ranking members of the gang were arrested after a five-year investigation. The FBI said several gang members were charged with conspiracy to commit assault on members of the Hells Angels Motorcycle Club in Indiana.

- On March 5, 2008, fighting broke out at a motorcycle meeting in Germany between Outlaws and Hells Angels members. Arrests were made.
- On March 10, 2008, a racial conflict broke out between the Outlaws and a group of African-Americans.
- On July 30, 2008, agents from the FBI and the ATF raided several facilities associated with the Outlaws in the Chicago area. The FBI brought in a SWAT team and an urban assault vehicle to the club-house on the city's west side in case violence broke out.

Coffin Cheaters originates from Australia, where there are ten departments with approximately one hundred seventy members. The members are involved in all kinds of criminality that generate income for the club and its members. Coffin Cheaters MC now has two full-worthy departments in Norway, one in Ringerike and the other in Stjørdal.

In Norway, an Outlaws member was shot and wounded in 1996. Six Hells Angels members were arrested, but charges were dismissed. Again in 1997, two Outlaws members were shot at (*Aftenbladet*, 2000):

- *1987.* Members of the MC club The Shabby Ones are involved in a number of violent episodes.
- *1988.* In June, four Shabby Ones members are accused of serious violence against a man. The crime occurred at a motorcycle gathering in Lyngdal. In August, three Shabby Ones members are searched for after a violent episode at the cinema in Bryne. In September, narcotics and weapons are found in an apartment belonging to one of the members of The Shabby Ones.
- *1989.* Two members of The Shabby Ones are arrested, suspected of drugs smuggling. Two are involved in insurance fraud.
- *1991.* The MC gang The Shabby Ones from Sandnes attack Ålgård Motorcycle Club members with bats.
- *1992.* Police action against the club localities of The Shabby Ones, weapons are confiscated and seven members arrested.
- *1993.* Member of MC club The Shabby Ones is put on trial because of violence against a policeman, which caused serious injuries.
- *1995.* In February, shooting between members of the Rabies MC (now Bandidos) and Customizers (now HA) in Oslo. Rabies MC members in a car were shot at. In August, five persons are arrested after illegal import of 25 kilos of hashish from Denmark to Norway. Two of the arrested are members of an MC club. In October, a member of the Hells Angels club at Braut is arrested. The police found narcotics and weapons. In December, a man from HA, Braut, is caught by police in Trondheim, with weapons, illegal spirits, and amphetamine. Also in

December, shots fired against a member of the Bronx-95 (Bandidos). Three HA members prosecuted, but released.

- *1996.* In January, two members of Back Guard MC W. Seaside are jailed for illegal import of a kilo of amphetamine to Norway. Also in January, Outlaws member shot and wounded. Ten HA members released after trial. In February, police find weapons in the clubhouse of Black Guard MC W. Seaside at Lomeland in Gjesdal. In March, Bandidos member shot and wounded at Oslo Airport. HAMC suspected of attempted murder. In May, two women in a car outside HA premises shot at, one hurt. In July, a Danish Bandidos member is shot and killed by Newcastle United in Bangkok. A Hells Angels member was imprisoned. In November, police found weapons, narcotics, user equipment, and stolen goods in the clubhouse of Hells Angels at Braut. In December, seven members of HA at Braut are arrested for using drugs.
- *1997.* In June, two persons in the HA club at Braut are arrested by police. One of them is jailed for possession of narcotics. Also in June, a woman is killed when a powerful bomb explodes in the Bandidos headquarters in Bangkok. In November, police action against Black Guard MC W. Seaside. The catch consists of weapons and narcotics. Two men in the criminal MC milieu are jailed after drug seizure.
- *1998.* In January, a member of the MC club Hogs Riders in Stavanger is jailed. He has been indicted in connection with 11 kilos of amphetamine seized in Oslo in December 1996. In July, after a police action against the Hells Angels in Braut, seven people reported use of drugs.
- *2000.* Four people linked to Bandidos were arrested and indicted in a serious violence case in Østfold.

The Norwegian departments are closely linked to international operations. All over the world, these criminal biker clubs make money on narcotics traffic, human smuggling, prostitution, debt collection, and violence tasks. The MC gangs are dependent on personal contacts across borders. At international gatherings and parties, organized crimes are agreed upon and planned, and international executives from the United States and Europe give their orders to each chapter or department. MC gatherings for these gangs are more than drinking and fun. Gang members have secret meetings in hotel rooms, camping wagons, and bars. An example is the international party held in the city of Kristiansand in Norway by Bandidos in 2007. Swedes came by ferry from Strømstad to Sandefjord, while groups of fifteen members arrived by plane from the continent at Kjevik airport outside Kristiansand, and some came by ferry from Hirtshals in Denmark. A total of two hundred guests took part in the Bandidos feast in Kristiansand.

Prison guards in Norwegian prisons are afraid of inmates from criminal motorcycle clubs. One guard expressed his concerns like this (*Dagsavisen*, 2007):

> Every time we get in someone from HA and Bandidos, it takes only two minutes and then they have control over all the prisoners in the section. They always have some assistants who do the work for them so that we never get a case against them, and they can follow regular progression as prisoners without red tags, while they in reality regulate all activities among prisoners. They recruit new ones that [*sic*] they can use when they get out, for various criminal activities. Prisoners do, of course, not want to get in conflict with these inmates, as it can have consequences for them when they get out, and it is always useful to get a bit of protection both inside and outside, and therefore they take on the role of assistants. This is a problem, and it becomes bigger and bigger.

Theories Applied to MC Crime

There are many theories about MC crime, but few empirical studies. One theory is the matrix theory, which claims that criminal projects are organized horizontally while the motorcycle club is managed vertically. This would imply that the Hells Angels MC, for example, is a matrix organization. A member initiates a criminal project by involving other members (colleagues) in the same club; this is a horizontal initiative. Management is not necessarily involved. The legal part of the motorcycle club is run by the vertical axis, while the criminal part of the motorcycle club is run by the horizontal axis in the matrix. This theory seems to find support in the MC crime practice in Norway.

Another theory is the newcomer theory, which implies that newcomers need to make themselves deserving of membership in the MC club through committing successful crimes. These freshmen need to convince MC club management that they are competent in carrying out criminal activities, such as smuggling of drugs and debt collection. Based on successful completion of organized crimes, newcomers expect to be enrolled in the MC club. This theory seems to find support in MC crime practice in Norway as well.

Swedish police recently carried out an intelligence-led action against Bandidos based on the newcomer theory. It was a coordinated action at ten locations in Sweden. A total of thirteen persons were arrested among Bandidos members. The arrests were a result of cooperation between several government authorities. The background was intelligence and analysis carried out by the Skåne police district and national criminal police in Sweden's national task force against MC groups (Rikskriminalpolisen, 2008, 33).

Bandidos has a strictly hierarchical structure while Hells Angels has a flat organization similar to a franchising business. Deepest down in the pyramid are the
criminals that apply for membership. To qualify, they must carry out crimes and
several specific activities, such as cleaning, shopping, guarding, chauffeuring, etc.
The benefit is protection and the prospect of future climbing in ranks. Already
before membership is actually achieved, prospect persons have normally become
regular criminals in organized crimes.

The suspicions against the thirteen Bandidos members were specifically
about organized transfer of illegal labor and tax withdrawal amounting to 15
million Swedish krona (US$6 million). The general impression at the national
criminal police in Sweden is that MC gangs are active in most or all crime
areas where there is money. The leaders are a special brand of entrepreneur
who consider the laws in society as not valid either for themselves or for their
business activities.

There are a number of more general theories that might be applied to
explain aspects of organized crime:

1. Theory of criminal market forces—cartel theory
2. Theory of unstable governments—regime theory
3. Theory of rivalry—competition theory
4. Theory of dominance—monopoly theory
5. Theory of external threats—conspiracy theory
6. Theory of rational choice—decision theory
7. Theory of fear—violence theory
8. Theory of market mechanisms—market theory
9. Theory of psychological deviance—behavioral theory
10. Theory of competence—learning theories
11. Theory of social environments—environment theory
12. Theory of deviant subcultures—subculture theory
13. Theory of decentralization—organizational theory
14. Theory of social control—control theory
15. Theory of prisoner's dilemma—game theory
16. Theory of entrepreneurship—innovation theory

Knowledge Matrix in Policing MC Crime

Police in Canada have put substantial efforts recently into fighting criminal
MC clubs. For several years, they have used expert witnesses in cases related
to MC crime. Expert witnesses are neutral experts who are able to explain
how these clubs and their members work in terms of, for example, signs and
signals used by debt collection where threats of violence are common. These

expert witnesses are independent of police intelligence and police investigations, and they explain in court the structure and culture in various MC clubs, such as Hells Angels, Bandidos, and Outlaws.

Norwegian police has very limited knowledge of MC-related crime. The limited knowledge available to the Norwegian police force is spread over many national police agencies and local police districts. We, therefore, assume that there is a need to develop knowledge in the police force about criminal motorcycle clubs in Norway. We further assume that there will be a new department established in the National Criminal Police Center (Kriminalpolitisentralen—Kripos) for intelligence and analysis in the country. We might label the new department the MC Crime Department (MCCD) within Kripos. MCCD's ultimate goal would be to eliminate criminal MC clubs in Norway by the year 2030 in cooperation with local police districts, national police agencies, and international police organizations, such as Europol and Interpol. We assume that MCCD will have ten knowledge workers, among them five police officers, three data technologists, and two lawyers. Police officers are intelligence and investigation experts, data technologists are computer experts, while lawyers are the legal experts. One of the police officers will head the department. It is assumed that the department will be in operation next year. The department's role is to contribute to more knowledge about MC crime and criminals in Norway.

The purpose of the remaining chapter is to illustrate potential preparations that need to be completed before establishing this thought department in terms of knowledge needs, information systems, work process, work dynamics, and causal relationships.

A knowledge matrix is a table that lists knowledge needs. The matrix shows knowledge categories and knowledge levels. Here, we make distinctions between these knowledge categories for policing MC crime:

1. *Administrative knowledge* is knowledge about police as an organization and workplace. It is knowledge about procedures, rules, and regulations.
2. *Policing knowledge* is knowledge about work processes and practices in police work when fighting crime. Police knowledge is based on police science, which includes all aspects of policing internally as well as externally. It includes external factors that influence the role and behavior of police in society.
3. *Investigative knowledge* is knowledge based on case-specific and case-oriented collection of information to confirm or disconfirm whether an act or no act is criminal. Included here are case documents and evidence in such a form to prove useful in a court case.

4. *Intelligence knowledge* is knowledge based on a systematic collection of information concerned with a certain topic, a certain domain, certain persons, or any other focused scope. Collected information is transformed and processed according to a transparent methodology to discover criminal capacity, dispositions, and goals. Transformation and processing generate new insights into criminality that guide the effectiveness and efficiency of policing. Included in intelligence knowledge is phenomenological knowledge, which is defined as knowledge about a phenomenon, in terms of what it is about (know what), how it works (know how), and why it works (know why). Phenomenological knowledge enables intelligence officers to "see" what "something" is about by understanding and not missing it when information emerges.

5. *Legal knowledge* is knowledge of the law, regulations, and legal procedures. It is based on access to a variety of legal sources both nationally and internationally, including court decisions. Legal knowledge is composed of declarative, procedural, and analytical knowledge. Declarative knowledge is law and other regulations. Procedural knowledge is the practice of law. Analytical knowledge is the link between case information and laws.

6. *Technological knowledge* is knowledge about the development, use, exploitation, and exploration of information and communication technology. It is knowledge about applications, systems, networks, and databases.

7. *Analytical knowledge* is knowledge about the strategies, tactics, and actions that police can implement to reach desired goals.

In addition to this classification in knowledge categories, we also make distinction between knowledge levels:

1. *Basic knowledge* is knowledge necessary to get work accomplished. Basic knowledge is required for an intelligence officer as a knowledge worker to understand and interpret information, and basic knowledge is required for an intelligence unit as a knowledge organization to receive input and produce output. However, basic knowledge alone produces only elementary and basic results of little value and low quality.

2. *Advanced knowledge* is knowledge necessary to get good work done. Advanced knowledge is required for an intelligence officer as a knowledge worker to achieve satisfactory work performance, and advanced knowledge is required for an intelligence unit as a knowledge organization to produce intelligence reports and crime analysis that are useful in policing. When advanced knowledge is combined

with basic knowledge, then we find professional knowledge workers and professional knowledge organizations in law enforcement.

3. *Innovative knowledge* is knowledge that makes a real difference. When intelligence officers apply innovative knowledge in intelligence and analysis of incoming and available information, then new insights are generated in terms of crime patterns, criminal profiles, and policing strategies. When intelligence units apply innovative knowledge, then new methodologies in intelligence and analysis are introduced that other parts of police forces can learn.

Based on these categories and levels, our knowledge matrix consists of seven knowledge categories and three knowledge levels, as illustrated in Table 9.3. The purpose of the table is to illustrate that there are a total of twenty-one knowledge requirements in policing criminal business enterprises. Based on the table, each intelligence unit has to identify and fill in the table for knowledge requirements.

Knowledge levels are defined as basic knowledge, advanced knowledge, and innovative knowledge. An alternative is to define knowledge levels in terms of knowledge depth: know what, know how, and know why. These knowledge depth levels represent the extent of insight and understanding about a phenomenon. While know what is simple perception of what is going on, know why is complicated insight into cause-and-effect relationships to why it is going on.

1. *Know what* is knowledge about what is happening and what is going on. A police officer perceives that something is going on that might need his or her attention. The officer's insight is limited to perception of something happening. The officer doesn't understand how it is happening or why it is happening.

3. *Know how* is knowledge about how a crime develops, how a criminal behaves, or how a criminal business enterprise is organized. The

Table 9.3   Knowledge Matrix for Knowledge Requirements in Policing Criminal Business Enterprises

	Basic Knowledge	Advanced Knowledge	Innovative Knowledge
Administrative Knowledge			
Policing Knowledge			
Investigative Knowledge			
Intelligence Knowledge			
Legal Knowledge			
Technological Knowledge			
Analytical Knowledge			

officer's insight is not limited to a perception of something that is happening; he or she also understands *how* it is happening.

3. *Know why* is the knowledge representing the deepest form of understanding and insight into a phenomenon. The officer does not only know that it occurs and how it occurs, he or she also has developed an understanding of why it occurs or why it is like this.

When HAMC is organized in a different way than Bandidos, an officer at the know what level only knows that they are different. An officer at the know how level knows how they are different, for example, in terms of recruiting new bikers with criminal experience. An officer at the know why level knows why Bandidos has a stronger tendency than Hells Angels to recruit bikers with criminal experience.

Based on these depth levels, our alternative knowledge matrix consists of seven knowledge categories and three knowledge depth levels, as illustrated in Table 9.4. Again the purpose of the table is to illustrate that there are a total of twenty-one knowledge requirements in policing criminal business enterprises. Based on the table, each intelligence unit has to identify and fill in the table for knowledge requirements.

Research Model for Policing MC Crime

We assume that the ambition and goal in Norway is to reduce MC crime and ultimately eliminate criminal motorcycle clubs. This is illustrated in Figure 9.3, where a time perspective is introduced. Starting in 2008, we assume that Norwegian police authorities will have to spend some years to develop knowledge. Then, more effective policing can take place, thereby reducing the number of crimes. Ultimately in 2030, there might still be a core of crimes that still exist.

Table 9.4 Alternative Knowledge Matrix for Knowledge Requirements in Policing Criminal Business Enterprises

	Know What	Know How	Know Why
Administrative Knowledge			
Policing Knowledge			
Investigative Knowledge			
Intelligence Knowledge			
Legal Knowledge			
Technological Knowledge			
Analytical Knowledge			

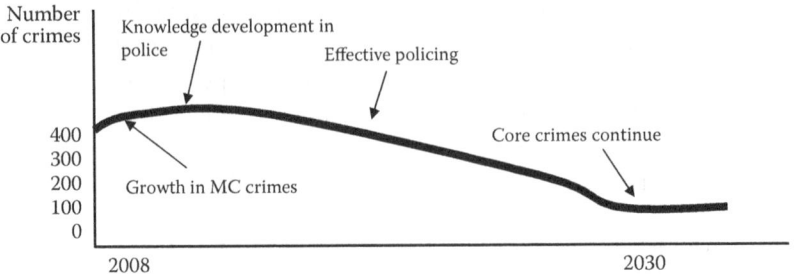

Figure 9.3 Possible development in crimes by criminal motorcycle clubs.

The reason for this positive projection into the future has to be found in causal relationships if the projection is to be trustworthy. In the research model in Figure 9.4, some potential causal relationships are illustrated. The dependent variable in the model is the number of crimes committed by criminals in MC clubs annually in Norway.

The next step in a research process is to formulate research hypotheses for each of the links in the research model. These hypotheses are labeled H1

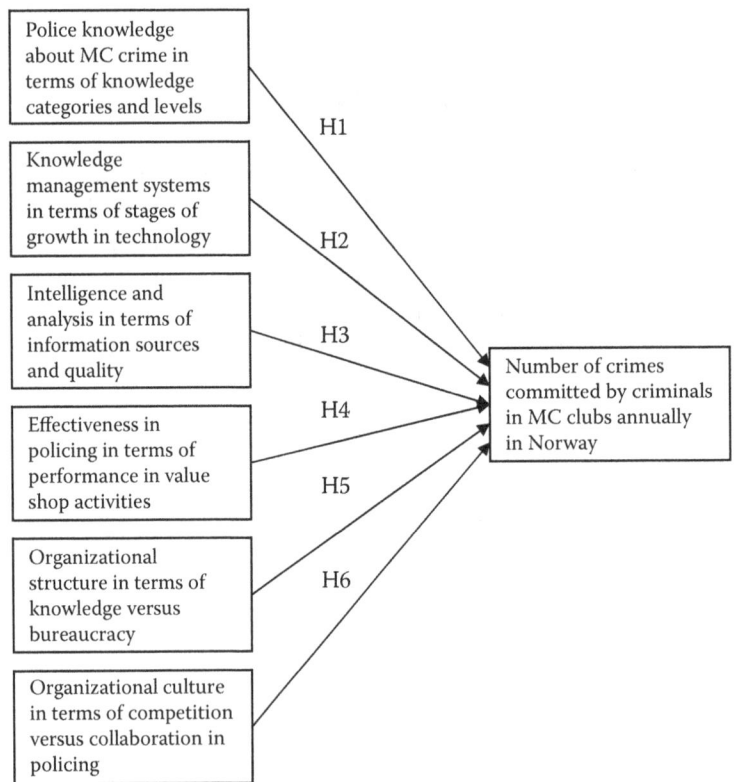

Figure 9.4 Research model explaining variation in the number of crimes.

to H6 in the research model. However, in this book, it is not appropriate to move beyond the stage of a research model in our presentation of policing criminal business organizations.

References

Adresseavisen newspaper. 2005. Maktkamp i Hells Angels (Power fight in Hells Angels). June 6, online at: www.adressa.no.

Aftenbladet newspaper. 2000. MC-krim—Rogaland (MC crime in Rogaland). July 11, online at: www.aftenbladet.no.

Aftenposten newspaper. 2001. Hells Angels-sjef med ny forretning (Hells Angels boss with new business). May 27, online at: www.aftenposten.no.

Aftenposten newspaper. 2007. Siste gang i Norge? (Last time in Norway?) October 14, p. 3, online at: www.aftenposten.no.

Dagsavisen newspaper. 2007. Fengselsansatte frykter MC-krim (Prison guards fear MC crime). February 20, online at: www.dagsavisen.no.

Lavigne, Y. 1996. *Hells Angels: Into the abyss*, New York: Harper Paperbacks, Harper Collins Publishers.

Nelen, H. and Lankhorst, F. 2008. Facilitating organized crime: The role of lawyers and notaries. In *Organized crime: Culture, markets and policies*, Eds. D. Siegel and H. Nelen, 127–142. New York: Springer-Verlag.

NRK News. 2007. Til kamp mot HA (To fight against HA), September 9, online at: www.nrk.no.

Quinn, J. and Koch, D.S. 2003. The nature of criminality within one-percent motorcycle clubs. *Deviant Behavior: An Interdisciplinary Journal* 24: 281–305.

Rikskriminalpolisen. 2008. *Rikskrim 07 (National Crime 07)*. Rikskriminalpolisen (National criminal police), Stockholm, Sweden.

Schein, E.H. 1990. Organizational culture. *American Psychologist* 45 (2): 109–119.

Schmidt, Ø. 2008. Frykter for at Hells Angels etablerer seg i Bergen (Fears that the Hells Angels establish in Bergen). *Hegnar Online*, October 30. www.hegnar.no.

von Rassel, J. and Komarnicki, J. 2007. Gangs ranked: Crazy Dragons head list of Alberta crime threats. *Calgary Herald*, Saturday, July 21.

Wolf, D.R. 1991. *The rebels: A brotherhood of outlaw bikers*, Toronto, Ontario: University of Toronto Press.

Applying Police Knowledge

10

The need for knowledge in policing criminal business enterprises has been stressed throughout this book. Knowledge has emerged as the most important resource in policing. So far, we have offered new insights into the understanding of organized crime based on the enterprise paradigm, the theory of profit-driven crimes, and theories of criminal entrepreneurship. This chapter now makes a contribution to intelligence-led and knowledge-based policing, an emerging area of interest that builds upon and enhances policing as knowledge work, police officers as knowledge workers, and police forces as knowledge organizations.

Policing criminal business enterprises requires police intelligence and investigations. Police intelligence has to be based on an *implemented* intelligence strategy.

Criminal organizations take on many different forms requiring different kinds of policing of criminal business enterprises. For example, Staring (2008, 165) tells the story of how Dutch police discovered a Chinese gang controlling human smuggling in The Netherlands:

> Just before the summer holidays of 2005, the Dutch National Criminal Investigation Service arrested ten members of a violent Chinese gang. All detainees were suspected of human smuggling, drug trafficking, extortion, and liquidations. Police not only found large amounts of drugs and money, but also came across twenty-four automatic firearms, among which [were] several Uzis. The Chinese gang members were allegedly heavily involved in smuggling Chinese from their home country through The Netherlands to the United Kingdom. Smuggled immigrants had to pay up to forty or even fifty thousand euros for their journey and, according to the police, the gang members were prepared to use violence towards defaulters. In addition, the police suspected some of the arrested gang members [of] being linked to previously apprehended snakeheads of other Chinese smuggling organizations. Since the turn of the millennium, the Chinese in The Netherlands have acquired the reputation of being involved in professionally organized human smuggling through Eastern European countries to the United Kingdom, using safe houses in harbor cities such as Rotterdam. The involvement of Chinese immigrants with human smuggling in The Netherlands became explicitly visible through the "Dover case." In this tragedy on June 18, 2000, fifty-eight Chinese smuggled immigrants on their way to the United Kingdom suffocated in a refrigerated cargo container. The "Dover case" put The Netherlands on the map as a transit country for human smuggling although it wrongly focused solely on Chinese smugglers. It turned out that Dutch citizens from different ethnic backgrounds and with different judicial status were involved in the lucrative business of human smuggling.

Contrary to public belief, organized crime by criminal organizations is not a new phenomenon. Felsen and Kalaitzidis (2005) describe historical cases, such as piracy, slavery, and opium smuggling. Piracy is a robbery committed at sea. The earliest documented incidences of piracy are the exploits of the Sea Peoples who threatened the Aegean in the thirteenth century BCE. The most famous and far-reaching pirates in medieval Europe were the Vikings, warriors and looters from Scandinavia. They raided the coasts, rivers, and inland cities of all Western Europe as far south as Seville in Spain.

Like slavery and piracy, smuggling has existed throughout history by criminal organizations of different sizes. Smuggling arises because of different laws and regulations that govern markets across borders. Whenever the flow of a commodity is controlled or prohibited by one state, it creates an environment that favors profits through smuggling (Felsen and Kalaitzidis, 2005).

Police Knowledge Organization

To fight organized crime and police criminal business enterprises, police officers need knowledge that is determined by their role or duties (Centrex, 2005, 18).

> The level of knowledge required by police staff will be determined by the specific role they perform or duties, which they are assigned. Staff profiling is a means of conducting a gap analysis. This analysis helps to determine the levels of staff knowledge required to meet organizational needs (in line with NIM [National Intelligence Model]) and also to assist with succession planning and the need for knowledge to be maintained.

Knowledge management is important and often critical in policing. Combating fraud and financial crime is an interesting example, where financial intelligence and interaction between public and private sectors is required. Identifying, reporting, and investigating suspected fraud and suspicious financial operations is essential for the effectiveness of antifraud measures and the protection of financial interests. This process, which can result in asset confiscation and prosecution, requires reliable intelligence, often received from reports on suspicious transactions made by the business sector (banks, intermediaries, notaries, audit firms, etc.) to financial intelligence units. At a conference on combating fraud and financial crime hosted by the Academy of European Law (ERA, 2008), several issues related to financial intelligence and interaction between public and private sectors were discussed:

- What are the practical results of the application of antimoney laundering legislation?
- What are the new trends and developments in the field of financial intelligence based on information from antimoney laundering agencies?
- How can financial intelligence help prevent financial crime in the first place?
- How is cooperation between financial intelligence units and other authorities developing?
- Is there a role for customs authorities in combating underground banking, enforcing cash controls, and other measures?
- Are there benefits to be drawn from wider intelligence, such as the analysis of trade data in order to identify trade-based money laundering?

Through the experience of national, European Union (EU), and international experts, the roles of private and public sectors in terms of handling requests, safeguarding information, and other aspects of the financial intelligence-gathering process were discussed at the conference (ERA, 2008). Intelligence provided by financial intelligence units is today an essential tool for investigation agencies in fulfilling the official mandate to fight fraud in organized crime, ensuring accuracy and relevance of the information received, disseminated, and processed for different user groups, such as criminal police.

Policing is normally left to law enforcement authorities in a region or nation. However, policing sometimes occurs in the private sector, such as corporate policing in the case of a press leak from Hewlett Packard's board of directors (Baer, 2008, 2).

When Hewlett Packard (HP) announced in September 2006 that its Board Chairman, Patricia Dunn, had authorized HP's security department to investigate a suspected Board-level press leak and that the investigation included tactics such as obtaining HP Board members' and reporters' telephone records through false pretences (conduct known as "pretexting"), observers vehemently condemned the operation as illegal and outrageous. In congressional testimony, however, Dunn defended the investigation as "old fashioned detective work." Although Dunn would later claim that she was unaware of key aspects of the investigation, her description was not so far off. The police routinely rely on deception to investigate and apprehend wrongdoers.

Deception is an activity where someone is to believe something that is not true. In law enforcement, deception in overt contacts is applied to extract information from witnesses and suspects. Deception is in direct opposition with the common norms associated with corporate governance, loyalty, trust, and transparency. Despite the risk of subsequent liability, Baer (2008) argues that corporations increasingly employ surveillance, undercover investigations, and deceptive techniques in interrogations.

Knowledge organization has emerged as the dominant structure of both public and private organizations in the transition from an industrial to a knowledge society (Lassen et al., 2006). Knowledge organization in the management sciences is concerned with structures within which knowledge workers solve knowledge problems (Bennet and Bennet, 2005a, 2005b; Lassen et al., 2006; Smith, 2003; Uretsky, 2001).

There are many definitions of knowledge. Nonaka et al. (2000) describe it as justified true belief. Definitions of organizational knowledge range from a complex, accumulated expertise that resides in individuals and is partly or largely inexpressible to a much more structured and explicit content. There are also several classifications of knowledge, e.g., far, explicit, embodied, encoded, embedded, event, procedural, and common. Knowledge has long been recognized as a valuable resource for the organizational growth and sustained competitive advantage, especially for organizations competing in uncertain environments. Recently, some researchers have argued that knowledge is an organization's most valuable resource because it represents intangible assets, operational routines, and creative processes that are hard to imitate (Wasko and Faraj, 2005). However, the effective management of knowledge is fundamental to the organization's ability to create and sustain a competitive advantage.

Knowledge management research has described organizational knowledge flows in terms of the knowledge circulation process that consist of five components: knowledge creation, accumulation, sharing, utilization, and internalization. Of these five parts, the knowledge-sharing process is what this book focuses on. Knowledge sharing within and between organizations is not a one-way activity, but a process of trial and error, feedback, and mutual adjustment of both the source and the recipient of knowledge. This mutuality in the knowledge sharing suggests that the process can be constructed as a sequence of collective actions in which the source and the recipient are involved. There are many different knowledge-sharing mechanisms: it can be informal and personal as well as formal and impersonal. Informal mechanisms include conversation, unscheduled meetings, electronic bulletin boards, and discussion databases. More formal knowledge-sharing channels include video conferencing, training sessions, organizational intranets, and databases.

Bennet and Bennet (2005a) define knowledge organizations as complex adaptive systems composed of a large number of self-organizing components that seek to maximize their own goals, but operate according to rules in the context of relationships with other components. In an intelligent complex adaptive system, the agents are people. The systems (organizations) are frequently composed of hierarchical levels of self-organizing agents (or knowledge workers), which can take the forms of teams, divisions, or other structures that have common bonds. Thus, while the components (knowledge workers) are self-organizing, they are not independent from the system they comprise (the professional organization).

Knowledge is often referred to as information combined with interpretation, reflection, and context. In cybernetics, knowledge is defined as a reducer of complexity or as a relation to predict and to select those actions that are necessary in establishing a competitive advantage for organizational survival. That is, knowledge is the capability to draw distinctions within a domain of actions (Laise et al., 2005). According to the knowledge-based view of the organization, the uniqueness of an organization's knowledge plays a fundamental role in its sustained ability to perform and succeed (Turner and Makhija, 2006).

According to the knowledge-based theory of the firm, knowledge is the main resource for a firm's competitive advantage. Knowledge is the primary driver of a firm's value. Performance differences across firms can be attributed to the variance in the firms' strategic knowledge. Strategic knowledge is characterized by being valuable, unique, rare, nonimitable, nonsubstitutable, nontransferable, combinable, and exploitable. Unlike other inert organizational resources, the application of existing knowledge has the potential to generate new knowledge (Garud and Kumaraswamy, 2005).

Inherently, however, knowledge resides within individuals and, more specifically, in the employees who create, recognize, archive, access, and apply knowledge in carrying out their tasks (Liu and Chen, 2005). Consequently, the movement of knowledge across individual and organizational boundaries is dependent on employees' knowledge-sharing behaviors (Liebowitz, 2004). Bock et al. (2005) found that extensive knowledge sharing within organizations still appears to be the exception rather than the rule.

The knowledge organization is very different from the bureaucratic organization. For example, the knowledge organization's focus on flexibility and customer response is very different from the bureaucracy's focus on organizational stability and the accuracy and repetitiveness of internal processes. In the knowledge organization, current practices emphasize using the ideas and capabilities of employees to improve decision making and organizational effectiveness. In contrast, bureaucracies utilize autocratic decision making by senior leadership with unquestioned execution by the workforce (Bennet and Bennet, 2005b).

In knowledge organizations, transformational and charismatic leadership is an influential mode of leadership that is associated with high levels of individual and organizational performance. Leadership effectiveness is critically contingent on, and often defined in terms of, leaders' ability to motivate followers toward collective goals or a collective mission or vision. (Kark and Dijk, 2007).

In the knowledge society, knowledge organizations are expected to play a vital role in local economic development. For example, knowledge institutions, such as universities, are expected to stimulate regional and local economic development. Knowledge transfer units in universities, such as Oxford in the United Kingdom and Grenoble in France, are responsible for local and regional innovations (Smith, 2003).

Uretsky (2001) argues that the real knowledge organization is the learning organization. A learning organization is one that changes as a result of its experiences. Under the best of circumstances, these changes result in performance improvements. The terms *knowledge organization* and *learning organization* are usually (but not necessarily) used to describe service organizations. This is because most, if not all, of the value of these organizations comes from how well their professionals learn from the environment, diagnose problems, and then work with clients or customers to improve their situations. The problems they work on are frequently ambiguous and unstructured. The information, skills, and experience needed to address these problems vary with work cases. A typical example is detectives in police investigations.

Similarly, Bennet and Bennet (2005b) argue that learning and knowledge will have become two of the three most important emergent characteristics of the future world-class organization. Learning will be continuous and widespread, utilizing mentoring, classroom, and distance learning, and will likely be self-managed with strong infrastructure support. The creation, storage, transfer, and application of knowledge will have been refined and developed such that it becomes a major resource of the organization as it satisfies customers and adapts to environmental competitive forces and opportunities.

The third characteristic of future knowledge organizations will be that of organizational intelligence. Organizational intelligence is the ability of an organization to perceive, interpret, and respond to its environment in a manner that meets its goals while satisfying multiple stakeholders. Intelligent behavior may be defined as being well prepared, providing excellent outcome-oriented thinking, choosing appropriate postures, and making outstanding decisions. Intelligent behavior includes acquiring knowledge continuously from all available resources and building it into an integrated picture, bringing together seemingly unrelated information to create new and unusual perspectives and to understand the surrounding world (Bennet and Bennet, 2005b).

In our context of policing and law enforcement, "intelligence" has another meaning as well. Brown (2007, 340) defined intelligence in this context as:

Intelligence is information, which is significant or potentially significant for an enquiry or potential enquiry.

What establishes information as intelligence is that it is a subset of information defined by the special quality of being significant and relevant. If information is significant, it has value and it has relevance. Analysis does not create intelligence, it merely discovers, attributes, and refines it.

According to Bennet and Bennet (2005a), designing the knowledge organization of the future implies development of an intelligent complex adaptive system. In response to an environment of rapid change, increasing complexity, and great uncertainty, the organization of the future must become an adaptive organic business. The intelligent complex adaptive system will enter into a symbiotic relationship with its cooperative enterprise, virtual alliances, and external environment, while simultaneously retaining unity of purpose and effective identification and selection of incoming threats and opportunities.

In the knowledge organization, innovation and creativity are of critical importance. The literature on creativity provides a view of organizing for innovation by focusing on how individuals and teams come to shape knowledge in unique ways. Innovation consists of the creative generation of a new idea and the implementation of the idea into a valuable product, and thus creativity feeds innovation and is particularly critical in complex and interdependent work. Taylor and Greve (2006) argue that creativity can be viewed as the first stage of the overall innovation process.

Innovative solutions in the knowledge organization arise from diverse knowledge, processes that allow for creativity, and tasks directed toward creative solutions. Creativity requires application of deep knowledge because knowledge workers must understand the knowledge domain to push its boundaries. Team creativity likewise relies on tapping into the diverse knowledge of a team's members (Taylor and Greve, 2006).

Within knowledge organizations, we often find communities of practice. Brown and Duguid (2001) argue that for a variety of reasons, communities of practice seem a useful organizational subset for examining organizational knowledge as well as identity. First, such communities are privileged sites for a tight, effective loop of insight, problem identification, learning, and knowledge production. Second, they are significant repositories for the development, maintenance, and reproduction of knowledge. Third, community knowledge is more than the sum of its parts. Fourth, organizational ability to adapt to environmental change is often determined by communities of practice.

Police Knowledge Resources

Knowledge is a renewable, reusable, and accumulating resource of value to the organization when applied in the production of products and services. Knowledge cannot as such be stored in computers, it can only be stored in the human brain. Knowledge is what a knower knows; there is no knowledge without someone knowing it.

The need for a knower in knowledge existence raises the question as to how knowledge can exist outside the heads of individuals. Although knowledge cannot originate outside the heads of individuals, it can be argued that knowledge can be represented in and often embedded in organizational processes, routines, and networks, and sometimes in document repositories. However, knowledge is seldom complete outside of an individual.

In this book, knowledge is defined as information combined with experience, context, interpretation, reflection, intuition, and creativity. Information becomes knowledge once it is processed in the mind of an individual. This knowledge then becomes information again once it is articulated or communicated to others in the form of text, computer output, spoken or written words, or other means. Six characteristics of knowledge can distinguish it from information: knowledge is a human act, knowledge is the residue of thinking, knowledge is created in the present moment, knowledge belongs to communities, knowledge circulates through communities in many ways, and new knowledge is created at the boundaries of old. This definition and these characteristics of knowledge are based on current research (e.g., Poston and Speier, 2005; Wasko and Faraj, 2005).

Today, any discussion of knowledge quickly leads to the issue of how knowledge is defined. A pragmatic definition defines the topic as the most valuable form of content in a continuum starting at data, encompassing information, and ending at knowledge. Typically, data is classified, summarized, transferred, or corrected in order to add value, and become information within a certain context. This conversion is relatively mechanical and has long been facilitated by storage, processing, and communication technologies. These technologies add place, time, and form utility to the data. In doing so, the information serves to inform or reduce uncertainty within the problem domain. Therefore, information is united with the context, that is, it only has utility within the context.

Knowledge has the highest value, the most human contribution, the greatest relevance to decisions and actions, and the greatest dependence on a specific situation or context. It is also the most difficult of content types to manage because it originates and is applied in the minds of human beings. People who are knowledgeable not only have information, but also have the ability to integrate and frame the information within the context of their experience, expertise, and judgment. In doing so, they can create new information that expands the state of possibilities and, in turn, allows for further interaction with experience, expertise, and judgment. Therefore, in an organizational context, all new knowledge stems from people. Some knowledge is incorporated in organizational artifacts like processes, structures, and technology. However, institutionalized knowledge often inhibits competition in a dynamic context, unless adaptability of people and processes (higher order learning) is built into the institutional mechanisms themselves.

Our concern with distinctions between information and knowledge is based on real differences as well as technology implications. Real differences between information and knowledge do exist, although for most practical purposes these differences are of no interest at all. Information technology implications are concerned with the argument that computers can only manipulate electronic information, not electronic knowledge. Business systems are loaded with information, but without knowledge.

Some have defined knowledge as a fluid mix of framed experience, values, contextual information, and expert insights that provides a framework for evaluating and incorporating new experiences and information. It originates and is applied in the minds of knowers. In organizations, it often becomes embedded not only in documents or repositories, but also in organizational routines, processes, practices, and norms. Distinctions are often made between data, information, knowledge, and wisdom.

- *Data* are letters and numbers without meaning. Data are independent, isolated measurements, characters, numerical characters, and symbols.
- *Information* is data that are included in a context that makes sense. For example, 40 degrees can have different meaning depending on the context. There can be a medical, geographical, or technical context. If a person has 40 degrees Celsius in fever, that is quite serious. If a city is located 40 degrees north, we know that it is far south of Norway. If an angle is 40 degrees, we know what it looks like. Information is data that make sense because it can be understood correctly. People turn data into information by organizing it into some unit of analysis, e.g., dollars, dates, or customers. Information is data endowed with relevance and purpose.
- *Knowledge* is information combined with experience, context, interpretation, and reflection. Knowledge is a renewable resource that can be used over and over, and that accumulates in an organization through use and in combination with employees' experiences. Humans have knowledge; knowledge cannot exist outside the heads of individuals in the company. Information becomes knowledge when it enters the human brain. This knowledge transforms into information again when it is articulated and communicated to others. Information is an explicit representation of knowledge; it is in itself not knowledge. Knowledge can be both truths and lies, perspectives and concepts, judgments and expectations. Knowledge is used to receive information by analyzing, understanding, and evaluating;

by combining, prioritizing, and decision making; and by planning, implementing, and controlling.

- *Wisdom* is knowledge combined with learning, insights, and judgmental abilities. Wisdom is more difficult to explain than knowledge because the levels of context become even more personal and, thus, the higher-level nature of wisdom renders it more obscure than knowledge. While knowledge is mainly sufficiently generalized solutions, wisdom is best thought of as sufficiently generalized approaches and values that can be applied in numerous and varied situations. Wisdom cannot be created like data and information, and it cannot be shared with others like knowledge. Because the context is so personal, it becomes almost exclusive to our own minds and incompatible with the minds of others without extensive transaction. This transaction requires not only a base of knowledge and opportunities for experiences that help create wisdom, but also the processes of introspection, retrospection, interpretation, and contemplation. We can value wisdom in others, but we can only create it ourselves.

It has been argued that expert systems using artificial intelligence are able to do knowledge work. The chess-playing computer called Deep Blue by IBM is frequently cited as an example. Deep Blue can compete with the best human players because chess, though complex, is a closed system of unchanging and codifiable rules. The size of the board never varies, the rules are unambiguous, the moves of the pieces are clearly defined, and there is absolute agreement about what it means to win or lose. Deep Blue is no knowledge worker; the computer only performs a series of computations at extremely high speed.

While knowledge workers develop knowledge, organizations learn. Therefore, the *learning organization* has become a term frequently used. The learning organization is similar to knowledge development. While knowledge development is taking place at the individual level, organizational learning is taking place at the firm level. Organizational learning occurs when the firm is able to exploit individual competence in new and innovative ways. Organizational learning also occurs when the collective memory, including local language, common history, and routines, expands. Organizational learning causes growth in the intellectual capital. Learning is a continuous, never-ending process of knowledge creation. A learning organization is a place where people are constantly driven to discover what has caused the current situation and how they can change the present. To maintain a competitive advantage, an organization's investment decisions related to knowledge creation are likely to be strategic in nature.

Police versus Criminal Knowledge

Police organizations are not the only entities developing into knowledge organizations with police officers developing into knowledge workers, but, criminal organizations are doing so as well, with criminals developing into knowledge workers.

Knowledge is a resource in organized crime. This chapter makes a contribution to existing theory. Using a resource-based theory approach, we attempt to develop new means of conceptualizing organized crime. It is timely in as much as this is a growing area of concern for researchers active in entrepreneurship. However, the developments suggested in this book need to be further explored in future research to make a significant contribution. As an early exploration into the possible fit between resource-based theories of the firm and criminal entrepreneurship, we do suggest some linkages that might be profitably researched.

The essence of the resource-based theory of the enterprise lies in its emphasis on the internal resources available to the enterprise, rather than on the external opportunities and threats dictated by industry conditions. Enterprises are considered to be highly heterogeneous, and the bundles of resources available to each enterprise are different. This is because enterprises have different initial resource endowments and because managerial decisions affect resource accumulation and the direction of enterprise growth as well as resource utilization.

Organized criminals apply their criminal entrepreneurship in resource allocation decisions. The business enterprise model of organized crime focuses on how economic considerations, rather than hierarchical or ethnic considerations, lie at the base of the formation and success of organized crime groups. Regardless of ethnicity or hierarchy, the enterprise model labels economic concerns as the primary cause of organized criminal behavior. A study of illicit drug sales in the Southwest United States found that the drug markets consisted of small organizations rather than massive, centralized bureaucracies that were competitive rather than monopolistic in nature. A study of bookmaking, loan sharking, and numbers gambling in New York City found that they were not monopolies in the classic sense or subject to control by some external organization (Albanese, 2004). Instead, economic forces arising from the illegality of the product tended to fragment the market, making it difficult to control or centralize these illegal activities on a large scale. The supply of illegal goods seems not marked by a tendency toward the development of large-scale criminal enterprises, due to the illegal nature of the product. Instead, smaller, more flexible, and efficient enterprises characterized this type of organized crime.

Illegal entrepreneurship knowledge might also be applied to legal business development. In a study by Aidis and Praag (2004), illegal entrepreneurship experience was found to be associated with business motivation. This is in line with human capital theory that maintains that knowledge provides individuals with increases in their cognitive abilities, leading to more productive and efficient potential activity.

Aidis and Praag (2004) found that the skills developed through illegal business activities under socialist systems in Eastern Europe were not acquired with the expectation that they would ultimately be useful in a completely different setting of transition to market economy. Nevertheless, such prior experience in the black market provides valuable human capital for entrepreneurs in a market-oriented setting, and thereby changing the perception of the "unofficial" or "black" economy. Illegal entrepreneurship experience within centrally planned economies is a unique and historical phenomenon.

Operational Knowledge Sectors

Criminal organizations are, to an increasing extent, knowledge organizations as they develop over time. Also police forces are, to an increasing extent, knowledge organizations, as policing is more and more about preventing crime and solving complicated criminality.

If the police have more knowledge, crime will be fought in an efficient and effective way, and the police will succeed. If the police know less than the criminals, crime will have freedom to expand and succeed. Hence, it is not the absolute level of knowledge in police that is important, rather it is the relative knowledge level, as illustrated in Figure 10.1, about knowledge war between the police and criminal organizations.

Distinctions can be made between core, advanced, and innovative knowledge. These knowledge categories indicate different levels of knowledge sophistication. Core knowledge is that minimum scope and level of knowledge required for daily operations, while advanced knowledge enables an organization to be competitively viable, and innovative knowledge is the knowledge that enables the organization to lead its industry and competitors.

Core Knowledge

Core knowledge is the basic knowledge required to stay in business. This is the type of knowledge that can create efficiency barriers for entry of new companies, as new competitors are not up to speed in basic business processes. Because core knowledge is present in all existing competitors, the firm must have this knowledge even though it will provide the firm with no advantage that distinguishes it from its competitors. Core knowledge is that minimum

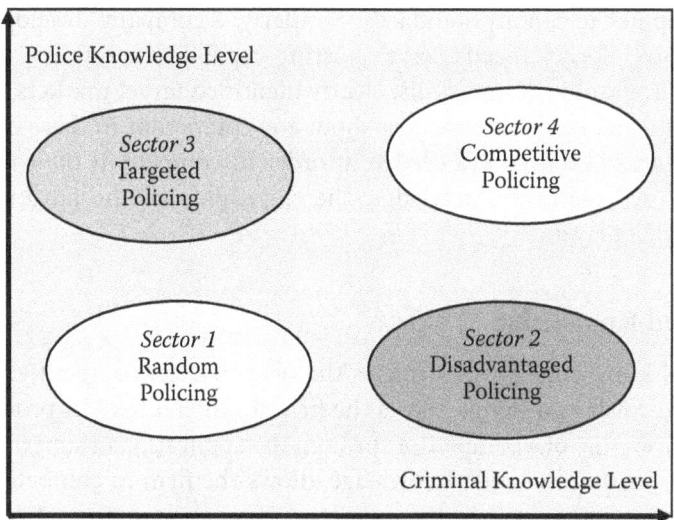

Figure 10.1 Knowledge war between the police and criminal organizations.

scope and level of knowledge required just playing the game. Having that level of knowledge and capability will not assure the long-term competitive viability of the firm, but does present a basic industry knowledge barrier to entry. Core knowledge tends to be commonly held by members of an industry and, therefore, provides little advantage other than over nonmembers (Zack, 1999).

In a law firm, examples of core knowledge include knowledge of the law, knowledge of the courts, knowledge of clients, and knowledge of procedures. For a student in the business school, core knowledge includes knowledge of what subjects to study this term and where the lectures take place. In a police organization, core knowledge includes knowledge of policing tasks and procedures. In a criminal organization, core knowledge includes knowledge of relevant crimes and procedures.

According to Tiwana (2002), core knowledge is the basic level of knowledge required just to play the game. This is the type of knowledge that creates a barrier for entry of new companies. Because this level of knowledge is expected of all competitors, you must have it even though it will provide your company with no advantage that distinguishes it from its competitors. Let us take two examples from the business world: one is from the consumer electronics (hard product) business and one from Internet programming (soft product). To enter the modem manufacturing market, a new company must have extensive knowledge of these aspects: a suitable circuit design, all electronic parts that go into a modem, fabricating surface mount (SMD) chip boards, how to write operating system drivers for modems, and familiarity with computer telephony standards. Similarly, a company developing Web sites for, say, florists, needs server hosting capabilities, Internet programming skills, graphic design skills, clearly identified target markets, and necessary software. In either case, just about any competitor in these businesses is assumed to have this knowledge in order to compete in their respective markets; such essential knowledge, therefore, provides no advantage over other market players.

Advanced Knowledge

Advanced knowledge is what makes the organization competitively visible and active. Such knowledge allows the firm to differentiate its products and services from that of a competitor through the application of superior knowledge in certain areas. Such knowledge allows the firm to compete head on with its competitors in the same market and for the same set of customers. Advanced knowledge enables a firm to be competitively viable. The firm may have generally the same level, scope, or quality of knowledge as its competitors, although the specific knowledge content will often vary among competitors, enabling knowledge differentiation. Firms may choose to compete on knowledge head on in the same strategic position, hoping to know more than a competitor. They instead may choose to compete for that position by differentiating their knowledge (Zack, 1999).

In a law firm, examples of advanced knowledge include knowledge of law applications, knowledge of important court rulings, and knowledge of successful procedural case handling. For a student in the business school, advanced knowledge includes knowledge of important articles and books, which are compulsory literature in subjects this term. In police organizations, examples of advanced knowledge include intelligence procedures and investigation techniques. In criminal organizations, examples of advanced knowledge include competitor intelligence and policing insights.

According to Tiwana (2002), advanced knowledge is what makes your company competitively viable. Such knowledge allows your company to differentiate its product from that of a competitor, arguably, through the application of superior knowledge in certain areas. Such knowledge allows your company to compete head on with its competitors in the same market and for the same set of customers. In the case of a company trying to compete in modem manufacturing markets, superior or user-friendly software or an additional capability in modems (such as warning online users of incoming telephone calls) represents such knowledge. In case of a Web site development firm, such knowledge might be about international flower markets and collaborative relationships in Dutch flower auctions that the company can use to improve Web sites delivered to its customers.

Innovative Knowledge

Innovative knowledge allows a firm to lead its entire industry to an extent that clearly differentiates it from competition. Such knowledge allows a firm to change the rules of the game by introducing new business practices. Such knowledge enables a firm to expand its market share by winning new customers and by increasing service levels to existing customers. Innovative knowledge is that knowledge that enables a firm to lead its industry and competitors and to significantly differentiate itself from its competitors. Innovative knowledge often enables a firm to change the rules of the game (Zack, 1999).

In a law firm, examples of innovative knowledge include knowledge of standardizing repetitive legal cases, knowledge of successful settlements, and knowledge of modern information technology to track and store vast amounts of information from various sources. For a student in the business school, innovative knowledge includes knowledge of important topics within subjects, links between subjects, typical exam questions, and knowledge of business cases where theory can be applied. In police organizations, innovative knowledge includes intelligence within the center of criminal organizations, such as the Cosa Nostra, Hells Angels, and Yakuza. In criminal organizations, innovative knowledge includes intelligence within the center of customs agencies, police authorities, and municipalities.

According to Tiwana (2002), innovative knowledge allows a company to lead its entire industry to an extent that clearly differentiates it from competition. Innovative knowledge allows a company to change the rules of the game. Patented technology is an applicable example of changing the rules. Patents cannot always protect innovative knowledge, as the lawsuit between Microsoft˚ and Apple˚ in the 1980s should serve to remind us. Apple sued Microsoft for copying the look and feel of its graphical user interface (GUI). The Supreme Court ruled that things like look and feel could not be patented; they can only be copyrighted. Microsoft won the case because it copied the look and feel, but used entirely different code to create it in the first place.

Knowledge Depth

Knowledge levels were here defined as basic knowledge, advanced knowledge, and innovative knowledge. An alternative is to define knowledge levels in terms of knowledge depth: *know what*, *know how*, and *know why*. These knowledge depth levels represent the extent of insight and understanding about a phenomenon. While know what is simple perception of what is going on, know why is complicated insight into cause-and-effect relationships about why things are going on.

- *Know what* is knowledge about what is happening and what is going on. A police officer perceives that something is going on that might need his or her attention. The officer's insight is limited to perception of something happening. The officer doesn't understand how it is happening or why it is happening. Similarly, a criminal knows what to do, but he does not know how to do it or why he is supposed to do it.
- *Know how* is police knowledge about how a crime develops, how a criminal behaves, how investigation can be carried out, or how a criminal business enterprise is organized. The officer's insight is not limited to a perception of something that is happening; he or she also understands how it is happening or why it is. Similarly, criminal know-how is present when the criminal understands how crime is to be carried out and how criminal competitors and the police will react to the crime.
- *Know why* is the knowledge representing the deepest form of understanding and insights into a phenomenon. The police officer and the police knowledge organization not only know that it occurs and how it occurs, but he/she also has developed an understanding of why it occurs or why it is like this. The criminal individual and the criminal organization not only know what is going on and how it is occurring, but an understanding of causality is also present.

A key point of this research article is that the relative knowledge level of police should determine policing strategy when forcing law enforcement on criminal enterprises. Variations in the relative knowledge level might be found between countries and regions, and it might be found between criminal industries.

For example, countries like Norway and Sweden may find themselves in sector 1 (see below) most of the time, mainly due to ignorant criminals, which does not require extremely knowledgeable police forces to fight them successfully. The United Kingdom may find itself in sector 4 (see below) most of the time, mainly because of the National Intelligence Model (NIM) and national control actions required in law enforcement against national and transnational organized crime. Countries such as Italy and Pakistan may find themselves in sector 2 (see below) of disadvantaged policing, where the relative knowledge level is higher in criminal organizations than in police organizations. We do not suggest any country in sector 3 (see below), although that is certainly a sector to strive for in all countries.

Variations may be found between criminal industries as well. In Norway, trafficking of women and children may be found in sector 1, smuggling and handling of narcotics in sector 2, smuggling of alcohol in sector 3, and armed robbery in sector 4. In the United Kingdom, the situation may be quite different with armed robbery in sector 1, protection business in sector 2, drug trade in sector 3, and trafficking in sector 4. These examples are just ideas to illustrate the situations that may differ within nations and among nations.

Sector 1: Random Policing

In this first sector, both police and criminals suffer from lack of knowledge. Therefore, it becomes random who succeeds and who fails. Both criminal entrepreneurs and investigating police officers only have basic knowledge of crime business. The *core knowledge* may consist of some basic insights into distribution channels and market places. The knowledge is limited to *know what*, where both sides know what is going on, but they do not know how it is going on, and they do not know why it is going on. Criminal entrepreneurs are not very sophisticated; they are typically opportunity-based without understanding how and why business performance does not improve. Similarly, police observe what is going on, but they do not understand how, and they certainly do not understand why. Also, police actions are only understood in terms of what is done in policing, as they do not know how their actions work and why some of their actions work while other do not work.

This situation causes randomness on both sides. Because they have so little knowledge, randomness occurs both among criminal entrepreneurs and police officers in their crime and law enforcement, respectively. Randomness is lack of order, purpose, cause, and predictability.

In sector 1, we suggest that the optimal law enforcement strategy has these characteristics:

- *Time frame*: Some weeks up to some months
- *Goal*: Imprisonment of nonimportant members of criminal organizations
- *Forecast*: Chaotic, turbulent, and dynamic criminal environment
- *Change*: Results in quantitative terms
- *Action*: Short-term gain rather than long-term prevention
- *Resources*: Division of labor based on need-to-know management
- *Analysis*: Identifying criminals
- *Decision*: Hierarchical organizational structure

Sector 2: Disadvantaged Policing

In this second sector, criminals are ahead of police. For example, criminal business enterprises may have knowledge of money laundering procedures and methods and knowledge of information and communication technology that are completely unfamiliar to law enforcement agencies.

In this sector, we suggest that the optimal law enforcement strategy has these characteristics:

- *Time frame*: A few days up to a few weeks
- *Goal*: Imprisonment of individuals associated with criminal organizations
- *Forecast*: Chaotic, turbulent, and dynamic criminal environment
- *Change*: Results in quantitative terms
- *Action*: Short-term gain rather than long-term prevention
- *Resources*: Division of labor based on need-to-know management
- *Analysis*: Identifying and solving crimes based on random policing opportunity
- *Decision*: Hierarchical organizational structure

Sector 3: Targeted Policing

In this third sector, police can be in charge of the situation and can prevent and solve crime because they are ahead of criminals in terms of relative knowledge level. Police have a better understanding of security, psychology, technology, and other factors influencing organized crime.

In this sector, we suggest that the optimal law enforcement strategy has these characteristics:

- *Time frame*: A few months up to a few years
- *Goal*: Closedown of criminal enterprises
- *Forecast*: Predictable environment
- *Change*: Results in society quality terms
- *Action*: Focus on criminal organization rather than criminals
- *Resources*: Knowledge management for knowledge sharing and knowledge development
- *Analysis*: Business analysis of criminal enterprises
- *Decision*: Knowledge organization structure

Sector 4: Competitive Policing

In this fourth and final sector, both criminals and police officers work in knowledge organizations characterized by innovative knowledge. Criminal knowledge organizations are able to adapt quickly to new market conditions, law enforcement strategies, customs control procedures, and other factors influencing business performance. Similarly, police knowledge organizations understand criminal business enterprises in terms of their structures, markets, roles, and relationships.

In this sector, we suggest that the optimal law enforcement strategy has these characteristics:

- *Time frame*: From weeks to years
- *Goal*: Limit criminal industries in terms of size in the legal economy
- *Forecast*: Stable environment
- *Change*: Results in quantitative terms
- *Action*: Short-term gain combined with long-term borders for crime
- *Resources*: Knowledge workers
- *Analysis*: Identifying criminal businesses and their performance
- *Decision*: Vertical knowledge-based decision making

Contingent Approach to Policing

The contingent approach to policing organized crime takes into account that policing strategy must be dependent on the relative position in the knowledge war with organized criminals. As such, this chapter has made a contribution to the emerging academic discipline of police science. According to Jaschke et al. (2007, 23),

> Police science is the scientific study of the police as an institution and of policing as a process. As an applied discipline, it combines methods and subjects of other neighboring disciplines within the field of policing. It includes all of what the police do and all aspects from outside that have an impact on policing and public order. Currently it is a working term to describe police studies on the way to an accepted and established discipline. Police science tries to explain facts and acquire knowledge about the reality of policing in order to generalize and to be able to predict possible scenarios.

Core topics of police science include strategies and styles of policing, police organizations and management, and policing specific crime types. This chapter is at the core of police science by studying the serious type of organized crime in the context of policing illegal business entrepreneurship.

Policing criminal business enterprises requires police intelligence and police investigations that is central to police science. Police intelligence has to be based on an implemented intelligence strategy.

This chapter so far has suggested that policing organized crime requires a contingent approach. The relative knowledge between police organizations and criminal organizations determines the optimal policing approach. Both police organizations and criminal organizations were identified as knowledge organizations, where the knowledge levels are core knowledge, advanced knowledge, and innovative knowledge in terms of know what, know how, and know why. Based on the relative knowledge of criminals versus police, four sectors emerge: random policing, disadvantaged policing, targeted policing, and competitive policing. Future research will need to evaluate the sector model and the relevant policing strategies suggested in this chapter.

Case: Social Intelligence and Investigation Service*

In The Netherlands, we find SIOD (the Social Intelligence and Investigation Service). Fighting criminal entrepreneurship is a priority task for SIOD, which defines criminal entrepreneurship as obtaining financial–economic gains through facilitating criminal offenses by delivering goods or services. This not only concerns the criminal entrepreneur who specializes in illegal activities in terms of organized crime, but also the entrepreneur who combines his role of bona fide entrepreneur with that of criminal entrepreneurship that represents forms of organization criminality. The social disturbance resulting from criminal entrepreneurship may take the form of financial damage, but also other forms of damage for society may result from it, such as false competition and human exploitation.

The investigation process of the SIOD is intelligence led. The SIOD deals with social disturbance thematically within the chain of work and income. The SIOD chooses a particular theme, in consultation with policy directorates of the Ministry of Social Affairs and Employment. This takes place on the basis of knowledge of the type, degree, and development of criminal entrepreneurship. Next, this theme is developed into an action plan, in which all investigations and external parties cooperate on this specific theme.

Since the SIOD fights criminal entrepreneurship, they invest in the development of financial and digital expertise. Based on this expertise, the service distinguishes itself as a special police force. It is the purpose of financial and digital investigation to uncover more financial damage and criminal capital and, eventually, recover it.

The SIOD makes knowledge of its employees transparent by registering information in a structured fashion in a centralized database. This should enable better use of available knowledge in the organization for investigation, policy, and analysis. Developing, retaining, and sharing expertise with respect to each investigation of fraud in the social security domain is important for success.

One of the reasons for establishing a special police force within social security was that it was considered desirable to add a final approach of heavy investigation to the regular inspection, control, and light investigation of entrepreneurship in organized crime. The Special Police Forces

---

* This case is based on information on the Web site: www.siod.nl.

Act (Wet op de BOD'en) determines the domain of the SIOD. In this act, and in the Parliamentary discussion of it, the area of activity of the SIOD is described in relation to the role of the special investigation as part of the antifraud measures within the sphere of the Ministry of Social Affairs and Employment.

The domain of the SIOD concerns, in principle, all legislation of the Ministry of Social Affairs and Employment. This mainly concerns subjects in the fields of employee insurance schemes, social assistance (benefits and getting people back to work), and the labor market (employment of illegal aliens, temporary work agencies, and labor market subsidies). In addition, other ministry-related subjects, such as labor conditions, belong to the domain of the SIOD.

Case: Criminal Intelligence Service Alberta*

"At a time when Hells Angels are gathering outside Calgary to celebrate the group's tenth anniversary in Alberta, law enforcement agencies are identifying another gang—the Crazy Dragons—as the province's top criminal threat.

The Criminal Intelligence Service Alberta's annual report, obtained Friday by the Herald, identifies 54 criminal groups of varying sophistication operating in the province.

Four groups are identified as 'mid-level' threats, meaning they have demonstrated some level of sophistication and are linked to multiple criminal groups.

The remaining 50 were classified as 'lower level' threats focused on a limited amount of activities and fewer links to other criminal organizations.

'The most noticeable criminal group in Alberta—with cocaine operations throughout the province as well as in parts of British Columbia, Saskatchewan, and the Northwest Territories—is known to police as the Crazy Dragons,' says the report, a collection of intelligence from Alberta's law enforcement agencies.

In another passage that doesn't refer to the Crazy Dragons by name, the document says nearly every law enforcement agency that contributed to the report has encountered the gang.

'Among competing groups there is one that surpasses all the others with their drug products being provided in some measure to virtually every

---

* This case is based on a newspaper article in the Calgary Herald in Canada entitled "Gangs ranked: Crazy Dragons head list of Alberta crime threats." (von Rassel and Komarnicki, 2007)

reporting city and town, even in the midst of activities by other criminal groups,' the report says.

Nothing is said about any specific activity in Calgary, but police in the past have linked the Crazy Dragons to the deadly feud between two street gangs, Fresh off the Boat (FOB) and FOB Killers (FK).

A previous Criminal Intelligence Service Alberta report said the Crazy Dragons may have supplied guns to one of the gangs. Violence between FOB and FK has killed nine members or associates since 2001.

This year's report said a second group, led by a Vietnamese organized crime figure, 'is involved in the large-scale production of marihuana [sic] in southern Alberta.'

The report bleakly predicts the province's booming economy will allow organized crime groups to maintain their grip on the underworld while police deal with the fallout among the working poor and drug addicted.

'It is suggested the bulk of police intervention will become increasingly necessary at the street level where social network breakdowns (domestic and labor-related) as well as competition among lower level criminals will manifest themselves with greater frequency,' reads the report.

The Hells Angels, meanwhile, are identified as being involved in the street-level drug trade.

The worldwide biker gang arrived in Alberta 10 years ago when it took over locally based independent gangs such as the Grim Reapers in Calgary.

Despite that history and three chapters in Alberta—Calgary, Edmonton, and a 'Nomad' chapter based in Red Deer—Criminal Intelligence Service Alberta says the gang has failed to make significant inroads in the province's criminal underworld.

'Without making light of their propensity for extreme violence—augmented by loyalty to the club's name—members of the Hells Angels continue to lack in criminal business savvy,' the report says.

'They have proven themselves to be an available source of 'muscle' either for their own endeavors or for other criminal organizations. They are preoccupied with the supremacy of their name within the criminal biker sub-culture.'

The Hells Angels' Calgary chapter has suffered some highly publicized setbacks, notably having to abandon a fortified clubhouse under construction in Bowness because it violated building codes.

The chapter's then-president, Ken Szczerba, was jailed in 2001 for trying to arrange a plot to bomb the homes of Ald. Dale Hodges and a community activist involved in getting construction halted.

Nevertheless, police agencies underestimate the Hells Angels in this province at their peril, said the author of several books on the gang.

'They weren't the best and brightest of the bikers, but they're still part of an international organization and they're dangerous,' said Yves Lavigne.

More than 50 Hells Angels from different chapters pulled up to the local clubhouse southeast of Calgary Friday evening as RCMP cruisers patrolled nearby roads.

Neighbor Nancy Gunn said the motorcycle gang has met at the clubhouse next door before, and she's never had any concerns.

'Rush hour traffic is worse than having a few bikes go by,' she said.

Monitoring Hells Angels parties has dubious value, Lavigne added, considering they take great care to behave in public.

'When the Hells Angels socialize, they know they're under scrutiny,' he said.

Although there are only three chapters in Alberta, the Hells Angels involvement in the drug trade is widespread, said Lavigne.

'Who do you think supplies Fort McMurray and Grande Prairie?'

Those boomtowns are evidence Alberta's robust economy has a downside, Criminal Intelligence Service Alberta says—growing demand for illegal drugs that will enrich organized crime groups and stretch police resources.

'The problems associated with harmful lifestyle choices facilitated by increased incomes may predominate law enforcement attention,' the report says."

References

Aidis, R. and von Praag, M. 2004. *Illegal entrepreneurship experience*. Tinbergen Institute Discussion paper TI 2004-105/3, Erasmus University, Rotterdam, The Netherlands.

Albanese, J.S. 2004. *Organized crime in our times*, 4th ed. Cincinnati, OH: LexisNexis, Anderson Publishing, LexisNexis Group.

Baer, M.H. 2008. Corporate policing and corporate governance: What can we learn from Hewlett-Packard's pretexting scandal? New York University Public Law and Legal Theory Working Paper 73, New York University School of Law, New York City.

Bennet, A. and Bennet, D. 2005a. Designing the knowledge organization of the future: The intelligent complex adaptive system. In *Handbook of knowledge management*, Vol. 2, Ed. C.W. Holsapple, 623–638. Dordrecht, The Netherlands: Springer Science & Business Media.

Bennet, D. and Bennet, A. (2005b). The rise of the knowledge organization. In *Handbook of knowledge management*, Ed. C.W. Holsapple, 5–20. Dordrecht, The Netherlands: Springer Science & Business Media.

Bock, G.W., Zmud, R.W., and Kim, Y.G. 2005. Behavioral intention formation in knowledge sharing: Examining the roles of extrinsic motivators, social-psychological forces, and organizational climate. *MIS Quarterly* 29 (1): 87–111.

Brown, J.S. and Duguid, P. 2001. Knowledge and organization: A social-practice perspective. *Organization Science* 12 (2): 198–213.

Brown, S.D. 2007. The meaning of criminal intelligence. *International Journal of Police Science & Management* 9 (4): 336–340.

Centrex. 2005. *Guidance on the national intelligence model*. Centrex, National Centre for Policing Excellence, Bedford, U.K.

ERA. 2008. *Combating fraud and financial crime.* Trier, Germany: Academy of European Law, online at www.era.int.

Felsen, D. and Kalaitzidis, A. 2005. A historical overview of transnational crime. In *Handbook of transnational crime and justice,* Ed. P. Reichel, 3–19. London: Sage Publications..

Garud, R. and Kumaraswamy, A. 2005. Vicious and virtuous circles in the management of knowledge: the case of Infosys Technologies. *MIS Quarterly* 29 (1): 9–33.

Gill, M. 2001. The craft of robbers of cash-in-transit vans: Crime facilitators and the entrepreneurial approach. *International Journal of the Sociology of Law* 29: 277–291.

Jaschke, H.G., Bjørgo, T., del Romero, F.B., Kwanten, C., Mawby, R., and Pogan, M. 2007. *Perspectives of police science in Europe.* Final report, European Police College, CEPOL, Collège Européen de Police, Hampshire, England.

Kark, R. and van Dijk, D. 2007. Motivation to lead, motivation to follow: The role of the self-regulatory focus in leadership processes. *Academy of Management Review* 32 (2): 500–528.

Laise, D., Migliarese, P., and Verteremo, S. 2005. Knowledge organization design: A diagnostic tool. *Human Systems Management* 24: 121–131.

Lassen, C., Laugen, B.T., and Næss, P. 2006. Virtual mobility and organizational reality: A note on the mobility needs in knowledge organizations. *Transportation Research* Part D, 11: 459–463.

Liebowitz, J. 2004. Will knowledge management work in the government? *Electronic Government: An International Journal* 1 (1): 1–7.

Liu, C.C. and Chen, S.Y. 2005. Determinants of knowledge sharing of e-learners. *International Journal of Innovation and Learning* 2 (4): 434–445.

Nonaka, I., Toyama, R., and Konno, N. 2000. SECI, ba and leadership: A unified model of dynamic knowledge creation. *Long Range Planning* 33 (1): 5–34.

Poston, R.S. and Speier, C. 2005. Effective use of knowledge management systems: A process model of content ratings and credibility indicators. *MIS Quarterly* 29 (2): 221–244.

Smith, H.L. 2003. Knowledge organization and local economic development: The cases of Oxford and Grenoble. *Regional Studies* 37 (9): 899–909.

Staring, R. 2008. Controlling human smuggling in the Netherlands: How the smuggling of human beings was transformed into a serious criminal offence. In *Organized crime: Culture, markets and policies,* Eds. D. Siegel and H. Nelen, 165–181. New York: Springer-Verlag.

Taylor, A. and Greve, H.R. 2006. Superman or the fantastic four? Knowledge combination and experience in innovative teams. *Academy of Management Journal* 49 (4): 723–740.

Tiwana, A. 2002. *The knowledge management toolkit: Practical techniques for building a knowledge management system,* 2nd ed. Upper Saddle River, NJ: Prentice Hall.

Turner, K.L. and Makhija, M.V. 2006. The role of organizational controls in managing knowledge. *Academy of Management Review* 31 (1): 197–217.

Uretsky, M. 2001. Preparing for the real knowledge organization. *Journal of Organizational Excellence* 21 (1): 87–93.

von Rassel, J. and Komarnicki, J. 2007. Gangs ranked: Crazy Dragons head list of Alberta crime threats. *Calgary Herald*, Saturday, July 21.

Wasko, M.M. and Faraj, S. 2005. Why should I share? Examining social capital and knowledge contribution in electronic networks of practice. *MIS Quarterly* 29 (1): 35–57.

Zack, M.H. 1999. Developing a knowledge strategy. *California Management Review* 41 (3): 125–145.

Policing Criminal Enterprises

11

Policing organized crime remains problematic. Harfield (2008) found that organized crime challenges long-held paradigms about policing delivery infrastructure and whether law enforcement (as opposed to other policing and regulatory interventions) is the most effective way of dealing with organized crime. Perceptions of organized crime have changed. It is now often viewed in terms of preventing harm caused rather than automatically prosecuting criminality.

With the creation of the Serious Organized Crime Agency (SOCA) in the United Kingdom, for example, government, in essence, is suggesting that organized crime has developed to become an issue beyond the competence of conventional policing. Policing organized crime has become a resource-intensive, technology-dependent, specialist skill activity, which challenges capacity and capability in organizations that are characterized more by bureaucracy than a knowledge organization of structure and culture. Techniques lawfully available when policing organized crime include human, audio and video surveillance, and the use of covert human intelligence sources, such as infiltration by undercover officers and the gathering of intelligence through informants (Harfield, 2008).

Given the making-money motivation based on the enterprise paradigm in organized crime, it seems like an obvious step to divest organized criminals of their ill gotten proceeds (Beare and Martens, 1998, 415).

> If taking the profit out of crime is a legitimate goal of law enforcement, it then seems only logical that criminal organizations that have the most assets as a result of their illegal endeavors should be high on the list of priorities.

Law enforcement agencies need advanced knowledge about crimes and criminal organizations to fight organized crime successfully. In addition, they need knowledge of tools for analysis of organized crime. For example, geographic information systems (GIS) can help identify hotspots and simulate activities of criminal organizations.

Knowledge Support Systems

The effective use of information in knowledge work is at the heart of successful policing (Home Office, 2008, 42).

> The analysis of information about offences and offenders enables investigation, analysis of crime patterns determines deployment and planning, good communication with the public is the basis of reassurance and can provide vital intelligence about criminal activity. Officers who are able to access accurate, timely information in an efficient way can deliver better service and achieve better outcomes.

The achievements and considerable investment in police information technology over the past decade has to be recognized. That investment has given the police service a number of capabilities. These include DNA database and fingerprint identification systems that support law enforcement.

The use of GIS by crime analysts in law enforcement is growing. In England and Wales, Weir and Bangs (2007) report that the large majority of crime analysts surveyed used GIS in their analysis, which, when used in crime reduction and community safety, can extend beyond crime data alone. Analysts make use of a large number of multiagency datasets in order to better understand crime problems and more effectively target interventions. Similarly, Johnson et al. (2007) report the use of GIS in crime mapping, where they found that crime (burglary and other types) develops clusters in space and time.

In the United States, the Shelby Police Department in North Carolina has built a GIS-based ComputerStatistics (CompuStat) system using ESRI ARcGIS® software that is helping to lower crime rates and better share information. Map-based tools help the agency see exactly where crimes have been reported and effectively respond to events in a dynamic fashion. The department implemented ESRI software-based Crime Analysis Tools® (CAT), an ArcGIS extension that analyzes crime patterns and calls for service. Viewing and analyzing incidents by crime type and on a weekly, monthly, and annual basis helps commanders comb through volumes of data stored in record management systems. They use GIS to look at district breakdowns of reported incidents, repeat calls, and areas where particular crimes have spiked above average. These analyses help district managers compare and contrast what is happening in other districts. Spatial analysis is used for all types of crimes, including homicide, sexual assault, robbery, larceny, and car theft. The query results, once visualized on a map, are then shared agency-wide.

A strategic move that makes prevention, detection, and repression of organized crime more effective has to do with strengthening the technological capabilities of the police force. When Italian police launched their recent anti-Mafia strategies, funding was provided for information and communication technology in terms of an integrated system of satellite telecommunication, modern sensors located in the area, and operative interconnected control rooms (Spina, 2008, 203).

A targeted and effective use of new technologies can be devastating to [M]afia activities. "Men of honor" usually speak very little, but they cannot avoid a certain amount of crucial communication, both between themselves as well as with their victims. In the past (and often still today) the [M]afia moved without anybody seeing or hearing anything, but if phone calls and conversations can be tapped and acts can be filmed, there is no need for witnesses anymore, and the work of [M]afia men becomes much more difficult. As is well known, Bernardo Provenzano—the boss of all bosses in Cosa Nostra—used an archaic medium (small slips of paper, so called pizzini), to avoid interception. But even small sheets need "postmen" to deliver them and postmen can be detected. Provenzano was caught in April 2006, after having spent more than 40 years on the run, because the police were able to monitor his relatives and the people who brought him clean underwear.

Another example of information and communication technology in intelligence and analysis is network analysis. Xu and Chen (2004) demonstrate how network analysis might be applied by using shortest path algorithms to identify associations in criminal networks. Effective and efficient link analysis techniques are needed to help law enforcement and intelligence agencies fight organized crimes, such as narcotics violation, terrorism, and kidnapping.

Knowledge organizations apply knowledge management systems in their knowledge work. Several knowledge management systems support detectives. One example is geographic information systems. In Sweden, the Hobit system is a geographic occurrences and crime information system used within the Swedish police. The system gives the police an improved opportunity to map out crimes. When and where crimes are committed can be processed and sought out much faster thanks to this new system.

Knowledge management is concerned with simplifying and improving the process of sharing, distributing, creating, capturing, and understanding knowledge. Information technology can play an important role in successful knowledge management initiatives. The extent of information technology can be defined in terms of growth stages for knowledge management systems.

A model consisting of four stages—officer-to-technology systems, officer-to-officer systems, officer-to-information systems, and officer-to-application systems—is discussed below (Figure 11.1).

Office-to-Technology Systems: Stage 1

In this stage, tools for end users are made available to knowledge workers. In the simplest stage, this means a capable networked PC on every desk or in every briefcase with standardized personal productivity tools (word processing, presentation software, etc.), so that documents can be exchanged easily throughout a company. More complex and functional desktop infrastructures can also be the basis for the same types of knowledge support. Stage 1 is recognized by widespread dissemination and use of end-user tools among

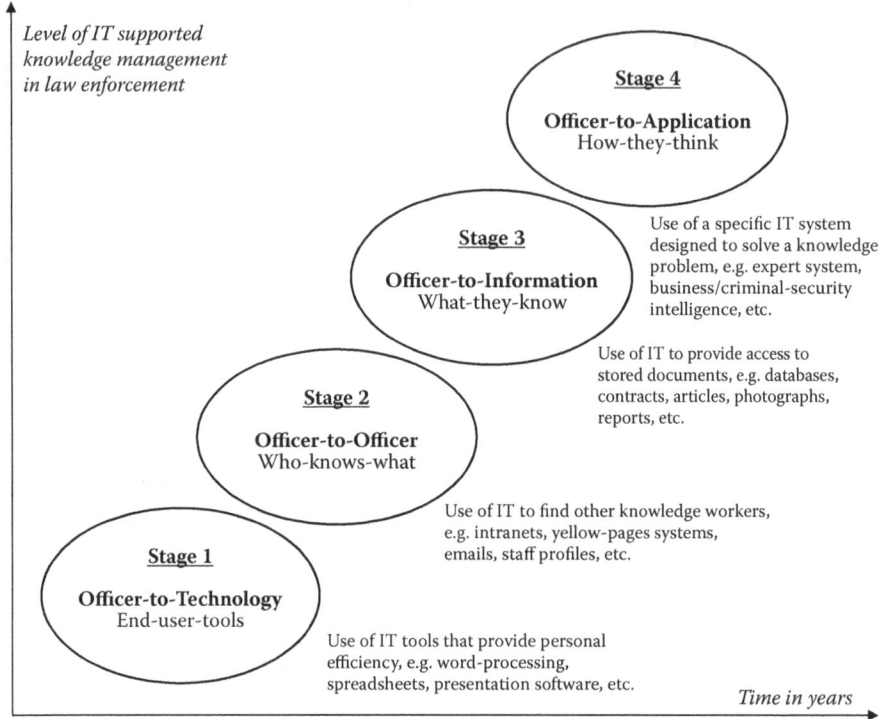

Figure 11.1 The knowledge management system's stage model for police intelligence.

knowledge workers in the company. For example, lawyers in a law firm will in this stage use word processing, spreadsheets, legal databases, presentation software, and scheduling programs.

Related to the new changes in computer technology is the transformation that has occurred in report writing and recordkeeping in police investigations. Every police activity or crime incident demands a report on some kind of form. The majority of police patrol reports written before 1975 were handwritten.

Today, officers can write reports on small notebook computers located in the front seat of the patrol unit; disks are handed in at the end of the shift for hard copy needs. Cursor keys and spell check functions in these report programs are useful, timesaving features.

An example of an officer-to-technology system is the Major Incident Policy Document in the United Kingdom (Home Office, 2005b). This document is maintained whenever a Major Incident Room using HOLMES (Home Office large major enquiry system) is in operation. Decisions, which should be recorded, are those that affect the practical or administrative features of the enquiry, and each entry must clearly show the reasoning for the decision.

When the HOLMES is used, the senior investigative officer (SIO) directs which policy decisions are recorded on the system.

The basic information entered into HOLMES includes location of incident, data and time of incident, victim(s), senior investigating officer, and date enquiry commenced. During the enquiry, which has been run on the HOLMES, a closing report is prepared and registered as another document linked to a category of Closing Report. The report will contain the following information: introduction, scene, the victim, and miscellaneous.

Stage 1 can be labeled *end user tools* or *people-to-technology* as information technology provides knowledge workers with tools that improve personal efficiency.

Officer-to-Officer Systems: Stage 2

This stage concerns information about who knows what knowledge is made available to all people in the firm and to selected outside partners. Search engines should enable work with a thesaurus because some expertise terminology may not always match the terms the expert uses to classify that expertise. The creation of corporate directories, also referred to as the mapping of internal expertise, is a common application of knowledge management technology. Because much knowledge in an organization remains noncodified, mapping the internal expertise is a potentially useful application of technology to enable easy identification of knowledgeable persons.

Here we find the cartographic school of knowledge management (Earl, 2001), which is concerned with mapping organizational knowledge. It aims to record and disclose who in the organization knows what by building knowledge directories. Often called Yellow Pages, the principal idea is to make sure knowledgeable people in the organization are accessible to others for advice, consultation, or knowledge exchange. Knowledge-oriented directories are not so much repositories of knowledge-based information as gateways to knowledge, and the knowledge is as likely to be tacit as explicit.

At stage 2, firms apply the personalization strategy in knowledge management. According to Hansen et al. (1999), the personalization strategy implies that knowledge is tied to the person who developed it and is shared mainly through direct person-to-person contact. This strategy focuses on dialog between individuals; knowledge is transferred mainly in personal e-mail, meetings, and one-on-one conversations.

Electronic networks of practice are computer-mediated discussion forums focused on problems of practice that enable individuals to exchange advice and ideas with others based on common interests. Electronic networks have been found to support organizational knowledge flows between geographically dispersed co-workers and distributed research and development efforts. These networks also assist cooperative open-source software development and open congregation on the Internet for individuals interested in a specific practice. Electronic networks make it possible to share information quickly, globally, and with large numbers of individuals (Wasko and Faraj, 2005).

Communication competence is important at stage 2. Communication competence is the ability to demonstrate skills in the appropriate communication behavior to effectively achieve one's goals. Communication between individuals requires both the decoding and encoding of messages (Ko et al., 2005). Lin et al. (2005) found that knowledge transfer depends on the completeness or incompleteness of the sender's and the receiver's information sets.

The dramatic reduction in electronic communication costs and ease of computer-to-computer linkages has resulted in opportunities to create new channel structures, fueling interest in interorganizational systems. These systems are planned and managed ventures to develop and use information technology (IT)-based information exchange systems to support collaboration and strategic alliances between otherwise independent actors. These systems allow for the exchange of information between partners for the purpose of coordination, communication, and cooperation.

While the access to organizational information and communication of knowledge with distant colleagues through mobile technology is a common phenomenon in the business world, the police have a long tradition of supporting geographically distributed work through the employment of state-of-the-art mobile technologies as well.

The typical system at stage 2 of knowledge management technology in police investigations is the intranet. Intranets provide a rich set of tools for creating collaborative environments in which members of an organization can exchange ideas, share information, and work together on common projects and assignments regardless of their physical location. Information from many different sources and media, including text, graphics, video, audio, and even digital slides can be displayed, shared, and accessed across an enterprise through a simple common interface.

Stage 2 can be labeled *who knows what* or *people-to-people* as knowledge workers use information technology to find other knowledge workers.

Office-to-Information Systems: Stage 3

In this stage, information from knowledge workers is stored and made available to everyone in the firm and to designated external partners. Data-mining techniques can be applied here to find relevant information and combine information in data warehouses (Srinivasa et al., 2007, 4295).

Data mining is a process of extracting nontrivial, valid, novel, and useful information from large databases. Hence, data mining can be viewed as a kind of search for meaningful patterns or rules from a large search space that is the database.

However, data mining as in any other computer software has limitations Lind et al. (2007).

Whenever huge masses of personal data are stored at one place, and especially when tied to a system with the intelligence to tailor this data, there is enormous privacy risk. The idea is that strict access control surround the data. Will that be the case? We can only hope. We see a risk of abuse from corrupted personnel and from hackers or other intruders. Also, there is a risk that data [may] be overly interpreted as true, and that end users be wrongly accused. With the ease in accessing and perhaps performing data mining on huge amounts of personal data, the risk that a police investigation might take the wrong turn is much greater.

On a broader basis, search engines are Web browsers and server software that operate with a thesaurus because the terminology in which expertise is sought may not always match the terms used by the expert to classify that expertise.

An essential contribution that IT can make is the provision of shared databases across tasks, levels, entities, and geographies to all knowledge workers throughout a process (Earl, 2001). For example, Infosys Technologies—a $3.2 billion Indian company with over 100,000 employees and globally distributed operations—created a central knowledge portal called KShop. The content of KShop was organized into different content types, for instance, case studies, reusable artifacts, and downloadable software. Every knowledge asset under a content type was associated with one or more nodes (representing areas of discourse) in a knowledge hierarchy or taxonomy (Garud and Kumaraswamy, 2005).

Sifting though the myriad content available through knowledge management systems can be challenging, and knowledge workers may be overwhelmed when trying to find the most relevant content for completing a new task. To address this problem, system designers often include rating schemes and credibility indicators to improve users' search and evaluation of knowledge management system content (Poston and Speier, 2005).

An enterprise information portal is viewed as a knowledge community. Enterprise information portals are of multiple forms, ranging from Internet-based data management tools that bring visibility to previously dormant data so that their users can compare, analyze, and share enterprise information to a knowledge portal, which enables its users to obtain specialized knowledge that is related to their specific tasks.

Electronic knowledge repositories are electronic stores of content acquired about all subjects for which the organization has decided to maintain knowledge. Such repositories can comprise multiple knowledge bases as well as the mechanisms for acquisition, control, and publication of the knowledge. The process of knowledge sharing through electronic knowledge repositories involves people contributing knowledge to populate repositories (e.g., customer and supplier knowledge, industry best practices, and product expertise) and people seeking knowledge from repositories for use.

Individuals' knowledge does not transform easily into organizational knowledge even with the implementation of knowledge repositories. According to Bock et al. (2005), individuals tend to hoard knowledge for various reasons. Empirical studies have shown that the greater the anticipated reciprocal relationships are, the more favorable the attitude toward knowledge sharing will be.

In stage 3, firms apply the codification strategy in knowledge management. According to Hansen et al. (1999), the codification strategy centers on information technology: Knowledge is carefully codified and stored in knowledge databases and can be accessed and used by anyone. With a codification strategy, knowledge is extracted from the person who developed it, is made independent from that person, and stored in the form of interview guides, work schedules, benchmark data, etc., and then searched and retrieved and used by many employees.

Two examples of knowledge management systems at stage 3 in law enforcement are COPLINK° and geodemographics. COPLINK has a relational database system for crime-specific cases, such as gang-related incidents and serious crimes, such as homicide, aggravated assault, and sexual crimes. Deliberately targeting these criminal areas allows a manageable amount of information to be entered into a database (Chen et al., 2002). Geodemographic profiles of the characteristics of individuals and small areas are central to efficient and effective deployment of law enforcement resources. Geocomputation is based on GISs.

Stage 3 can be labeled *what they know* or *people-to-docs* as information technology provides knowledge workers with access to information that is typically stored in documents. Examples of documents are contracts and agreements, reports, manuals and handbooks, business forms, letters, memos, articles, drawings, blueprints, photographs, e-mail and voice mail messages, video clips, script and visuals from presentations, policy statements, computer printouts, and transcripts from meetings.

At stage 3, police management gets access to electronic information that can be used for managing police performance. At this stage, sufficient information is electronically stored to apply performance management systems. An example of such a system is iQuanta in the United Kingdom, which is a Web-based data analysis tool that provides its users with easy access to unified policing performance information based on common data and agreed analysis. iQuanta arose from a system developed to provide the Home Office with accurate and timely assessment of police performance at different organizational levels. The system iQuanta supports the comparison of performance in three main ways: (1) comparison with peers (similar areas elsewhere), (2) comparison across time, and (3) progress toward targets/direction of travel (Home Office, 2005a).

Another example from the United Kingdom is the CORA system. CORA (Crime Objective Results and Analysis) is implemented at the Lancashire Police for performance management. CORA provides access to crime and detection data at several organizational levels. Several comparisons and forecasts are made and presented using a variety of different graphical displays. Navigation between views and drilling into the data is a matter of on-screen button presses. Printable versions of the views have been predefined (Home Office, 2005a).

Officer-to-Application Systems: Stage 4

In stage 4, information systems solving knowledge problems are made available to knowledge workers and solution seekers. Artificial intelligence is applied in these systems. For example, neural networks are statistically oriented tools that excel at using data to classify cases into one category or another. Another example is expert systems that can enable the knowledge of one or a few experts to be used by a much broader group of workers requiring the knowledge. Officer-to-application systems will only be successful if they are built on a thorough understanding of law enforcement.

Artificial intelligence (AI) is an area of computer science that endeavors to build machines exhibiting human-like cognitive capabilities. Most modern AI systems are founded on the realization that intelligence is tightly intertwined with knowledge. Knowledge is associated with the symbols we manipulate.

Knowledge-based systems deal with solving problems by exercising knowledge. The most important parts of these systems are the knowledge base and the inference engine. The former holds the domain-specific knowledge, whereas the latter contains the functions to exercise the knowledge in the knowledge base. Knowledge can be represented as either rules or frames. Rules are a natural choice for representing conditional knowledge, which is in the form of "if–when" statements. Inference engines supply the motive power to the knowledge. There are several ways to exercise knowledge, depending on the nature of the knowledge. For example, backward-chaining systems work backward from the conclusions to the inputs. These systems attempt to validate the conclusions by finding evidence to support them. In law enforcement, this is an important system feature, as evidence determines whether a person is charged or not for a crime.

Case-based reasoning systems are a different way to represent knowledge through explicit historical cases. This approach differs from the rule-based approach because the knowledge is not complied and interpreted by an expert. Instead, the experiences that possibly shaped the expert's knowledge are directly used to make decisions. Learning is an important issue in case-based reasoning because with the mere addition of new cases to the library, the system learns. In law enforcement, police officers are looking for similar cases to learn how they were handled in the past, making case-based reasoning systems an attractive application in policing.

Use of expert systems in law enforcement includes systems that attempt to aid in information retrieval by drawing upon human heuristics or rules and procedures to investigate tasks. The AICAMS (artificial intelligence crime analysis management system) project is a knowledge-based system for identifying suspects, which was developed by Prof. K.P. Lam of the Chinese University of Hong Kong. AICAMS also includes a component to fulfill the needs for a simple but effective facial identification procedure based on a library of facial components. The system provides a capability for assembling an infinite number of possible facial composites by varying the position and size of the components. AICAMS also provides a geomapping component by incorporating a map-based user interface (Chen et al., 2002).

Another example is the SSMT (Scientific Support Modeling Tool) in the United Kingdom. This tool is aimed at enabling rapid process analysis and improvement of scientific support processes. The SSMT comprises two linked modules. First, the identification module covers the process from scene attendance through to generating a fingerprint or DNA match. Next, the detections module covers the steps after an identification has been generated through to detection of the crime. SSMT is a simulation tool applied to different situations, such as testing the impact of alternative scene attendance policies on resource requirements and identifying bottlenecks in the process (Home Office, 2005a).

Stage 4 can be labeled *how they think* or *people-to-systems* where the system is intended to help solve a knowledge problem.

Improving Knowledge Support

Information technology to support knowledge work of police officers is improving (Hughes and Jackson, 2004). For example, new information systems supporting police investigations are evolving. Police investigation is an information-rich (Fahsing et al., 2004) and knowledge-intensive practice (Chen, et al., 2002; Sheptycki, 2002). Its success depends on turning information into evidence. However, the process of turning information into evidence is neither simple nor straightforward. The raw information that is gathered through the investigative process is often required to be transformed into usable knowledge before its value as potential evidence can be realized

(Hughes and Jackson, 2004). Hence, in an investigative context, knowledge acts as an intervening variable in this transformative process of converting information via knowledge into evidence.

Decision Chart for Crime Investigation

Policing organized crime requires a structured, yet flexible procedure as illustrated in the organized crime investigation flow chart in Figure 11.2. It represents a checklist in a certain sequence to determine whether it is organized crime as well as the crime severity. A distinction is made between absolute requirements and questions guiding the investigation.

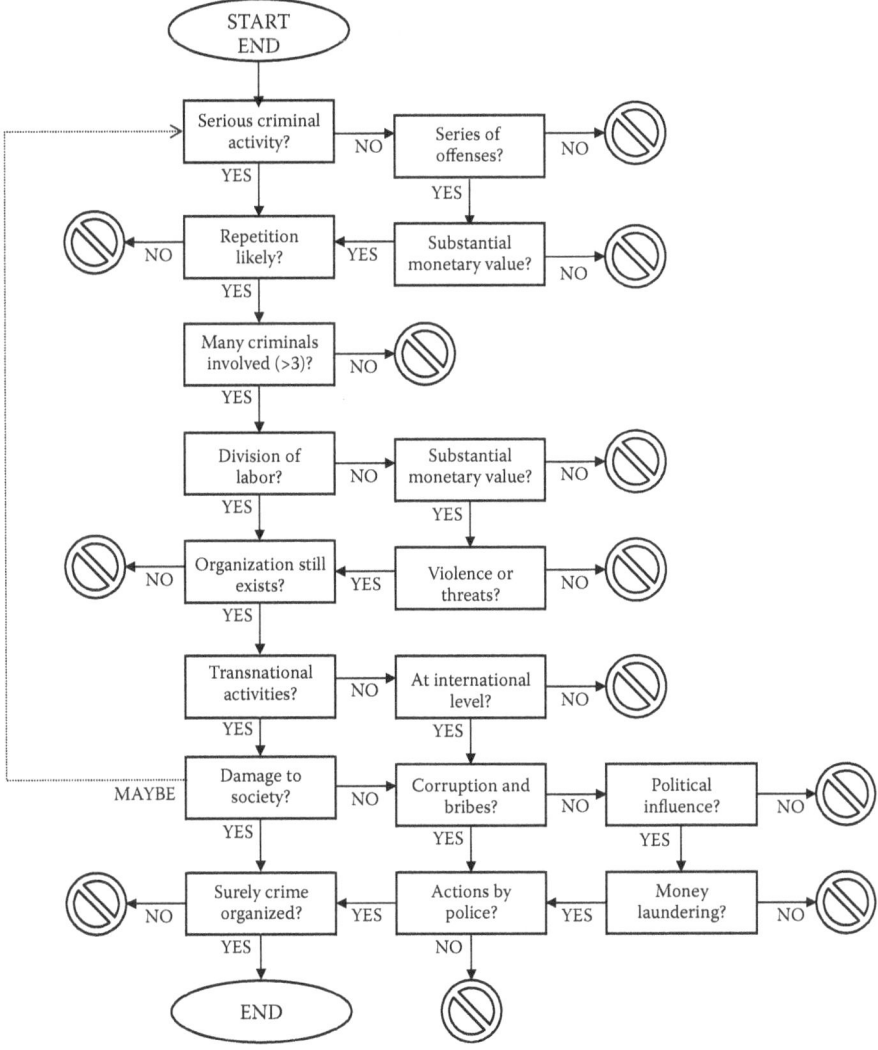

Figure 11.2 Organized crime investigation flow chart.

A flow chart is a schematic representation of an algorithm or a process. A flow chart also is a method to monitor a process. It typically has a start and an end. Arrows represent flow of control, while boxes represent processing steps. In the flow chart, each processing step results in a conditional question, where Yes and No are alternative answers leading to different paths in the flow chart.

The first question—"Serious criminal activity?"—refers to a single incident, where a No answer would lead to the next question: "Series of offenses?" A Yes answer would lead to the question: "Repetition likely?" This initial decision sequence in the flow diagram indicates that either one, single criminal activity is serious or there is a series of minor offenses for one to move on in the diagram. Exit from the diagram will occur if there is only a single, minor criminal activity. Exits are indicated by a circular symbol.

The proposed flow chart is not universal. Rather, it is contingent on expertise and situation. Experts in law enforcement in a country or region may have different decision texts in the decision boxes. We do not argue with them, as the text in the boxes in our flow chart represents *examples* of Yes–No decision points rather than a universal template.

Therefore, our idea is to present the flow chart approach in general to law enforcement. Because of the definitional problems of organized crime and criminal organizations that have plagued both theory and practice for several decades, the flow chart represents an alternative approach to identify organized crime in a structured and sequential fashion.

If we start randomly in the middle of the flow chart at "Violence or threats?" (assuming that the investigation of a criminal activity has led to this decision point), a No answer would lead to termination in the sense of rejecting the organized crime hypothesis. On the other hand, a Yes answer would maintain the organized crime hypothesis into the next decision question—"Organization still exists?"—meaning the existence of involved criminals still being active.

At the end of the flow chart, the final control question is phrased: "Surely organized crime?" If the answer is Yes, investigators might be completely sure that the initial crime observed is part of organized crime by a criminal organization.

Road Map for Law Enforcement

In addition to the flow chart determining the extent and severity of organized crime, there is a need for a systematic approach to fight organized crime by law enforcement. We call it a road map, where law enforcement starts by determining an ambition level for policing organized crime. An extreme, ultimate ambition would be to prevent organized crime from developing into criminal organizations, as illustrated in Figure 11.3.

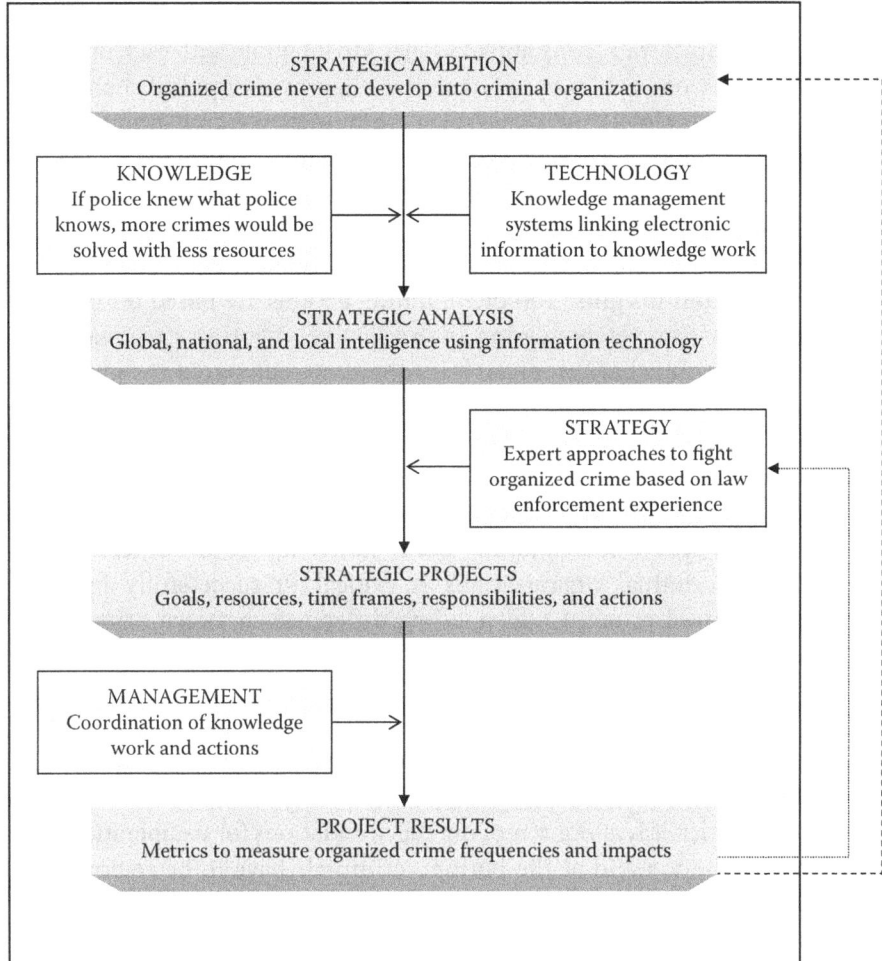

Figure 11.3 Law enforcement road map.

A road map represents a diagnostic- and assessment-based framework for consolidating efforts, reflecting the collective engagement experiences of all law enforcement stakeholders. A road map is a visual representation of phases and factors in a plan. The road map for fighting organized crime consists of four phases, and it is characterized by four critical success factors. The four phases are:

1. *Ambition phase.* The strategic ambition phase is where politicians and executive police management develop a strategy to fight organized crime. Several documents may result in this phase. For example, the government may supply the Parliament with a document where the issues and priorities are lined up. Often, such a document is so generally formulated that it is of little value to policing. However, the political document might be followed by a more specific document by the Police Directorate formulating goals and local documents in

police districts formulating actions. The different document levels—politics, directorate, constabulary—need to integrate with each other, which they often do not do. To secure alignment of political ambitions, criminology ambitions, social ambitions, policing ambitions, and other ambitions related to organized crime, alignment mechanisms, such as content analysis, milestones, goals, and evaluations, should be institutionalized.

2. *Analysis phase.* The strategic analysis phase is concerned with understanding and insights. Too often, failing actions are based on fragmented or completely missing analysis. When fighting street gangs based on ethnic backgrounds, it is sometimes compared to fighting local Hells Angels chapters. Nothing could be more wrong. While street gangs have to be understood in a context of temporary and dynamically changing relationships and finances, motorcycle club (MC) groups have to be understood as more permanent structures and finances. Understanding both similarities and differences between criminal organizations is critical in successfully fighting organized crime. Understanding differences between criminal industries, such as commerce versus robbery, is crucial in selecting appropriate and contingent policing actions.

3. *Project phase.* Before moving into operations, policing actions should be organized as projects. Fighting a criminal organization successfully is normally not a matter of quick policing raids and interrogations. Rather, it is about removing the foundations for its operations. Both at the top and at the bottom, criminals have to be removed. Valuables belonging to the criminal organization have to be removed, and the markets, on which it operates, have to be closed down. To coordinate such a diversity of actions, a project structure should be put in place. A project has a goal, it is a coordinated undertaking of interrelated activities, it has limited duration, and it is unique in the sense of fighting a specific criminal organization or a specific kind of organized crime.

4. *Evaluation phase.* In the evaluation phase, project results are evaluated. Evaluation does not have to wait until the project duration is expired. Rather, all major deviations from a project plan should be studied. If the goal was to close down a criminal Hells Angels MC chapter in one city, and this goal was achieved, it may not be satisfactory if a new chapter is established in another city with the same gang members. Therefore, one needs not only to look at project goals, but also at ambitions from the ambition phase when evaluating project performance, as the project is just one stone in building a safe and noncriminal society.

The road map consists of four critical success factors:

1. *Knowledge.* Basic knowledge in policing includes criminology, psychology, sociology, and law. To fight organized crime, required knowledge includes management science, organizational theory, accounting, finance, and business administration.
2. *Technology.* Information systems have to be available to both analysts and project participants. Systems should cover all four stages in the knowledge management technology stage model: officer-to-tools systems, officer-to-officer systems, officer-to-information systems, and officer-to-application systems. For example, GISs with information from various sources might be combined into a complete picture of activities for simulation and prediction of organized crime.
4. *Strategy.* Based on experience, police officers have an understanding of what works and what does not work. Strategy is about approaches that work. For example, the national intelligence model in the United Kingdom represents a collection of approaches based on experience. Strategy is here a choice of approaches to fighting organized crime, where the choice is a selection from a wider set of alternatives.
4. *Management.* Leadership is required to coordinate knowledge work and policing actions when fighting organized crime. Management is about both individuals and tasks. Individuals may be both experts and newcomers who are in need of very different kinds of coaching and feedback. Tasks may be both small and large, which are in need of very different kinds of planning and evaluation.

Knowledge Matrix with Categories and Levels

The types of knowledge involved in the practice of law enforcement can be categorized as administrative, policing, legal, procedural, and analytical knowledge (Gottschalk, 2007).

- *Administrative knowledge* is knowledge about the operations of the crime areas, offices, services, locations, uniforms, budgets, and statistics.
- *Policing knowledge* is knowledge about actions, behavior, procedures, and rules.
- *Legal knowledge* is knowledge of the law and court rulings.
- *Procedural knowledge* is knowledge of evidence and rights of suspects.
- *Analytical knowledge* is knowledge of investigative behavior, including investigative thinking styles.

Distinctions can be made between core, advanced, and innovative knowledge. These knowledge categories indicate different levels of knowledge sophistication (Gottschalk, 2007).

- *Core knowledge* is that minimum scope and level of knowledge required for daily operations.
- *Advanced knowledge* enables an intelligence unit to be competitively viable.
- *Innovative knowledge* is the knowledge that enables the intelligence unit to take the lead in the police district or force.

To identify knowledge needs in policing, we can combine knowledge levels with knowledge categories. Core knowledge, advanced knowledge, and innovative knowledge are combined with administrative knowledge, policing knowledge, legal knowledge, procedural knowledge, and analytical knowledge, as illustrated in Table 11.1.

Knowledge-Based Systems

The use of knowledge-based systems in intelligence and analysis has always been somewhat limited. One reason for the limited use might be that these systems often bring along changes. These changes can be limited to adaptation of working methods and procedures, but structural changes might also be unavoidable. Changes can cause uncertainty among knowledge workers, such as intelligence officers and detectives. This uncertainty, for example, could be related to possible future shifts in the balance of power between office workers and patrolling officers.

Table 11.1 Knowledge Matrix to Identify Knowledge Needs in Police Intelligence

Levels Categories	Core Knowledge	Advanced Knowledge	Innovative Knowledge
Administrative Knowledge			
Policing Knowledge			
Legal Knowledge			
Procedural Knowledge			
Analytical Knowledge			

Knowledge-based policing systems are systems that represent knowledge relevant to law enforcement, usually combined with knowledge of methods and processes of a specific police domain. These systems are capable of executing or supporting (some segments) of police tasks, using the available knowledge representations in terms of data and information in the systems. Two well-known classes of knowledge-based systems are rule-based systems and case-based reasoning systems.

In a rule-based system, knowledge is represented and stored in the form of police rules. These rules often have the form of action rules, which are sets of conditions and connected actions. A rule says that if a certain situation occurs, or a certain condition occurs, then a specific action is to be executed. By reasoning, with rules the knowledge-based system can answer intelligence and other police questions. Rule-based systems offer the possibility to store and apply well-defined procedures within an organization. Besides legal, policing, and intelligence rules, police officers often use rules of thumb, heuristics, and implicitly developed criteria in their crime analysis. Rule-based systems facilitate the application of such knowledge by explicating the decision rules.

Case-based reasoning systems use a database containing solutions to problems in order to solve new problems. Examples from intelligence include undercover operations, interrogations, and informants. In these systems, known case positions are compared with a new problem; the comparison is based on theoretical assumptions and hypotheses, and arguments both pro and con are evaluated. A case-based reasoning system facilitates the application of semistructured information representing knowledge by intentionally reusing past experiences when solving problems. A case-based reasoning system uses problems from the past to facilitate the solving of new problems by comparing patterns. As time goes by, a collection of problems and solutions for these problems are constructed, thereby reaching a critical mass of cases, which makes it interesting for comparison with new problems. Each problem is classified with the help of already specified attributes. The user specifies a problem and assigns weights to various attributes to indicate their relative importance in solving problems.

Case: Criminal Money Management

The need for knowledge in policing will be exemplified in the following by criminal money management. In December 2005, the European Union commissioned the EDGE project on criminal financing. This project was a report into the disguising or laundering of illegally derived money or, more accurately defined by the project team, as about criminal money management (CMM).

The term CMM is presented in the final report of the EDGE project as the link and cutting edge between profit-oriented crime and terrorism. Furthermore, the term *profit-oriented crime* is viewed as any money derived from the various activities of what has academically been considered as related yet different fields of study into organized crime, white collar, and gang crime (AGIS, 2005). The link with terrorism of CMM relates to the extent to which legal and/or crime money is used to finance terrorist attacks and activities.

The EDGE project identified 20 influential factors that impact to varying degrees on CMM. These factors were defined and given projection weightings by the experts involved in the EDGE project as to the relative impact of these factors occurring in the foreseeable future, up to and until the year 2012, on the world stage.

Each of these influential factors and the experts' relative projections are presented and discussed below. These factors are presented as a way of summarizing a number of the themes on criminal financing involved in organized crime as well as foreshadowing a range of other issues connected to crime financing in general. The factors are (AGIS, 2005):

1. *Global Migration: Significant increase (70 percent projection).* The movement of people across and between countries will significantly increase in the near future as a result of increasing birth rates, social inequalities, and worldwide climate changes.

2. *Criminal Underground Markets: Substantial increase (80 percent projection).* Criminal underground markets will substantially expand due to increasing demand for illegal goods and services that are driven by globalized economy and global social disparity between rich and poor countries.

3. *Political Perceptions: Sizeable increase (60 percent projection).* Politicians will become increasing aware of the huge financial impact that CMM has on their national economies and the pressure this exerts on public confidence in the financial sector as well as national security issues, such as international terrorism threats and environmental disasters.

4. *World Economy: Steady increase (45 percent projection).* The development of global trade will continue at a steady pace over the longer term. This projection takes into account the occasional market corrections and fluctuations that occur from time to time on the world economy. Hence, as global trading increases so does crime development in terms of expanding criminal markets and, as a consequence, money laundering or the more accurate term: criminal money management.

5. *International Movement of Goods, Services, and Values: Substantial increase (80 percent projection).* In line with the steady development of the world economy into a borderless global community, or at the very least, more liberalized and, hence, porous border control mechanisms, there is a corresponding increased flow of goods, services, and values across the international landscape. Such a substantially increasing international movement of goods, services, and values creates multiple opportunities for criminal entrepreneurs to use a wide variety of means for the transportation and distribution of their illegal products and activities, in particular, people and drug trafficking.

6. *Development of Extremism: Extensive increase (90 percent projection).* Several factors on the global horizon (social and economic inequalities; difficult democratization process in Afghanistan, Iraq, and the Middle East; increasing racial segregation in many countries and cities, particularly in Europe) make extremist behavior in its many forms, especially political and religiously inspired extremism, increasing likely and extensive in the foreseeable future.

7. *Flexibility of Criminal Actors: Significant increase (70 percent projection).* Criminals who are profit-oriented are quick to respond to and exploit new business opportunities resulting from new technologies, new products, and new markets. Also, the movement in organized crime trends is away from the more traditional notions of hierarchical structures, like the Italian Mafia, to more transnational networks and loose alliances of criminal groups working together for particular criminal operations. Such criminal flexibility will present increasing new challenges for policing international security.

8. *Corruption Development: Moderate increase (40 percent projection).* Corruption is a major issue for police and security services worldwide because of the vast amount of money available to organized crime groups to bribe and corrupt police and public officials. This is especially significant in developing countries where law enforcement is weak and police are not well paid. Hence, corruption as a strategy used by organized crime to further their business aims will continue to increase at a moderate rate in the foreseeable future.

9. *Development of Criminal Upper World Markets: Moderate increase (45 percent projection).* Criminal businesses exist in an underworld market and work as a black economy. The movement by the criminal underworld into upper world markets via legal business enterprises holds significant advantages for them; for example, by using such enterprises where organized criminals can launder their illegally derived money, as well as reinvest laundered money and also facilitate other criminal activities. This can happen through product

piracy in the IT area, and construction companies can undertake fraudulent contracts and so forth.

10. *Citizens' Loyalty: Stable (60 percent projection).* This factor is considered as an important crime enabling influence. That is, if citizens care little about the financial burden that CMM places on the legitimate economy of their country then there will be little incentive by politicians and the government of the day to pass new laws and aggressively enforce and proactively seek out and prosecute profit-oriented criminality. It is projected that studies of the current level of citizen acceptance of laws and legal regulations related to profit-oriented crimes will remain relatively stable for the near future at around 60 percent.

11. *Influence of Media: Substantive increase (100 percent projection).* The media is a powerful shaper of opinion and beliefs. Hence, its influence will continue to be a central and substantive factor for better or worse in the field of CMM.

12. *Social Polarization: Substantive increase (100 percent projection).* The global distribution of income in terms of inequalities between countries and continents, as well as disparities of income in individual countries and regions, is growing significantly. Hence, there is a global trend toward an increasing and sharply rising gap between the rich and the poor. Such a global bifurcation into rich and poor results in social polarization and, as a consequence, opens up substantial opportunities for criminal markets to exploit this income gap.

13. *Development of International Standards for Combating CMM: Moderate increase (60 percent projection).* Further development toward internationally accepted and enforceable global standards of a high quality and easily understandable nature with regard to national and international CMM is expected to continue at a moderate rate in the near future. Clearly, the influence of other factors like global migration, political perceptions, citizens' acceptance of the need for new CMM-type laws, and the media will affect considerably the projected rate in terms of the speed of development of this factor.

14. *Digital Development: Substantial increase (80 percent projection).* The rapid development in the digital world of new technologies in relation to money management strategies will offer substantial new opportunities for profit-oriented criminality. New electronic means of money transfer and management, such as e-payment online systems (e.g., paypal, e-gold, e-dinar, and mobile transfer systems using cell phones and other electronic devices), make it easier, faster, and, importantly for criminals, to more anonymously engage in CMM.

15. *Misuse of New Technologies: Significant increase (70 percent projection).* The diversity of new technologies in terms of a wide range of

media—computerized word, image, film, and sound files and formats—will also exponentially open up new opportunities for criminal misuse. It is likely that other types and new forms of profit-oriented crime will emerge that will involve not just traditional organized crime activities, but also white-collar criminality and especially large-scale criminal frauds.

16. *National and International Cooperation: Stable (60 percent projection).* The level of information sharing and collaboration between national and international law enforcement agencies has considerably increased since the world-changing events of 9/11 and the advent of a new wave of extremist terrorism. The EDGE report predicts this will remain stable for the near future at around a 60 percent projection level. However, given the massive slip-ups by police and intelligence agencies prior to 9/11, there is no guarantee that this situation of knowledge sharing as opposed to just sharing information has substantially increased to match the size of the threat, not only from terrorism, but also by the growth of CMM. Clearly, this projection may need to be revised in the future.

17. *Management of Natural Disasters: Moderate increase (60 percent projection).* Natural disasters present profit-oriented criminals with evolving situations to exploit donated funding opportunities in a range of ways. The Asian tsunami and Hurricane Katrina in New Orleans are good examples of how organized criminal groups can reap huge amounts of donated money into criminal channels. Hence, this projection indicates that a moderate increase should be expected in how well criminal groups can get organized to respond to natural disaster appeals in respect to CMM strategies for this type of event.

18. *Development of Education: Stagnates (50 percent projection).* A lack of educational opportunities is often associated with the onset of criminal behavior as a person's future prospects in the legal–economic context to earn a reasonable living can be sometimes severely curtailed. Therefore, the appeal to engage in profit-oriented crime is enhanced for individuals with little future earning capacity.

Alternately, well-educated professionals can be corrupted through greed to use their skills to either engage in or assist in profit-oriented crimes. Either way, education plays a vital role in both the quantity and quality of future crime, especially crimes to do with CMM.

Furthermore, training law enforcement agencies to remain educationally competent in dealing with high-end crimes like sophisticated frauds, cyber crimes, and the like is a constant challenge. Hence, the EDGE experts' projection is that overall education levels for countries will remain constant in the medium time for at least the next five years. Thus, no significant changes to the status quo are expected in the realm of education for either criminals or law enforcement agencies.

19. *Conflicts of Interests: Moderate convergence (45 percent projection).* The world of finance is full of conflicting interests that manifest themselves politically, socially, culturally, as well as economically. Thus, it is a substantial challenge to law enforcement agencies working in the CMM field to establish a holistic, well-integrated, global plan of attack on CMM. The multiplicity of interdependences, sociocultural and geopolitical, makes a moderate convergence of views toward such a holistic global agenda on CMM the only likely outcome in the foreseeable future.

20. *Nongovernment Organizations (NGOs): Substantive increase (100 percent* projection). The nongovernment sector occupies a central location in the global economy, for it is often the case that NGOs are able to respond more rapidly and with more flexibility to changes in global conditions than the more bureaucratic instruments and agencies of government. Hence, the influence of NGOs is highly likely to rise substantially especially when global conditions are in a state of flux or suffering from environmental shocks.

To conclude, these 20 influential factors involved in CMM should not be considered in isolation. Each is linked in multiple ways and at multiple levels and, therefore, will have multiple realizations in how both profit-oriented criminals and law enforcement agencies deal with CMM. Which side is winning in this fight about CMM will unfold in the future. But one thing is certain, the role of criminal finance will be central in this fight against organized crime.

References

AGIS. 2005. *Criminal money management as a cutting edge between profit oriented crime and terrorism.* A European Interdisciplinary Analysis Project, Landeskriminalamt Nordrhein-Westfalen, Germany. Online at: www.lka.nrw.de.

Beare, M.E. and Martens, F.T. 1998. Policing organized crime. *Journal of Contemporary Criminal Justice* 14 (4): 398–427.

Bock, G.W., Zmud, R.W., and Kim, Y.G. 2005. Behavioral intention formation in knowledge sharing: Examining the roles of extrinsic motivators, social-psychological forces, and organizational climate. *MIS Quarterly* 29 (1): 87–111.

Chen, H., Schroeder, J., Hauck, R.V., Ridgeway, L., Atabakhsh, H., Gupta, H., Boarman, C., Rasmussen, K., and Clements, A.W. 2002. COPLINK connect: Information and knowledge management for law enforcement. *Decision Support Systems* 34: 271–285.

Earl, M.J. 2001. Knowledge management strategies: Toward a taxonomy. *Journal of Management Information Systems* 18 (1): 215–233.

Fahsing, I., Ask, K., and Granhag, P.A. 2004. The man behind the mask: Accuracy and predictors of eyewitness offender descriptions. *Journal of Applied Psychology* 89 (4): 722–729.

Garud, R. and Kumaraswamy, A. 2005. Vicious and virtuous circles in the management of knowledge: The case of Infosys Technologies. *MIS Quarterly* 29 (1): 9–33.

Gottschalk, P. 2007. *Knowledge management in law enforcement: Technologies and techniques.* Hershey, PA: Idea Group Publishing.

Hansen, M.T., Nohria, N., and Tierney, T. 1999. What's your strategy for managing knowledge? *Harvard Business Review* (March-April) 106–116.

Harfield, C. 2008. Paradigms, pathologies, and practicalities: Policing organized crime in England and Wales. *Policing* 2 (1): 63–73.

Home Office. 2005a. *Guidance on statutory performance indicators for policing 2005/2006.* Police Standards Unit, Home Office of the U.K. Government. Online at: www.policereform.gov.uk.

Home Office. 2005b. *Senior investigating officer development programme.* Police Standards Unit, Home Office of the U.K. Government. Online at: www.policere form.gov.uk.

Home Office. 2008. *From the neighbourhood to the national: policing our communities together.* Home Office, London. Online at: police.homeoffice.gov.uk.

Hughes, V. and Jackson, P. 2004. The influence of technical, social and structural factors on the effective use of information in a policing environment. *The Electronic Journal of Knowledge Management* 2 (1): 65–76.

Johnson, S.D., Birks, D.J., McLaughlin, L., Bowers, K.J., and Pease, K. 2007. *Prospective crime mapping in operational context,* Home Office, U.K. Online report July 19: www.homeoffice.gov.uk.

Ko, D.G., Kirsch, L.J., and King, W.R. 2005. Antecedents of knowledge transfer from consultants to clients in enterprise system implementations. *MIS Quarterly* 29 (1): 59–85.

Lin, L., Geng, X., and Whinston, A.B. 2005. A sender-receiver framework for knowledge transfer. *MIS Quarterly* 29 (2): 197–219.

Lind, H., Hjelm, J., and Lind, M. 2007. Privacy surviving data retention in Europe? Paper presented at the W3C Workshop on Languages for Privacy Policy Negotiation and Semantics-Driven Enforcement. Online at: www.w3.org.

Poston, R.S. and Speier, C. 2005. Effective use of knowledge management systems: A process model of content ratings and credibility indicators. *MIS Quarterly* 29 (2): 221–244.

Sheptycki, J. 2002. *In search of transnational policing: Towards a sociology of global policing,* Aldershot, U.K.: Ashgate Publishing.

Spina, A.L. 2008. Recent anti-Mafia strategies: The Italian experience. In *Organized crime: Culture, markets and policies,* Eds. D. Siegel and H. Nelen, 195–206. New York: Springer.

Srinivasa, K.G., Venugopal, K.R., and Patnaik, L.M. 2007. A self-adaptive migration model genetic algorithm for data mining applications. *Information Sciences* 177: 4295–4313.

Wasko, M.M. and Faraj, S. 2005. Why should I share? Examining social capital and knowledge contribution in electronic networks of practice. *MIS Quarterly* 29 (1): 35–57.

Weir, R. and Bangs, M. 2007. The use of geographic information systems by crime analysts in England and Wales, U.K. Home Office. Online report July 3: www.homeoffice.gov.uk.

Xu, J.J. and H. Chen 2004. Fighting organized crimes: Using shortest-path algorithms to identify associations in criminal networks. *Decision Support Systems* 38: 473–487.

Performance Management in Policing 12

Performance management should enable the police to deliver the level of service required by society, so it is an important component of the overall approach to policing organized crime. However, it may seem that where performance is poorly managed or where performance management is carried out with an insufficient understanding of the ways in which it will impact on the practice of enforcing law on criminal organizations, it can have a dysfunctional effect. This can be seen in police organizations where achieving performance targets has become the sole objective of many managers. This pressure to achieve targets tends to lead to an ever-diminishing intelligence capacity. The mechanism by which this happens is not difficult to understand. The need to achieve short-term goals, according to Stelfox (2008), leads managers to make choices that favor quick wins, low cost, and simplicity in performance management. These choices are carried out even when longer-term or higher-cost measures would lead to better outcomes. Over time, this reduces not only the standards of intelligence and investigation, but also the opportunities that investigators have to develop their skills.

Performance Management Standards

Given that performance management is here to stay and that the pressures are likely to remain, Stelfox (2008) argues that the police service needs to adopt some mechanisms to ensure that its capability to investigate crime is not eroded. Four areas seem important:

1. *Development of targets.* Targets have to be both short-term and long-term. They need to include both performance goals and performance processes.
2. *Responsibility for targets.* Responsibility for targets has to match the power to meet targets. Power is present when the responsible manager has decision-making authority to allocate resources to meet targets.
3. *Revision of targets.* When a target becomes irrelevant or nonachievable, a process of revision should take place.
4. *Achievement of targets.* Targets have to be formulated such that it is indisputable when a target has been achieved.

Surveying trends and debates in the measurement of police performance since 1970, Neyroud (2008, 345) considered what lessons from the past in the United Kingdom should inform how we determine "good" or "successful" policing.

> Over the last 30 years there have been some very significant shifts in the way that performance information is used and deployed within the police service. In the late 1970s and early 1980s, the focus on "doing the numbers" meant that the data available to the average Criminal Investigation Department consisted largely of the number of crimes recorded by Home Office categories and the number of detected crimes (the latter simply presented as "detected" and not divided into primary and secondary detections). There was a substantial flexibility within the system that allowed serious crimes to be detected through "secondary" means, by coding the detections to a series of Home Office classifications or through prison visits. Additionally, in the case of minor offences, a decision could be taken to "no crime," and this was particularly common practice in relation to minor criminal damage where, if the value of the damage was judged to be below £20, an incident was not eligible for a crime report. Indeed, the determining factor as to whether a reported offence would be "crimed" or not in many forces was whether it was likely to result in a detection.

National Crime Recording Standards put an end to such practices in 2007, which led to improved consistency of crime recording across the United Kingdom. Good quality data about levels of crime are essential, not only for police performance to be measured externally, but also for use internally by a police service that has moved to an intelligence-led approach. Neyroud found that the debate about performance targets often neglects to attend to the fact that performance data are used by the police service itself to target resources, understand problems, and measure local success.

Comparative Statistics in CompStat

It is to this end that CompStat (COMPuter STATistics or COMParative STATistics) has been deployed in the United Kingdom. Originally developed within the New York Police Department under the leadership of Police Commissioner William Bratton and his team, CompStat has been described as a goal-oriented strategic management process that uses computer technology, operational strategy, and managerial accountability to structure the manner in which a police department provides crime-control services. CompStat is a tool for presenting performance data and holding managers to account for performance against targets (Neyroud, 2008).

CompStat is a management tool for police departments. It represents a dynamic approach to crime reduction, quality of life improvement, and personnel and resource management. CompStat employs geographic information systems (GISs) and was intended to map crime and identity problems. Often on a weekly basis, personnel from different police departments in a police district compile a statistical summary of the week's crime complaints, arrests and summons activity as well as a written report of significant cases, crime patterns, and police activities. This information, with specific crime and enforcement locations and times, is forwarded to the chief of the department's CompStat unit where information is collated and loaded into a district-wide database. The unit runs computer analysis on the data and generates a weekly CompStat report.

However, there is a major contrast between the United States and the United Kingdom in the deployment of CompStat (Neyroud, 2008, 346).

> In the USA, CompStat has been utilized by Chiefs and Mayors to focus local, municipal policing on local priorities. In the UK, where its adoption has been patchy, CompStat has operated in a framework of national targets and national comparison.

In the United States, the CompStat program involves weekly crime control strategy meetings. These gatherings increase information flow between the agency's executives and the commanders of operational units, with particular emphasis on crime and quality of life enforcement information. In the department's vernacular, these briefings are referred to as CompStat (computerized statistics) meetings because many of the discussions are based on the statistical analysis and maps contained within the weekly CompStat reports. These meetings and the information sharing they generate are an important part of Commissioner Bratton's comprehensive, interactive management strategy: Enhancing accountability by providing local commanders with considerable discretion and resources. The program also ensures that precinct commanders remain aware of crime and quality of life conditions within their areas of responsibility. By meeting frequently and discussing the department's ten crime and quality of life strategies, the initiatives are fully implemented throughout the agency. Precinct and other operational unit commanders use this forum to communicate with the agency's top executives and other commanders, sharing the problems they face and successful crime reduction tactics. The process allows top executives to monitor issues and activities within precincts and operational units, evaluating the skills and effectiveness of middle managers. By keeping abreast of situations "on the ground," departmental leaders can properly allocate resources to most effectively reduce crime and improve police performance (www.wikipedia.org [search CompStat]).

In contrast, the national approach to CompStat use in the United Kingdom is strongly in the direction of top-down performance measures imposed nationally. The emphasis is on a small number of performance indicators, in particular, offenses brought to justice (Neyroud, 2008, 346).

> The marked increase in the use of fixed penalty notices as a result of the focus on "sanctions detections" is an example of the effects of such a national performance management regime and the well-documented lesson that pushing any performance indicator beyond a sensible point can potentially have adverse consequences.

Thus, it is argued that in a number of respects, the CompStat framework in the United Kingdom has become an obstacle to progress because the focus is too strongly in the direction of top-down performance measures imposed nationally. At the same time, there are substantial strengths to a national performance framework that seeks to understand the comparative performance of different areas and different forces.

William Bratton was chief of the Los Angeles Police Department in 2008 and former chief of the New York Police Department. He is best known for leading the development and expansion of CompStat, the internationally acclaimed command accountability system that uses computer-mapping technology and crime analysis to target emerging crime patterns and coordinate police response.

In February 1994, Bratton was appointed police commissioner of New York City. The odds were against him. The New York Police Department, with a $2 billion budget and a workforce of 35,000 police officers, was notoriously difficult to manage. Yet, in less than two years and without an increase in his budget, Bratton turned New York into the safest large city in the nation, according to Kim and Mauborgne (2003).

Research conducted by Kim and Mauborgne led them to conclude that Bratton's turnaround was an example of tipping point leadership. The theory of tipping point hinges on the insight that in any organization, once the beliefs and energies of a critical mass of people are engaged, conversion to a new idea will spread like an epidemic, bringing about fundamental change very quickly. The theory suggests that such a movement can be unleashed only by agents who make unforgettable and unarguable calls for change, who concentrate their resources on what really matters, who mobilize the commitment of the organization's key players, and who succeed in silencing the most vocal naysayers. Bratton did all of these things.

Kim and Maugorgne find that in many turnarounds, the hardest battle is simply getting people to agree on the causes of current problems and the need for change. Most CEOs try to make the case for change simply by pointing to the numbers and insisting that the company can achieve better ones. However, messages communicated through numbers seldom stick. Bratton (1998, 310) writes in his own book on the turnaround in New York:

The system my team and I installed continues to bring success. New York City is a much safer place now and will remain so.

Tipping point leaders do not rely on numbers to break through the organization's cognitive hurdles. Instead, they put their key managers face-to-face with the operational problems so that the managers cannot evade reality. Poor performance becomes something they witness rather than hear about. Communicating in this way means that the message—performance is poor and needs to be fixed—sticks with people, which is essential if they are to be convinced not only that a turnaround is necessary, but also that it is something they can achieve.

Leaders like Bratton use a four-step process to bring about rapid, dramatic, and lasting change with limited resources. Tipping all four hurdles leads to rapid strategy reorientation and execution.

- *Cognitive Hurdle.* Put managers face-to-face with problems and customers. Find new ways to communicate.
- *Resource Hurdle.* Focus on the hot spots and bargain with partner organizations.
- *Motivational Hurdle.* Put the stage lights on and frame the challenge to match the organization's various levels.
- *Political* Hurdle. Identify and silence internal opponents; isolate external ones.

By addressing these hurdles to tipping point change, leaders will stand a chance of achieving the same kind of results as Bratton delivered to the citizens of New York. Between 1994 and 1996, felony crime fell 39 percent, murders 50 percent, and theft 35 percent. Gallup polls reported that public confidence in the NYPD jumped from 37 to 73 percent in the 1990s (Kim and Mauborgne, 2003).

The tool for Bratton's success was CompStat. In 2008, he argued for taking CompStat to the next level after summarizing his experiences in Los Angeles so far (Bratton and Malinowski, 2008, 261).

It is important to note, however, that one size does not fit all. The process as it played out in New York City was very different from the way it now works in Los Angeles. Cultural differences, budget limitations, and bureaucratic constraints have caused the process to morph. The CompStat model as employed in Los Angeles, although different from its East Coast cousin, has also led to dramatic crime reductions over the last five years. Indeed, an inherent strength of CompStat and performance management is that they can be modified to direct and control significantly different environments.

A major performance management change in Los Angeles was a management philosophy that encourages and rewards risk taking and innovation. In this philosophy, vision, goals, and expectations are clearly defined from the top, while line managers are given more freedom and resources to manage their commands in exchange for results responsive to police department goals. This philosophy argues that line managers should have enhanced accountability, as accountability brings a capacity to explain what was done and why it succeeded or failed (Bratton and Malinowski, 2008).

Taking CompStat to the next level implies the implementation of CompStat Plus, which represents an enhanced application of principles of inspection and accountability, as well as the use of more in-depth auditing methods, mentorship, and close collaboration (Bratton and Malinowski, 2008, 262).

> To proceed with the inspection, we assembled an inspection team composed of proven experts in the fields that were the subject of CompStat Plus' focus (patrol and detective operations, the crime analysis section, community-related crime prevention efforts, and management and supervision). The group developed a set of inspection protocols to help uncover performance inhibitors with a clear focus on helping the area in reducing Part I Crimes. This goal would be achieved by implementing procedural efficiencies and creating an all-encompassing crime-fighting blue print designed to bring the various stakeholders together with a clear mission.

The potential effectiveness of CompStat Plus is based on three complementary approaches (Bratton and Malinowski, 2008):

1. Under CompStat Plus, a diagnostic exercise is conducted to identify accurately the causes for the underperformance. The temptation of wanting to provide easy and simple solutions to complex multilayered problems was avoided.
2. A clearly focused dialog was established among the stakeholders to assess the results of the diagnostic inspection and create a universally accepted conclusion of what the findings meant. It has been theorized that for the next step, the solution step, to be successful key stakeholders, had to come to an agreement about what the problems were.
3. The affected commands were given the task of creating their own plan of action. We created an environment where key stakeholders became full partners in the process. Gascón and his CompStat Plus team made it clear that the strategies and the results belonged to people doing the work. CompStat Plus is simply a catalyst, a means to achieve an end.

Based on an emphasis on targeted performance management strategies and a new and improved version of CompStat, Los Angeles became the second-safest large city in the United States in 2008.

Value Shop Performance

In this chapter, we suggest the value shop for performance assessment. The value shop is a value configuration that describes how value is created in an organization for its stakeholders. A value configuration shows how the most important business processes function to create value for its stakeholders. A value configuration represents the way a particular organization conducts business.

In the value shop, activities are scheduled and resources are applied in a fashion that is dimensioned and appropriate to the needs of the policing problem. The value shop is an organization that creates value by solving unique problems for society. Knowledge is the most important resource, and reputation is critical to organizational success.

A value shop is characterized by five primary activities: problem finding and acquisition, problem solving, choice, execution, and control and evaluation, as illustrated in Figure 12.1. *Problem finding and acquisition* involves

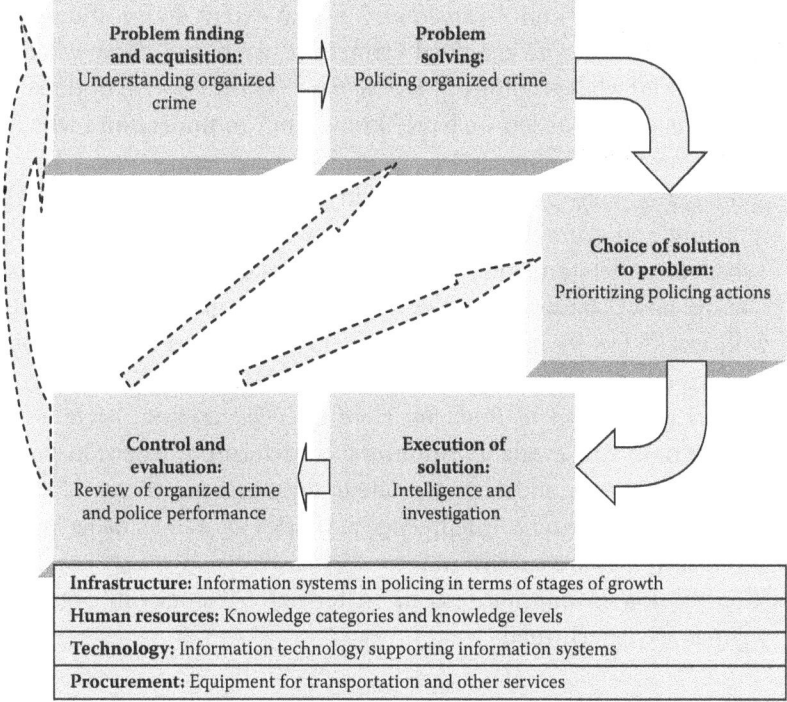

Figure 12.1 Primary and secondary activities in the value shop.

working with the victims and others to determine the exact nature of the problem or need. It involves deciding on the overall plan for approaching the problem. *Problem solving* is the actual generation of ideas and action (or treatment) plans.

Choice represents the decision of choosing between alternatives. While the least important primary activity of the value shop in terms of time and effort, it is also the most important in terms of value. *Execution* represents communicating, organizing, and implementing the decision, or performing the treatment. *Control and evaluation* activities involve monitoring and measurement of how well the solution solved the original problem or met the original need. Evaluation may feed back into the first activity (problem finding and acquisition) for two reasons. First, if the proposed solution is inadequate or did not work, it feeds back into learning why it was inadequate and begins the problem-solving phase anew. Second, if the problem solution was successful, the organization might enlarge the scope of the problem-solving process to solve a bigger problem related to or dependent upon the first problem being solved.

Performance management is carried out in the value shop by setting targets and evaluating goal achievement for each primary activity.

1. *Problem Finding and Acquisition.* To what extent do we understand the exact nature of organized crime? Do we have "know what" to understand what is going on? Do we have "know how" to understand how it is going on? Do we have "know why" to understand why it is going on? (See Chapter 10.)

2. *Problem Solving.* To what extent do we know how to do effective policing and enforce law on organized crime? Do we have "know what" to understand alternative approaches in policing? Do we have "know how" to understand how alternative approaches in policing will work? Do we have "know why" to understand how our police actions affect and possibly change criminal behaviors?

3. *Choice of Solution to Problem.* Here we need criteria, such as risk willingness and available resources, to determine what alternative actions may seem most appropriate to fight organized crime.

4. *Execution of Solution.* Intelligence activities as well as other prioritized activities are carried out.

5. *Control and Evaluation.* Effects in terms of changes in organized crimes are determined.

Performance management implies that the quality of each of these five primary activities is measured.

Detective Thinking Styles

In criminal investigations, detectives apply different thinking styles, such as method style, challenge style, skill style, and risk style. In a survey in Norway, detectives were asked to list the five most important characteristics of effective investigators. This was done in a free format, requiring content analysis to categorize responses. Responses were categorized according to thinking styles. While creativity was the most frequently mentioned characteristic, content analysis shows that the skill style of detectives is the most effective thinking style. To be effective, detectives need to practice good empathic communication, open-minded curiosity, logical reasoning, creative thinking, and dogged determination.

Creativity is often mentioned as a characteristic of effective detectives. Detectives can be creative in their job by generating new ways to perform their work, by coming up with novel procedures and innovative ideas, and by reconfiguring known approaches into new alternatives (Perry-Smith and Shalley, 2003). Yet, detectives are often told to work by the book, forgetting the importance of creative thinking and the importance of creative persons (Dean et al., 2008).

We distinguish between four thinking styles in police investigations (Dean et al., 2008). The *method* style is driven by procedural steps and conceptual processes for gathering information. The *challenge* style is driven by intensity of the job, the victim, the criminal, and the crime. The *skill* style is driven by personal qualities and abilities of relating to people at different levels. The *risk* style is driven by creativity in discovering and developing information into evidence. All four styles are illustrated in Figure 12.2 along the axis of complexity and time.

These four investigative thinking styles were introduced in this research to classify characteristics of effective detectives into relevant thinking styles. Such classification enables identification of important thinking styles and learning (Garcia-Morales et al., 2006).

The study was concerned with how police detectives experience, understand, and think about the process of doing serious and complex criminal investigations. In police investigations, the experience of investigation begins for detectives when they are given a crime to solve. When handed a case, detectives apply the basics of the procedural method in which they were trained.

There are a variety of procedural steps within the criminal investigation training literature for various types of crimes, but, in essence, all such steps follow a logical sequence that can be subsumed under a set of basic steps, referred to as the "5 Cs" of the police procedural method of investigation. The 5 Cs are the procedural steps of collecting, checking, considering, connecting, and constructing information into evidence.

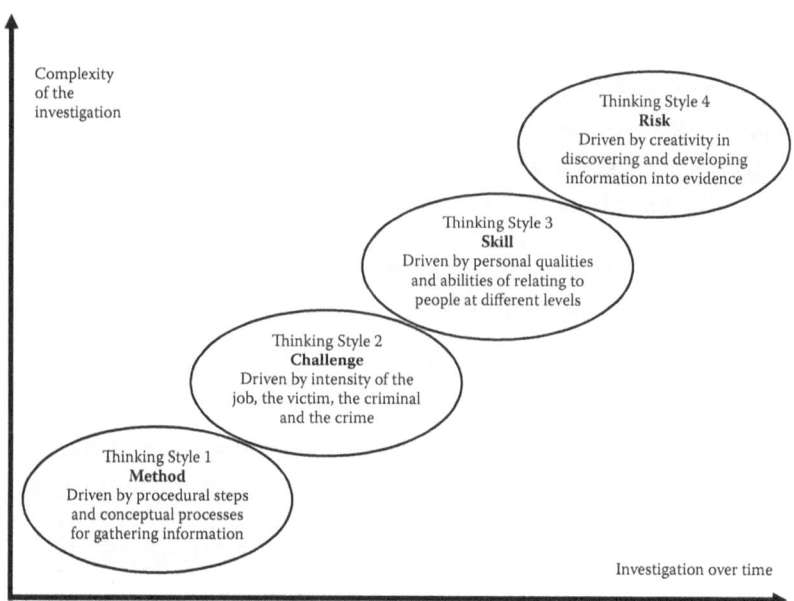

Figure 12.2 Ways of thinking about the investigation process.

Conceptually, this "procedural method" presents a problem for detectives in that since their formal investigative training only equips them with this one way of "thinking" investigation, the question becomes: How do they learn to think in any other way or do they when investigating?

Previous empirical research has identified that apart from the above mentioned "method" style of investigative thinking there are three other qualitatively different ways or styles of thinking that potentially can come into play when experienced detectives investigate a serious or complex crime: challenge style, the skill style, and the risk style of investigative thinking. How each of these other three investigative thinking styles works in conjunction with the basic method style is briefly outlined below.

As detectives conduct a serious and/or complex investigation, they become driven by the intensity of the challenge, which motivates them to do the best job they can for the victim(s) by catching the criminal(s) and solving the crime through the application of the "basic 5Cs" of the investigative method style of thinking in which they were trained. This challenge style of thinking is all about what motivates and drive detectives to do the best they can do in a particular investigation. At this level, detectives think about the job, the victim, the crime, and the criminal. These four elements (job–victim–crime–criminal) are the key sources of intensity (Home Office, 2005).

In meeting this investigative challenge, detectives require skill to relate and communicate effectively to a variety of people to obtain information so as to establish a workable investigative focus (Kiely and Peek, 2002). Such skill also requires detectives to be flexible in the how they approach people and the case, while maintaining an appropriate level of emotional involvement toward victims, witnesses, informants, and suspects. With this skill style of investigative thinking, detectives are concerned with how they relate to people. Detectives must think about how they are going to relate to the victim, witnesses, possible suspects, the local community, and the wider general public in order to get the information they need to make the case.

When exercising their investigative skill, detectives seek to maximize the possibilities of a good result by taking legally sanctioned and logically justifiable risks across a wide latitude of influence. Such justifiable risk taking requires detectives to be proactive in applying creativity to how they seek to discover new information and, if necessary, how they develop such information into evidence. This risk style revolves around how detectives think through being proactively creative enough to discover new information and, if necessary, develop it into evidence that will stand up to testing in a court of law.

Although experienced detectives and investigators intuitively use these four levels of thinking in an investigation, it is rare that any one detective will give equal weight to all four styles of investigative thinking in a particular case because detectives, like everyone else, have a preference for maybe one or two particular styles or ways of thinking.

This phenomenon is about the cognitive psychology of police investigators. At its core, investigation is a mind game. When it comes to solving a crime, a detective's ability to think as an investigator is everything. Four distinctively different ways of thinking are investigation as method, investigation as challenge, investigation as skill, and investigation as risk. All four ways of describing a criminal investigation can be seen as more or less partial understandings of the whole phenomenon of investigation.

The four distinctively different ways of thinking (styles) about the investigation process by detectives are illustrated in Figure 12.2. As can be seen in the figure, there is a hierarchical structure to how investigators think. Not all cases will require the use of all four investigation-thinking styles to solve them. However, as time marches on in an investigation without a result, then other styles of investigative thinking will need to come into play to increase the likelihood of a successful outcome. In essence, the more complex the crime, the higher the investigative thinking style required in solving it.

References

Bratton, W. 1998. Turnaround: How America's top cop reversed the crime epidemic. New York: Random House.

Bratton, W.J. and Malinowski, S.W. 2008. Police performance management in practice: Taking COMPSTAT to the next level. *Policing* 2 (3): 259–265.

Dean, G., Fahsing, I.A., Gottschalk, P., and Solli-Sæther, H. 2008. Investigative thinking and creativity: An empirical study of police detectives in Norway. *International Journal of Innovation and Learning* 5 (2): 170–185.

Garcia-Morales, V.J., Llorens-Montes, F.J., and Verdu-Jover, A.J. 2006. Organizational learning categories: their influence on organizational performance. *International Journal of Innovation and Learning* 3 (5): 518–536.

Home Office. 2005. Senior investigating officer development programme. Police Standards Unit, U.K. Government Home Office. Online at: www.policereform.gov.uk.

Kiely, J.A. and Peek, G.S. 2002. The culture of the British police: Views of police officers. *The Service Industries Journal* 22 (1): 167–183.

Kim, C.W. and Mauborgne, R. 2003. Tipping point leadership. *Harvard Business Review* (April) 61–69.

Neyroud, P. 2008. Past, present and future performance: Lessons and prospects for the measurement of police performance. *Policing* 2 (3): 340–348.

Perry-Smith, J.E. and Shalley, C.E. 2003. The social side of creativity: A static and dynamic social network perspective. *Academy of Management Review* 29 (1): 89–106.

Stelfox, P. 2008. Investigative practice and performance management: Making the marriage work. *Policing* 2 (3): 303–310.

Performance Measurement in Policing

13

In this chapter, we will introduce an empirical study of performance measurement in the police value shop. Also, we will present more results from the survey on intelligence strategy implementation.

Empirical Study of Police Investigations

To measure performance in the primary activities of the value shop, a survey instrument was developed. The questionnaire was e-mailed in 2005 to approximately 500 police officers in charge of criminal investigations in Norway. A total of 101 questionnaires were returned. This represents an approximate response rate of 20 percent. We have to write approximate, as police chiefs were asked to distribute the questionnaire link to their police investigations managers. The sample consisted of police officers in charge of criminal investigations in Norway with personnel, budget, outcome, knowledge, and investigation responsibilities.

The primary activities of the intelligence and investigation value shop were all measured on multiple item scales, as listed in Table 13.1. We developed all items by interviewing senior investigation officers in Norway. Therefore, an exploratory factor analysis had to be conducted before the confirmatory factor analysis was completed. The exploratory factor analysis suggested only three factors rather than five. However, since the statistically suggested, three-factor model was found to be without theoretical implications, a confirmatory factor analysis with five factors was conducted.

All five scales had acceptable reliability in terms of the Cronbach alpha. Therefore, means for each item were averaged into means for each primary activity. Out of the five primary activities in the value shop, performance in police investigations was best in problem understanding (5.0) and alternative solutions (5.0), while evaluation achieved the lowest score (4.0).

Empirical Study of Intelligence Work

The national strategy for intelligence and analysis in Norway was to be implemented in 2007. An empirical study of the implementation was carried out one year later. As described in Chapter 4, the extent of implementation in 2008 after one year was approximately one-third of the strategy. The survey indicated substantial variation in the extent of implementation among police districts.

Table 13.1   Investigation Performance in Value Shop Activities

Police Investigation Performance in the Value Shop	Average	Alpha
Understanding the case, what it is all about: problem finding and acquisition	**5.0**	**.934**
Channel the case to the right investigator	5.1	
Assess initial case information and other relevant information	5.2	
Collect additional historical information	4.3	
Evaluate whether there is suspicion of a criminal offense	5.5	
Assess the police task in the case	5.4	
Inform parties and stakeholders of the case	4.6	
Identifying investigation alternatives; which investigative steps are potentially relevant to the case: problem solutions	**5.0**	**.956**
Determine the purpose of the investigation	5.1	
Assess the extent to which there is experience from similar cases	5.0	
Discuss with colleagues what potential investigation schemes are appropriate	4.9	
Assess the seriousness of the criminal offense	5.1	
Find methods for investigative steps	5.0	
Plan for alternative investigative steps	4.6	
Investigation plan derived from alternatives by use of criteria for success: choice of solution to the problem	**4.8**	**.942**
Identify criteria for choice of investigation program	4.6	
Discuss with colleagues which investigation program is the best	4.8	
Check routines and guidelines for police work	4.4	
Check resources for investigative actions	4.7	
Find a qualified investigation leader	4.8	
Determine what the police must do in the case	5.2	
Work on the case, carrying out the investigation plan: execution of solution to solve problem	**4.8**	**.915**
Collect information from files	4.6	
Collect information from persons	5.0	
Secure leads	4.9	
Interrogate potential suspects	5.4	
Interrogate potential witnesses	5.3	
Inform involved persons (such as relatives) about the future	4.3	
Determining how the investigation has progressed so far and possible changes in the future: control and evaluation	**4.0**	**.926**
Evaluate the quality of police work in the case	*4.1*	
Evaluate the quality of legal work in the case	*4.0*	
Involve in the evaluation everyone who has participated in the investigation	*3.7*	

Table 13.1   Investigation Performance in Value Shop Activities (Continued)

Police Investigation Performance in the Value Shop	Average	Alpha
Assess how the investigation of the case was managed	*3.7*	
Control the use of resources in the case	*4.0*	
Learn from the case	*4.6*	
Average overall performance in the value shop	**4.7**	**.965**

Note: Scale from 1 = not clever to 7 = very clever.

In the survey research, organization structure and organization culture were applied as predictors of implementation extent. In separate regressions, it was found that both structure and culture have a significant influence on implementation, where a knowledge-oriented structure and a knowledge-oriented culture lead to more implementation than a bureaucracy-oriented structure and bureaucracy-oriented culture. When the two predictors were combined in one regression, the explanatory power of structure was stronger than culture, making culture a nonsignificant predictor in the regression analysis.

When looking at empirical results concerning intelligence work from this study, we can select some items from the questionnaire, as listed in Table 13.2. The scale ranges from 1 (completely disagree) to 7 (completely agree). The highest score (4.33) can be found for the statement: "We have implemented

Table 13.2   Measurement of Strategy Implementation

No.	Statements Concerning Implementation of National Strategy	Mean	Dev
01	We have implemented intelligence and analysis unit	4.11	1.986
02	We have implemented operational analysis function	3.98	2.099
03	We have implemented operational intelligence function	4.33	1.957
04	We have implemented strategic analysis function	3.99	2.064
05	We have implemented strategic intelligence function	3.70	1.895
06	We now prioritize knowledge-based police work	3.91	1.681
07	We have adapted the strategy to our own strategy	3.74	1.671
08	We have created environment to succeed with the strategy	3.41	1.568
09	A change process according to the strategy is going on	3.90	1.657
10	We have planned when to evaluate the implementation	2.30	1.506
11	Critical success factors for implementation have been identified	2.54	1.500
12	Goals have been set for the implementation process	2.76	1.707
13	Deadlines for implementation have been set	2.42	1.697
14	Resources have been allocated to strategy implementation	2.70	1.634
15	Measurement parameters according to strategy are developed	2.49	1.496
	Average	3.33	1.332

operational intelligence function." The lowest score (2.30) can be found for the statement: "We have planned when to evaluate the implementation."

On a scale from 1 to 7, the median is 4. All average scores below 4 represent disagreement, while all scores above 4 represent agreement. Only two statements have an average score above 4, i.e., "We have implemented intelligence and analysis unit" and "We have implemented operational intelligence unit." The average score for all items is 3.33, which indicates slight disagreement.

All statements have a standard deviation above 1, which indicates substantial variation among respondents. The greatest variation among respondents can be found for the statement: "We have implemented operational analysis function," with a standard deviation of 2.064.

The significant determinant of implementation extent of the national strategy for intelligence and analysis was organizational structure. A more knowledge-oriented organizational structure leads to a greater extent of implementation. A more bureaucratic structure leads to a lower degree of implementation. Items measuring organization structure are listed in Table 13.3.

The reliability of this scale was not satisfactory with all eighteen items included. An acceptable reliability was achieved by eliminating items 1, 2, 5,

Table 13.3 Measurement of Organization Structure

#	Statements Concerning Implementation of National Strategy	Mean	Dev
01	We do not work sequentially with one case at a time	4.66	1.748
02	We are free to choose how to solve our assignments	3.34	1.748
03	We have good routines for transferring knowledge internally	3.80	1.546
04	We have good routines for transferring knowledge externally	3.53	1.486
05	We do not always follow institutional routines	4.42	1.400
06	We do not always have to follow lines of command	3.87	1.622
07	Program management is important in our organization	3.35	1.325
08	We do not have a bureaucratic decision-making system	3.77	1.746
09	There is not always consistency between authority and responsibility	4.64	1.499
10	We are not always dependent on superiors' decisions	3.85	1.468
11	We change organizational structure in pace with the environment	3.68	1.602
12	Our organization is not characterized by hierarchy	3.32	1.594
13	In our organization, is it not always formal authority that counts	3.75	1.674
14	Our organization changes continuously	4.01	1.688
15	We are a knowledge organization	4.31	1.743
16	We have a flexible organization structure	3.54	1.584
17	We have an integrated cooperation internally	3.96	1.526
18	We have an integrated cooperation with partners externally	4.03	1.419
	Average	3.76	1.029

6, 9, and 10. By eliminating these six items, thirteen items with a reliability of 0.885 remained.

Characteristics of Effective Detectives

A survey instrument was applied in this research where respondents filled in a space. In the open electronic space, respondents could write five characteristics in their own wording. To classify these responses, content analysis was needed. According to Riffe and Freitag (1997), seven features of content analysis distinguish poor studies from excellent studies. First, an explicit theoretical framework is needed. In this research, the theoretical framework of investigative thinking styles as developed by Dean et al. (2008) is applied. Second, hypotheses or research questions are needed. In this research, the research question "what" is concerned with descriptions of characteristics. Third, other research methods should also be applied. In this research, a survey is supplemented with content analysis. Forth, extra-media data should be incorporated. In this research, results from another investigation survey were incorporated (Glomseth et al., 2007). Fifth, intercoder reliability should be reported. In this research, the characteristics content construct was coded by two researchers independently. Sixth, reliability based on a random sample of coded content was not relevant in this research, as there is a complete set of responses. Finally, presentations of only descriptive statistics should be avoided. In this research, two independent researchers coded characteristics by respondents.

The questionnaire was sent to 325 detectives by e-mail. With 110 responses returned, this gave a response rate of 34 percent. However, only seventy-one detectives filled in the open space for characteristics of effective detectives, thereby reducing the response rate to 22 percent. Because each detective wrote five characteristics each, a total of 355 characteristics were collected, as listed in Table 13.4.

Two raters were involved in the classification of responses. There was no need to develop key words in this research (Gottschalk, 2001) because respondents provided responses in terms of key words. Acceptable interrater judgment reliability (IJR) of 0.94 was achieved. Reliability is an assessment of the degree of consistency between multiple raters of a variable (Hair et al., 2006).

As can be seen in the table, 55 percent of the respondents wrote *creativity* as one of the five characteristics of effective detectives. The word "creativity" comes from the Latin concept *creare* that means "to make" or "to create." Creative activity appears to be an affectively charged event, one in which complex cognitive processes are shaped by, co-occur with, and shape emotional experience (Amabile et al., 2005). Novelty is a key defining criterion of

Table 13.4   Characteristics Responses (five characteristics by seventy-one respondents)

Objectivity	Creativity	Involvement	Patience	Initiative
Professional	Systematic	Creative	Cooperative	Motivated
Interested	Knowledgeable	Hardworking	Collegial	Organized
Curious	Detailed	Knowledge of law	Human intelligence	Not giving up
Patience	Good writing skills	Creative	Involved	Overview
Good to communicate	Good at listening	Open mind	Social abilities	Some curiosity
Be curious	Be positive	Update oneself	Positive to new methods	Ethic attitude
Analytic abilities	Simultaneous capacity	Good judgment	Knowledge	Intelligent
Human knowledge	Professional	Objective	Honest	Flexible
Curious	Human knower	Honest	Detailed	Open mind
Open mind	Professional	Systematic	Respect for people	Logic ability
Analytic	Creative	Structured	Empathy	Working correctly
Intelligent	Structured	Offensive	Listening to ideas	Creative
Tactical	Creative	Offensive	Information seeking	Objective
Experienced	Work independent	Motivated	Analytic abilities	Cooperative
Mature thinking	Hardworking	Focus on goal	Cooperative attitude	Empathy
Organized	Honest	Knowledge	Creative	Cooperative
Structure	Communicative skills	Analytic ability	Patience	Humane
Detailed	Persistent	Creative	Judge of character	Cooperative abilities
Ability to communicate	Systematic	Ability to be objective	Positive attitude	Action oriented
Creative	Involved	Structure	Goal oriented	Social
Motivated	Detail oriented	Analytical	Systematic	Professional
Holistic	Creative	Empathetic	Involved	Good writing skills
Creative	Offensive	Human	General knowledge	Interested
Correct	Organized	Objective	Effective	Hardworking

Table 13.4 Characteristics Responses (five characteristics by seventy-one respondents) (Continued)

Objectivity	Creativity	Involvement	Patience	Initiative
Honest	Systematic	Thorough	Identify important issues	Empathetic
Good to cooperate	Communication	Organized	Social skills	Knowledge of task
Good to communicate	Goal oriented	Creative	Good cooperative skills	Willing to work hard
Persistent	Thorough	Open mind	Creativity	Communicative
Listening	Work in team	Curious	Think about issues	Being present
Taking responsibility	High moral	Creative	Communicative skills	Analytic
Initiative	Curious	Listening	Open mind	Fair
Creative	Engaged	Good communicator	Structured	Positive
Being objective	Analytic	Systematic	Creative	Good to communicate
Structured	Analytic	Curious	Good to formulate	Awake for new things
Objective	Creative	Patient	Offensive	Honesty
Honest and fair	Communicating well	Awake and creative	Curious and interested	Creative
Interested in new ideas	Interested in knowledge	Concentrated	Methodical	Creative
Open	Organized	Detailed	Creative	Taking initiative
Good in communication	Observant	Human	Smart	Tactical
Knowledgeable	Open and humble	Creative	Objective	Communicative
Take good interviews	Se more options	Putting question marks	Communicate	Creative
Knowledgeable	Fair	Ambitious	Patient	Thorough
Professional	Patient	Curious	Good cooperative skills	Good to communicate
Ability to socialize	Treat with respect	Patience	Interested to learn	Creative and open
Professionally interested	Good to communicate	Curious	Structured	Honest
Detailed	Trustworthy	Create confidence	Communicate	Creative

Table 13.4   Characteristics Responses (five characteristics by seventy-one respondents) (Continued)

Objectivity	Creativity	Involvement	Patience	Initiative
Patience	Structured	Goal oriented	Feel satisfied	Feeling sympathy
Emphatic	Communication skills	Good listener	Professional	Honesty
Creative	Analytical	Staying ability	Results oriented	Personal integrity
Systematic	Analytical	Creative	Offensive	Professional
Independent	Socially skilled	Team worker	Creative	Professionally updated
Creative	Methodological	Structured	Professional competent	Social intelligence
Thorough	Professional ability	Ability to care	Moving on	Ability to cooperate
Communication skills	Empathy	Conscious ethics	Objectivity	Thorough
Professional knowledge	Thinking creatively	Independent	Learn new things	Critical reflection
Honest	Creative	Good cooperative skills	Systematically	Good formulating skills
Objective	Professionally involved	Creative	Structured	Empathy
Wide mind	Objective	Patient	Can communicate	Creative
Open	Involved	Creative	Good communicator	Independent
See connections	Active contributor	Loyal to the case	Logic thinking	Good communication
Creativity	Motivating	Professional	Investigative	Social
High integrity	Reliable	Ability to use experience	Cooperative skills	Ability to change
Structured	Objective	Professional	Curious	Creative
Knowledge	Experience	Attitude	Overview	Patience
Personal skills	See connections	Professional	Work in teams	Creative thinking
Ability to communicate	Structured	Open mind	Decision oriented	Persistent
Different perspectives	Thoroughly	Creativity	Empathy	Good communication
Ability to think logically	Ability to see pattern	Creative and intuitive	Social	Hunting instinct
Patient	Action driven	Communicative	Creative	Not conclusive
Honesty	Respect	Loyalty	Communication	Open mind

creativity, which means original to the individual or team producing the idea or solution (Kaufmann, 2004).

Second to creativity, *professionalism* was mentioned by 24 percent of the investigators. Other characteristics frequently mentioned were *objectivity, structure,* and *organization.*

Out of 355 characteristics, 60 characteristics were classified by the raters into the method style of thinking for detectives in police investigations. Fifty-five characteristics were classified into the challenge style, 165 into the skill style, and 75 into the risk style.

Survey results show that the most important thinking style for effective detectives is the skill style. Examples of characteristics classified as skill style include objectivity, proficiency in communication, analytic abilities, an open mind, and listening skills. At the skill level of investigative thinking, detectives are concerned with how they relate to people while collecting potential evidence. Detectives must think how they are going to relate to the victim, witnesses, possible suspects, the local community, and the wider general public in order to get the information they need to make the case.

Investigation as skill emphasizes the human dimension in investigative work, particularly the personal qualities of detectives. Hence, the central characteristic in this conception is a detective's ability to relate skillfully to a wide variety of people and, in conformity with prevailing law and regulation, collect the information vital to the matter under investigation.

Although experienced detectives and investigators intuitively use all four thinking styles in an investigation, it is rare that any one detective will give equal weight to all four styles of investigative thinking in a particular case because detectives, like everyone else, have a preference for maybe one or two particular styles or ways of thinking.

To summarize the findings in our survey in our own words, we will suggest that the five most important characteristics of a good detective are:

1. *Good empathic communication (skill style)*: A detective should be a "people person" or else he/she will not be able to get the most valuable information out of a person (witness, victim, suspect, etc.). However, at the same time, he or she must know and follow the law in detail so that the acquired information is applicable in court.
2. *Open-minded curiosity (skill style and, perhaps, a bit of risk style)*: A detective should have a mind that is curious about things and open to new ways of doing things to, not only discover information by making connections through being curious, but also to be open enough to avoid tunnel vision and conforming to stereotypical ideas.
3. *Creative thinking (risk style)*: A detective should be able to think creatively about the information/evidence by putting it together in different ways or looking at it from different perspectives. This outlook

forms the basis for further creative thought in how to go about getting other information/evidence needed to solve a case. Creative thinking also correlates highly with curiosity and being open-minded (characteristic 2).

4. *Logical, methodical reasoning (method style)*: A detective should be able to logically derive what piece of evidence is available and useful in a particular case/situation and how legally to get hold of it. Hence, a detective must think things through in a methodical manner without jumping to unwarranted conclusions or developing tunnel vision about a situation or person that cannot be supported with legal and logical inferences.

5. *Dogged determination, persistence (challenge style)*: A detective should be able to hang in for the long haul on a difficult and protracted investigation as persistence can often crack a case. However, the reason it is the last characteristic is that just being "determined" will not in itself necessarily find the information or evidence needed in an investigation. Hence, the reason for listing the other characteristics in priority order. If a detective has enough of the other characteristics, then determination is more likely to diminish in the long run.

From a management point of view, police investigation units need to be managed as knowledge organizations rather than bureaucratic organizations. When managed as a knowledge organization, the skill style of detective thinking is more likely to grow and succeed in police investigations.

While the responses to the question of characteristics of good investigators indicate that the skill style is the most important, responses to another question indicate that the risk style is the one they actually apply the most, as seen in Table 13.5.

Thus, there seems to be a discrepancy between what detectives practice and what they think is a good practice. They practice the risk style most extensively, followed by the skill style. At the same time, they argue that the skill style is the most important one. This can perhaps be explained by research design limitations, assuming that it normally would seem safer to define oneself as a skilled rather than a risky detective when performing self assessment by responding to an open-ended question. Nevertheless, they are able to rate the importance of risk when it is liked to a situation and not to their own personality.

The most effective thinking style of detectives as knowledge workers was empirically found to be the skill level. While an investigation involves an evidence-gathering enterprise by human beings, the conception of a detective in the knowledge organization emphasizes the quality of who is doing the gathering. Surprisingly, the same detectives claim that they apply the risk style more than the skill style. Detectives see an investigation as going nowhere

Table 13.5 Response to Thinking Style Items in the Survey

In Police Investigations	Mean	Deviation
Method style of investigative thinking		
When faced with a difficult case, I prefer to figure out how to solve the crime by following the basics of police procedure	3.5	0.97
Challenge style of investigative thinking		
I get a lot of satisfaction out of helping victims to achieve some sort of justice by bringing an alleged offender before a court	4.1	0.92
Skill style of investigative thinking		
I keep an open mind when investigating even when certain information suggests a possible suspect or course of action	4.6	0.58
Risk style of investigative thinking		
I keep an open mind and keep exploring various angles to find evidence	4.8	0.53

Note: 1 = completely disagree to 5 = completely agree.

unless they are able to extract good quality information out of people and their ability to do that depends on the quality of detectives' relational skill, particularly with regard to communicating well with people.

Other Performance Indicators

Police performance is a complicated construct. The police reform in the United Kingdom has developed some performance indicators for policing within an assessment framework. The policing performance assessment framework is an initiative led by the Home Office (2005), with the support of the Association of Chief Police Officers and the Association of Police Authorities. Some examples of performance indicators for 2005/2006 include:

- Satisfaction of victims of domestic burglary, violent crime, vehicle crime, and road traffic collisions
- Using the British Crime Survey, the percentage of people who think their local police do a good job
- Satisfaction of victims of racist incidents with respect to the overall service provided
- Using the British Crime Survey, the risk of personal crime
- Domestic burglaries per 1,000 households
- Number of offenses brought to justice
- Percentage of notifiable offenses resulting in a sanction detection
- Percentage of domestic violence incidents with a power of arrest

- Number of people killed
- Using the British Crime Survey, fear of crime
- Percentage of police officer time spent on frontline duties
- Delivery of cashable and noncashable efficiency target
- Average number of working hours lost per annum due to sickness per police officer

The guidance on statutory performance indicators for policing includes user satisfaction measures, confidence measures, fairness, equality and diversity measures, measures of crime level, offenses brought to justice measures, sanction detection measures, domestic violence measures, traffic measures, quality of life measures, frontline policing measures, and resource use measures.

One of the resource use measures is delivery of cashable and noncashable efficiency target. A cashable gain is where a particular level of output of a particular quality is achieved for less cost. A noncashable gain is where more output and/or output of better quality is achieved for the same cost.

In 1993, there was a debate in the United Kingdom whether to allow and stimulate direct entry into police management. According to Leishman and Savage (1993), it was a fundamental fact of the British police service that everyone had to start at the bottom, at the "lowest" rank of constable, in which office all entrants must serve a minimum period of two years. On the surface, then, the police service may appear to occupy a unique position among public sector organizations, as an apparently egalitarian meritocracy in which all confirmed constables could be said to have the opportunity to aspire to senior management positions.

At that time, chief constables were the first generation of completely self-made chiefs, lacking even the middle-class socialization of a university degree, although most went to grammar schools. Leishman and Savage (1993) argue that there are two important reasons in favor of direct entry. First, direct entry offers potential for the active furtherance of equal opportunities in the British police service. Whereas in Britain, target attainment would depend on the numbers of officers remaining in the service beyond their two-year probationary period, and then progressing through the rank of sergeant, this was not the case in Holland. Its system of direct entry, coupled with an explicit policy of positive action, allowed the recruitment and training of sufficient numbers of women and ethnic minority candidates directly into the rank of inspector, to achieve minimum targets within the agreed-upon time scale.

A second argument in favor of direct entry followed, in a sense, part of the rationale for "civilianization" within the service. While much of this process had been driven by the pursuit of economies, behind it also was the question of competences and specialist skills. For example, staff with backgrounds in personnel management have been appointed to head the personnel department in place of police officers (Leishman and Savage, 1993).

According to Jackson and Wade (2005), the understanding of police behavior, especially proactive behavior, has been pursued throughout policing history. Researchers have examined the impact of environmental factors (i.e., weapons, crime, etc.), individual factors (i.e., attitude, personality, etc.), police subculture, and organizational and departmental management on police behavior. Despite all of these research efforts, most if not all of the authors contributing to this line of research have concluded that the categorization, understanding, and predicting of police behavior is arduous (if not impossible), or that the relationship between police attitudes and their behavior is weak at best.

Researchers have examined empirically and conceptually the impact of social capital and police sense of responsibility on police behavior. For example, community social capital has been identified in the literature as having a significant impact on police behavior mainly because social capital serves as a measure of the community's ability to solve its own problems. In communities with low social capital, police may perceive themselves as the only form of social order and, therefore, may develop a higher sense of responsibility toward protecting citizens and themselves as well as preventing crime.

Jackson and Wade (2005) suggest that the examination of police sense of responsibility toward the community may be important in understanding police behavior. This assertion implies that police sense of responsibility may serve as an influential variable in explaining why police may demonstrate higher levels of proactive policing in communities with low social capital in comparison to those with high social capital. Police sense of responsibility toward the community seems important for understanding how police function in areas under their command. In communities where crime is commonplace, police can become overwhelmed and, thus, may focus on more serious crimes that pose a greater threat to police and citizen safety and ignore the lower-level crimes that do not.

Given these arguments, the major purpose of the study conducted by Jackson and Wade was to examine the relationship between police officers perception of their community's social capital and their sense of responsibility toward the provision of public safety, and, in turn, to assess empirically the impact of sense of responsibility on their propensity to engage in proactive policing.

By studying police perceptions of social capital and their sense of responsibility, it was possible to not only understand why community policing is or is not successful, but, more importantly, it was possible to understand police behavior in environments that, by their structural and demographic makeup, complicate the task of effective policing.

Jackson and Wade's findings support the hypothesis that police who indicate a more negative perception of community social capital are more likely to indicate a higher sense of responsibility toward the community. This finding suggests that as the police perception of community social capital becomes negative, they are more likely to rely upon their own resources to solve community problems. Generally, the only real resources that police possess in low social capital communities are their law enforcement powers.

Another finding was police who express a more negative perception of community social capital were more likely to indicate higher levels of proactive behavior. This finding suggests that, in communities with low social capital, police officers may utilize their law enforcement powers more in comparison to communities that possess higher levels of social capital.

The data gathered through a questionnaire distributed throughout the Kansas City Police Department in the United States suggested that the amount of crime occurring within the community is the most important variable for the explanation of police proactive behavior. Police proactive behavior includes new patrol techniques, increased utilization of technology, the organization of specialized units, and the use of criminal profiling. By being more proactive, police are conducting more stop-and-frisk contacts, requesting proof of identification more frequently, conducting more drug sweeps, and dispersing citizens who gather to protest public policies of various kinds (Jackson and Wade, 2005).

Proactive policing might perpetuate and exacerbate the social distance rift between the police and their community, and it also increases the likelihood that an officer may abuse his or her authority. In a time period of three years, Prince George's County, Maryland paid out $8 million dollars in jury awards and settlements in lawsuits that involved police misconduct and excessive force. The increasing costs resulting from payouts in police litigation cases and liability claims, coupled with increased pressure from public insurance pools to cut losses, are a few of the reasons that some U.S. law enforcement agencies are beginning to implement risk management programs (Archbold, 2005).

Risk management is a process used to identify and control exposure to potential risks and liabilities in both private and public organizations. Almost all of the basic duties of police work expose police officers to liability incidents on a daily basis. One aspect of police work that makes it unique to all other professions is the ability of police officers to use lethal and nonlethal force. This unique aspect of police work also contributes to police officer exposure to high levels of risk, which could lead to litigation, liability claims, or citizen complaints (Archbold, 2005).

Police personnel face some of society's most serious problems, often work in dangerous settings, and are typically expected to react quickly, and at the same time correctly. They must adapt to an occupation in which one moment may bring the threat of death, while other extended periods bring routine and boredom. They are expected to maintain control in chaotic situations involving injustice, public apathy, conflicting roles, injuries, and fatalities. Yet they are expected by both the public and their peers to approach these situations in an objective and professional manner, and to be effective decision makers and independent problems solvers while working in a system that encourages dependency by its quasimilitary structure (Kelley, 2005).

The nature of work in police professions requires optimal mental health. When their mental functioning is compromised, police professionals can lose touch with the common sense and resilience they need to minimize stress, enjoy their work, and operate at peak performance. Over time, Kelley (2005) finds that poor mental health can dramatically increase police officers proneness to physical illness, emotional disorders, accidents, marital and family problems, excessive drinking and drug use, suicide, and litigation ranging from excessive force and false arrest to failure to provide appropriate protection and services.

Performance Leadership

Although the appropriate measurement of police performance has long perplexed police practitioners, Coleman (2008) found that there has been a growing consensus that the traditional measurement of only "outputs" is insufficient. Authorities in Britain, the United States, and Canada have concluded that traditional police organizations have been focused mainly on the processes and outputs achieved through rigid adherence to bureaucratic processes and the finite measurement of easily determined performance indicators.

Coleman (2008, 307) phrased the question: "Managing strategic knowledge in policing: Do police leaders have sufficient knowledge about organizational performance to make informed strategic decisions?" He argues that there is a need for strategic management and, thus, the strategic performance measurements necessary to generate knowledge with which to make strategic decisions. Consequently, his study explored the extent to which Canadian police organizations have strategic performance measurement systems in place that are congruent with modern policing.

Because the goal of his study was to determine the extent to which Canadian police organizations were operating strategically and had implemented SPM (strategic performance measurement), a self-report survey of 128 questions was derived from the literature. The questions were created to identify whether respondents understood the concept of strategic management and SPM, whether they designed output measures and outcome measures to assist in organizational decision making, whether they collected and analyzed the appropriate data so that knowledge can be generated to assist strategic decision making, and whether they used this resultant knowledge when making strategic decisions.

The resulting comprehensive survey was distributed to leaders—chiefs of police, chief constables, or the equivalents—of seventy-five Canadian police organizations. All of these organizations, which were selected from the Police Resources in Canada 2004 report, were police agencies staffed with fifty or more police officers. Of the seventy-five surveys distributed, thirty-nine responses were received (52 percent) from police leaders in all provinces.

In order to determine the extent of the implementation of strategic management and the establishment of SPM in Canadian policing, the questions and responses were grouped into categories. Because policing must be implemented and managed strategically, the first category that was analyzed related to respondents' perception of what is meant by policing as organizational strategy. Most respondents did not appear to understand the concept of organizational strategy or had only a partial understanding. The second category addressed the question of whether the police organization had a corporate business plan. According to the literature, organizations that are led and managed strategically have a corporate plan or business plan with which to communicate the strategy and to guide their achievement of organizational goals. When respondents were asked to articulate the organizational strategy of their organization, half of the responding police leaders whose organizations reportedly had a corporate business plan suggested that they did not understand the concept of an organizational strategy.

Of the twenty-three organizations represented in the study (n = 39) that reportedly had a performance measurement system to determine organizational success, twenty-one of these used community surveys to measure performance.

References

Amabile, T.M., Barsade, S.G., Mueller, J.S., and Staw, B.M. 2005. Affect and creativity at work. *Administrative Science Quarterly* 50: 367–403.

Archbold, C.A. 2005. Managing the bottom line: Risk management in policing. *Policing: An International Journal of Police Strategies & Management* 28 (1): 30–48.

Coleman, T.G. 2008. Managing strategic knowledge in policing: Do police leaders have sufficient knowledge about organizational performance to make informed strategic decisions? *Police Practice and Research* 9 (4): 307–322.

Dean, G., Fahsing, I.A., Gottschalk, P., and Solli-Sæther, H. 2008. Investigative thinking and creativity: An empirical study of police detectives in Norway. *International Journal of Innovation and Learning* 5 (2): 170–185.

Glomseth, R., Gottschalk, P., and Solli-Sæther, H. 2007. Occupational culture as determinant of knowledge sharing and performance in police investigations. *International Journal of the Sociology of Law* 35: 96–107.

Gottschalk, P. 2001. Descriptions of responsibility for implementation: A content analysis of strategic information systems/technology planning documents. *Technological Forecasting and Social Change* 68: 207–221.

Hair, J.F., Black, W.C., Babin, B.J., Anderson, R.E., and Tatham, R.L. 2006. *Multivariate data analysis*, 6th ed. Upper Saddle River, NJ: Prentice Hall.

Home Office. 2005. *Guidance on statutory performance indicators for policing 2005/2006*. Police Standards Unit, U.K. Government Home Office. Online at: www.policereform.gov.uk.

Jackson, A.L. and Wade, J.E. 2005. Police perceptions of social capital and sense of responsibility. *Policing: An International Journal of Police Strategies & Management* 28 (1): 49–68.

Kaufmann, G. 2004. Two kinds of creativity—But which ones? *Creativity and Innovation Management* 13 (3): 154–165.

Kelley, T.M. 2005. Mental health and prospective police professionals. *Policing: An International Journal of Police Strategies & Management* 28 (1): 6–29.

Leishman, F. and Savage, S.P. 1993. Officers or managers? Direct entry into British police management. *International Journal of Public Sector Management* 6 (5): 4–11.

Riffe, D. and Freitag, A. 1997. A content analysis of content analyses, twenty-five years of journalism quarterly. *Journalism Mass Communication Quarterly.* 74: 873–882.

Index

A Call for Authors

Introducing a New Book Series from CRC Press

Advances in Police Theory and Practice

AIMS AND SCOPE:

This cutting-edge series is designed to promote publication of books on contemporary advances in police theory and practice. We are especially interested in volumes that focus on the nexus between research and practice, with the end goal of disseminating innovations in policing. We will consider collections of expert contributions as well as individually authored works. Books in this series will be marketed internationally to both academic and professional audiences. This series also seeks to —

- Bridge the gap in knowledge about advances in theory and practice regarding who the police are, what they do, and how they maintain order, administer laws, and serve their communities

- Improve cooperation between those who are active in the field and those who are involved in academic research so as to facilitate the application of innovative advances in theory and practice

The series especially encourages the contribution of works coauthored by police practitioners and researchers. We are also interested in works comparing policing approaches and methods globally, examining such areas as the policing of transitional states, democratic policing, policing and minorities, preventive policing, investigation, patrolling and response, terrorism, organized crime and drug enforcement. In fact, every aspect of policing, public safety, and security, as well as public order is relevant for the series. Manuscripts should be between 300 and 600 printed pages. If you have a proposal for an original work or for a contributed volume, please be in touch.

Series Editor
Dilip Das, Ph.D.,
Ph: 802-598-3680 E-mail: dilipkd@aol.com

Dr. Das is a professor of criminal justice and Human Rights Consultant to the United Nations. He is a former chief of police and, founding president of the International Police Executive Symposium, IPES, www.ipes.info. He is also founding editor-in-chief of *Police Practice and Research: An International Journal* (PPR), (Routledge/Taylor & Francis), www.tandf.co.uk/journals. In addition to editing the *World Police Encyclopedia* (Taylor & Francis, 2006), Dr. Das has published numerous books and articles during his many years of involvement in police practice, research, writing, and education.

Proposals for the series may be submitted to the series editor or directly to –

Carolyn Spence
Acquisitions Editor • CRC Press / Taylor & Francis Group
561-998-2515 • 561-997-7249 (fax)
carolyn.spence@taylorandfrancis.com • www.crcpress.com
6000 Broken Sound Parkway NW, Suite 300, Boca Raton, FL 33487

CRC Press
Taylor & Francis Group